THE
ISRAELI
MIND

ALSO BY ALON GRATCH

If Men Could Talk

If Love Could Think

THE ISRAELI MIND

HOW THE ISRAELI

NATIONAL CHARACTER

SHAPES OUR WORLD

ALON GRATCH

ST. MARTIN'S PRESS 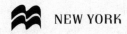 NEW YORK

www.stmartins.com

Design by Greg Collins

The Library of Congress Cataloging-in-Publication Data
is available upon request.

ISBN 978-1-250-06780-7 (hardcover)
ISBN 978-1-4668-8201-0 (e-book)

St. Martin's Press books may be purchased for educational, business,
or promotional use. For information on bulk purchases, please contact the
Macmillan Corporate and Premium Sales Department at 1-800-221-7945,
extension 5442, or write to specialmarkets@macmillan.com.

First Edition: September 2015

10 9 8 7 6 5 4 3 2 1

TO MY MOTHER,
HAYA GRATCH,

AND MY LATE FATHER,
AVRAHAM GRATCH

CONTENTS

INTRODUCTION: RABBI, I OBJECT   1

ONE. WHO IS AN ISRAELI?   29

TWO. IT'S EASIER TO CHANGE A SONG
THAN A CITY   61

THREE. THE WHOLE WORLD IS AGAINST US
AND THE WORLD IS SILENT   93

FOUR. CRYING WHILE SHOOTING   112

FIVE. ANATOMY OF A CLICHÉ: SABRAS AT WAR   159

SIX. THERE'S NO PLACE LIKE MASADA   185

CONCLUSION: SAYING NO, GETTING TO YES   206

EPILOGUE: DINNER IN JERUSALEM   241

ACKNOWLEDGMENTS   251

NOTES   253

INDEX   261

THE
ISRAELI
MIND

INTRODUCTION

RABBI, I OBJECT

The rabbi took to the podium. He blessed and praised the bar mitzvah boy, my son. Then, asking the congregants to be seated, he proceeded to deliver a sermon on Israel's recent military excursion into Gaza. Explaining and justifying Israel's behavior, he concluded with an emotional pitch, declaring that the 1967 Middle East war was Israel's finest hour.

At that moment one of the bar mitzvah's guests, an Israeli businessman in his fifties, stood up. "Rabbi," he implored with urgency, "I object to these statements!"

A hush fell over the large, ornate sanctuary. Unflustered, the rabbi respectfully replied, "My friend, why don't the two of us schmooze about this after the service."

But the man, who sat right behind my wife and me and who happened to be my brother, shot back, "No, Rabbi, I'd like to address the congregation."

"Sorry, I can't let you do that."

"I just want to say one word," my brother insisted.

As I was contemplating what that one word could possibly be,

I heard my wife—an exceptionally gracious and well-mannered American—mouthing to my brother, "Ariel, if you don't stop this, I'm going to kill you!"

Not skipping a beat, Ariel retorted, "Some causes are worth dying for."

But he took his order, sat down, and allowed the service to resume. As you may have gathered by now, my brother shares little more than a first name with the former Israeli prime minister who had sent those troops into the Gaza Strip. Except for one thing, of course—they are both Israelis.

I suspect this confrontation was a first for this rabbi, as well as for the congregation as a whole, which resides peacefully in an upscale suburb just north of New York City. It certainly provided for a lively background conversation for the rest of the day, when the festivities reconstituted in a tranquil, waterfront country club a couple of miles away. But there, too, notwithstanding the genteel ambience of the Waspy venue, the Israeli mind continued to make itself present.

Perhaps because my wife and I are both psychologists, or simply because we are not religious people, our son's bar mitzvah celebration did not follow the standard format. Among other things, we had asked seven men who had played an important role in our family life to say to our son a few public words of advice about becoming a man, which is what a bar mitzvah is supposedly about. We chose my father-in-law, my two brothers, three family friends, and my father and gave them some rather specific instructions. My father-in-law and our three American friends followed the directions. They recited some well-prepared, truly memorable crumbs of touching, funny, and adolescent-friendly advice.

You already met one of my brothers, Ariel. His advice, true to form, was "always follow your gut." But now it was my other brother's turn to follow his gut or, more accurately, march to his own tune. Taking his turn, Eli proudly announced he did not prepare anything. He congratulated my son warmly and sat down. Unlike Ariel, he made no political proclamations, yet that was hardly outside his repertoire. Ten years my senior, Eli was twenty-one in 1969 when he campaigned for Israel's perpetual right-wing candidate Menachem Begin, heading up one of his Jerusalem offices. Shortly thereafter he changed his last name from Gratch to Gadot. This was not inconsistent with common practice at that time, as many Israelis hebraized their European last names to conform to the ideal of the new Israeli Jew. But in a personal demonstration of his love for Greater Israel, Eli chose a name that translates to "riverbanks," referring to both banks of the Jordan River. It was taken from the right-wing revisionist school of Zionism, which envisioned not only the West Bank, but also the rest of historical Palestine, including the territory of the sovereign state of Jordan, as part of Israel. Years later, after he got married and passed his name on to his children, Mr. Gadot had a complete change of heart, ending up on the extreme left, where ceding the West Bank and even East Jerusalem to the Palestinians was acceptable. But he and his like-minded offspring are now stuck with the Gadot name.

Last but not least on the speakers list came—or more accurately didn't come—my father. Earlier he had told me he was going to tell the following tale from his own bar mitzvah. Shortly before he was born in Turkish-ruled Palestine of 1918, his own father was expelled to Syria because, not wanting to fight against the Allies in World War I, he had dodged the Turkish draft. His father therefore could not attend his bris, the religious ritual of circumcision performed on Jewish boys. But while in Damascus he had vowed that he would at least make it to his son's bar mitzvah. Well, he did, and on that occasion he told my father this whole story. "Now when I came to your son's—my youngest grandson's—bris," my father told me, "I vowed that I would make it to his bar mitzvah, to complete the cycle." Which he would, by traveling from Jerusalem to New York at age eighty-six, and preparing to tell this tale. Except that after he ran this by my mother, she apparently vetoed it, ruling that the story had nothing to do with my son's bar mitzvah and therefore was inappropriate. So notwithstanding my encouragement, my father decided against this speech. Instead, my mother helped him write something appropriately didactic about my son's coming of age, which he was going to read. But at the event, after the first six men spoke and my wife introduced my father as a man who survived five wars, three boys, and a fifty-eight-year-long marriage, my mother stood up and walked to the podium. Explaining that my father was not feeling well, she proceeded to read "his" speech.

Now lest you think my mother was an anomaly and it was principally the men in my family who "followed their gut" or marched to whatever tune came out of it, I should also mention a sister-in-law who announced she would not wear any "shmatte" on her head as required by the synagogue, and a niece who told my son she did not believe in God and would therefore not accept the honor of opening the ark, and also, why was he going through this entire charade if he, too, as he responded, did not believe in God . . . ?

I am a New York–based clinical psychologist and author. I was born and grew up in Jerusalem, the third and youngest son in a family with unusually deep roots in the Holy Land. One of my most vivid childhood memories was from the morning of June 5, 1967. A fourth grader at the time, I was on my way to school, pushing uphill on Ussishkin Street—named after an early, Russian-born Zionist leader—when a loud siren sounded. It was not the long, single-pitch siren used to signal a moment of silent standing on Holocaust and Memorial days, but rather the continuous ascending and descending one signaling war. I paused and looked around. Several other pedestrians did the same. Then, as if by unspoken consensus, we decided it was a false alarm or just another drill. We resumed walking. But when I arrived at school, it turned out to have been the real thing. War was coming, and some four hundred kids were gathered in the basement gym waiting to be picked up by their parents. By noon, when all but me and a friend who lived across the street from me had been picked up, our teacher paired us up and told us to walk home together. About halfway through our fifteen-minute walk home we started hearing explosions. Loud booms of mortar rounds were punctuated by more distant echoes from semiautomatic guns. We knew that a couple of blocks away from our street, in the Valley of the Cross, which lay beneath the Israeli Museum, the Israeli Defense Forces stationed a camouflaged artillery unit. We also knew that the prime minister's house, also nearby, was a potential target for Jordanian shelling. All this did not stop my father—who pulled over in his car driving back from work just as my friend and I reached our block—from suggesting that I accompany him to the corner grocery store. So only after we had bought food for several days did my father and I join our neighbors in the small shelter of our five-story apartment building. Some of our neighbors also took their time trickling into the shelter, whose entrance had only recently been secured by a few of us with a wall of sandbags.

During the night, the shelling continued and the building next door suffered a direct hit, shaking and shattering the windows in ours. In the morning, the shelling quieted down and my parents discussed moving from the shelter to the empty, second-floor apartment of a neighbor. We lived on the third floor and they somehow deemed the second floor safer.

"Why don't we just stay here?" I asked.

"What, are you scared?" replied my mother.

What I later came to see as her attempt at empathy and reassurance came across at the time as a bemused, almost contemptuous dismissal of my supposed fear. Strangely, through this entire day I was not aware of any feelings of fear. As I remember it, when

I suggested we stay in the shelter, it was a cognitive conclusion, akin, perhaps, to a parent's thinking that dressing up his or her baby with a sweater, coat, and hat on a cold day is merely logical. The same analytical detachment, accompanied perhaps by some excitement and pride, I experienced the following day when we emerged from the shelter and strolled up the street to observe Israeli jets bombing a Palestinian village or a Jordanian position a few miles away in the West Bank. As for my mother's experience, I understood it better many years later when she shared with me a memory from her life in Jerusalem under siege during the 1948 Arab-Israeli War, or Israel's War of Independence. A mother at the age of twenty-three, with limited food rations at her disposal, she searched the neighborhood for something to feed her growing, one-year-old baby, my eldest brother. She found a woman nearby who raised chickens in her backyard, and they ended up bartering a can of sardines for eggs. So amid artillery shelling, she walked back home, eggs in hand, caring more about not breaking them than about her own life. In a parallel memory from just a few months earlier, my father recalled how, as a foot soldier in one of the pre-state Jewish security forces, he found himself face-to-face with a British artillery unit aiming a mortar at him from merely fifty yards away. In other words, for my parents, empathizing with fear had long been a luxury they couldn't afford.

For better and for worse, in the history of my family this kind of drama was hardly the exception. And the particulars of the dramas—and traumas—the family endured in the span of two centuries, along with what appeared to have been its idiosyncratic fables and foibles, were intricately woven into the Jewish and Zionist narrative that gave rise to the Israeli national character. From the shtetls of Eastern Europe, through the holy cities of Safed and Jerusalem, to the shores of North America, with loss and renewal marking every turn in its story, the family had its share of devout men and secular rebels, self-made or self-declared geniuses, dreamers, schemers, charmers and charlatans, freedom fighters, terrorists and prisoners of war, petty peddlers and businessmen, and of course, ordinary men and women caught in a historical web of shifting, clashing realities. As we shall see, this family history not only formed and informed this storyteller, but also exemplified and foreshadowed the complexities and contradictions of life in contemporary Israel.

My mother was of the sixth generation of Jews in the Old City of Jerusalem. Her maternal ancestors were disciples of the "Genius from Vilna," an eighteenth-century, Polish-Lithuanian, ultraorthodox rabbi and scholar who inspired his pupils to travel to the Holy Land and study the Torah there. These religious pilgrims were not Zionists. In fact, some of their descendants were members of the anti-Zionist Neturei Karta, or Guardians of the City sect. Like the larger ultraorthodox community in Palestine of the time, this tiny, if loud, group believed that only the Messiah could restore Jewish sovereignty in Jerusalem. But unlike the larger community, after the establishment of the Jewish state it set itself apart by seeking strategic affiliations with Palestinian terrorist groups and later on with virulently anti-Israeli Iranian officials. One of the founders and the eventual leader of this sect was a cousin of my maternal grandmother.

The majority of the Genius' pupils, however, were apolitical, and the grandson of one of these pupils was my mother's maternal grandfather. A serious student of religion and a self-taught architect, this man designed, among other things, the cathedral ceiling of one of Jerusalem's largest synagogues. He was also a local chess legend, once playing and beating a wealthy rival in a bet to finance an overseas surgery for one of his children. My maternal grandmother was the youngest of eleven children, six of whom died in childhood. Of the remaining five, three boys and two girls, only my grandmother and one sister made it beyond their twenties or thirties. As my mother put it, "There were no medicines and doctors in Palestine back then."

My mother's paternal grandfather, also an ultraorthodox man, came to Palestine from Russia as a young boy. His family, too, settled in the Old City, and as a young man he opened a small winery there. To avoid being drafted into the Turkish army during World War I, he left the city and settled outside its walls, opening a grocery store in what was gradually becoming known as West Jerusalem. His wife died when his son, my grandfather, was fifteen. As he did not get along with his stepmother, my grandfather left home at seventeen. He studied to become a teacher but ended up a branch manager of a bank. He married my grandmother by matchmaking. He had two full and four half siblings. His sister married into the family of Yehoshua Stampfer, a celebrated early Zionist who in 1878 had been one of the founders of Petah Tikva, the first new Jewish city in Palestine. His half brother, Meir Feinstein, was a member of the Irgun, a militant underground organization fighting to expel the British army from Palestine after it had wrestled it from Turkish control in the aftermath of the Great War. In 1946, barely nineteen years old, Meir participated in an Irgun operation, planting a bomb in a Jerusalem rail station serving British soldiers. He lost an arm in the operation and retreated, but the British police followed his blood trail and arrested him and his coconspirator. They were tried and sentenced to death by hanging. Refusing to recognize the British authority over Palestine, Meir declined legal representation and refused to sign a petition for pardon. While visiting him on death row, his girlfriend smuggled him two hand grenades in hollowed-out oranges. The prisoners' plan was to use one grenade to attack the executioner and the other to kill themselves. But when they learned that the prison's rabbi would attend the hanging, they changed their plan and, a few hours before the execution, blew themselves up in their cells. When Meir's lawyer called my father with this news—my grandparents did not yet have a telephone—he consoled him with the idea that Meir died at his own hands rather than those of the illegitimate ruler. My grandfather's other half siblings also died at a young age, and all in tragic circumstances of various kinds.

As a young couple, my maternal grandparents lived in the Jewish Quarter of the Old City. On the first night of Passover in 1920 they were awoken late at night by the cries *Itbach al yahood,* or "Slaughter the Jews," and the sounds of a gathering Arab mob outside their window. This was in the aftermath of the Balfour Declaration, in which the British government announced its intention to facilitate the establishment of a national homeland for the Jewish people in Palestine. It was also a short time after right-wing Zionist leader Ze'ev Jabotinsky had arrived in Jerusalem and started training local Jews in the use of firearms. All this contributed to Arab resentment of the Jewish presence in the land. Earlier that evening, though, and reflecting another reality on the ground, when my grandparents were locked out of their gated courtyard upon returning from the seder, gracious Arab shopkeepers invited them in and offered them coffee and cake. Being kosher, however, they were unable to accept the invitation. Just before dawn, as the threat from the mob increased, the British police were summoned and all the Jews in the area were evacuated. My grandparents were thus forced to leave their home with literally nothing in hand and to start a new life in a nascent West Jerusalem neighborhood.

Here, my mother and her younger brother were born. After the birth of my uncle, my grandmother struggled with infertility. Years later her gynecologist treated her with antibiotic injections he stole from a hospital supply kept exclusively for British soldiers. The treatment cured what turned out to be tuberculosis of the uterus, but my grandmother was too old by that time to get pregnant again. In 1947, just before Israel gained its independence, my then twenty-two-year-old uncle, who was a member of the leading Jewish security force in Palestine, the Haganah, took part in an operation aiming to break into the Old City and support its dwindling and isolated Jewish population. Emerging from a tunnel they'd dug to avoid enemy fire from the city's walls, my uncle and his comrades were met and captured by the superior Jordanian army. My uncle was taken to Aman, Transjordan, now Jordan, where he remained a prisoner of war for nine months. A second or third cousin of my mother's was in the same prisoner-of-war camp. Sometime during that period the parents of this cousin—the father was the chief rabbi of the Kotel, or Western Wall—were killed in a terrorist bombing in Jerusalem. My uncle and his cousin were released and returned home in a prisoner exchange during a cease-fire in the subsequent 1948 war.

As for my father, on his mother's side he, too, was a descendant of the followers of the Genius of Vilna, though this group had settled far north of Jerusalem, in the holy city of Safed. My father's great-great-grandmother was found at the age of three or four amid a mass of volcanic rocks after a large earthquake demolished much of the town and killed her entire family. On the other side, my father's paternal grandfather was the son of a religious-community leader in a small village on the border of Russia and Poland. During the 1880s, a series of anti-Jewish pogroms in the area led the Jews to start leaving. While two of his siblings emigrated to America, my grandfather, a young teenager at the time, fell under the spell of Zionism. He was fifteen years old when he left home and joined another family who made their way to Palestine, settling in Jerusalem. His father followed him a few years later. Once established in Palestine, my father's grandfather made a living by traveling overseas to collect donations for Jewish families in Jerusalem. Using his earnings, his wife bought a house as well as a small grocery store that served the entire neighborhood. One story my father would tell was that his grandmother was amazed to discover that an oil barrel she bought to dispense cooking oil for her customers never ran out. "It's a miracle," she insisted over the years. When my father asked his grandfather about it, he found out that unbeknownst to her, his grandfather had arranged for an oil-importer buddy of his to refill the barrel when she was out of the store.

As noted earlier, my grandfather was exiled to Syria after avoiding the Turkish military draft. But the story was a bit more complicated. Before he was expelled, he had avoided the Ottoman military authorities by hiding in the attic of his synagogue for two years. He then further avoided the draft by getting an American passport through the help of a friendly consul in the American consulate in Jerusalem. Little did he know that when America joined World War I to fight against Turkey, he would once again be pursued by the Turkish authorities, only this time for being an American citizen. When caught, he was treated as a prisoner of war, which is why he was merely exiled. A fellow draft dodger who was caught with him was less lucky: he was executed by hanging.

My father had eight siblings. One of them died at eight and another at twenty-seven. Another close relative, a cousin, was a pilot in the Russian air force. He was killed in action in World War II. Later, in the late 1960s, my father's oldest brother and his family left Israel for Canada. At the time, leaving Israel—popularly and officially referred to as yerida, the opposite of aliyah, or ascending, which is the term still used for immigrating to Israel from the Diaspora—was something akin to a betrayal, so my grandfather disapproved. He did not talk to my uncle for seven years before reconciling. Though he was strictly orthodox, when his religious practice came into conflict with the Zionist agenda, my grandfather opted for the latter. So he approved of my father's performing work for the Haganah on Shabbat. He also allowed the Haganah to build a "slick," a secret cache of firearms, inside the sacred Torah ark of his synagogue. Having been a manager in a large building-supplies company, my grandfather actually built that synagogue and later served as its treasurer.

While my father ultimately had a successful career in the insurance business, like many Israeli men of his generation his early career was disrupted by the 1948 war. He started out working in an uncle's appliance store, but business was so slow that pretty soon the uncle needed an out. He set his store on fire, collected insurance, and used that money to open an insurance agency himself. My father joined and worked in the agency for ten years, then the uncle suffered a serious heart attack. It was the end of 1947 and Jerusalem was under siege by the surrounding Arab villagers and militias. Since he was in critical condition, my great-uncle was allowed into the last convoy to leave Jerusalem before the only road out of the city was cut off. He died before arriving at the Tel Aviv hospital, however, and soon thereafter the war erupted. My father was drafted into the newly formed Israeli Defense Forces, and the insurance agency closed down. After a year of service in a crude combat-engineering unit, my father restarted the business, signing up his military buddies as his first clients. In time, his firm became the largest independent insurance agency in Jerusalem.

My parents were the first generation in their families to not be introduced by a religious matchmaker. They met in 1946 in a popular coffee shop in downtown West Jerusalem. Both my father and his best friend, so goes the story, set their sights on my mother, who was seated a couple of tables away with her friends. Arguing over who would get to ask her out, they agreed to toss a coin, and my father won. Since both my parents came from orthodox families, their own parents approved of the courting and the subsequent marriage. However, while we only lived a few minutes away from my grandparents and saw them weekly, my parents never disclosed to them how fully secular they had gradually become. They did not tell them they drove on Shabbat, which was a problem because my maternal grandparents' house was on top of a small hill overlooking the main road leading out of Jerusalem. So whenever we drove out of town late on Saturday mornings, which tended to coincide with my grandparents' postsynagogue ritual of coffee and cake on the veranda, the three boys in the backseat had to duck so that we could not be recognized by our family configuration.

As we have seen, my own childhood was touched by war, too, though not nearly as dramatically as my parents'. As a young teen in the aftermath of the 1967 war, I was drawn to the political vision of Greater Israel. But my daily life was all about soccer, friends, and school. On many Saturdays as well as on Yom Kippur and other Jewish holidays, when everything in West Jerusalem was shut down for religious observation, my friends and I would go to Arab East Jerusalem, to bargain in the Old City's souk and feast on hummus and labane. During that time, Israel's economy, along with its self-confidence, was booming. My father's business flourished and my parents expanded their modest two-bedroom apartment, where previously the three boys shared a bedroom. When my oldest brother left for the army, we not only had a family room but I also had my own small bedroom. When I was sixteen, I made some news in our quiet, middle- to upper-middle-class neighborhood, consisting mostly of European Jews and academics. For the equivalent of a couple of dollars I bought a donkey from an Arab merchant in the souk and brought it home. Now, a boy on a donkey—though not a fair-skinned Jewish boy from our neighborhood—was not a rare sight on the streets of Jerusalem at that time. But when the donkey started hee-hawing in the middle of the night, and the neighbors in our building and the surrounding homes realized a donkey was in our backyard, all hell broke loose.

A year later, the 1973 Arab-Israeli or Yom Kippur War erupted. There was no fighting in the Jerusalem area this time, but there was no school for three weeks. To help with the national manpower shortage resulting from the calling of military reserves, I volunteered in a large bakery, making bread. By this time, I was in the midst of a stormy adolescence, accompanied by a political and cultural rebellion. My friends, most of whom had an intellectual or artistic bent, and I did not approve of government policies. We questioned whether it was committed to peace or under the grip of a growing military-industrial complex. As we reached the age of compulsory service, a couple of my friends avoided the draft by feigning, or perhaps merely exhibiting, psychiatric conditions. While avoidance was theoretically tempting, for me it was never an option, so two months after graduating high school, I was in the army. Yet with the exception of a six-month period guarding a lone settlement in Gaza, I was not even close to seeing action. After several other assignments, I eventually settled at a desk job, providing financial and vocational counseling to disabled veterans and bereaved families. The people I serviced appreciated my work, but much of what I felt, even if I was not always aware of it at the time, was shame. Though I felt justified by my opposition to the government's war and peace policies, I couldn't help but feeling ashamed that I was a "jobnik" rather then a real, combat-unit soldier. While my political views have undergone various permutations over the years, this sense of shame remained a constant. So even though I have no emotional affinity to military culture, I will always admire and envy those who are willing to put their lives on the line to defend their country.

Another unattractive emotion triggered by my military service was the one denied or repressed since fourth grade: fear. It re-emerged in full force during basic training when I was confronted by the prospect of having to throw a hand grenade. I was terrified by the thought that after pulling the safety pin I would somehow fail to throw the grenade fast enough and it would explode in my hand. On the whole, however, these kinds of fears remained muted for me, as during my three years of service Israel was not at war. By and large the same was true in my brothers' service, though one of them did see action on the eastern bank of Egypt's Suez Canal during the low-grade War of Attrition between Israel and Egypt in the late 1960s.

One of the most pronounced aspects of military service for me was what I experienced as the loss of personal freedom. Many years later, I realized that, not unlike college in the United States, the army for most Israeli youth is a transitional place between home and the "real world"; a place with reassuringly limited choices but also vast opportunities for personal growth. While for most Israeli youth of my generation the loss of personal freedom was eclipsed by feelings of pride and a sense of national duty, for me it was oppressive. At a time when every inch of my body was craving freedom and autonomy, I was a literally a property of the state. I was constrained by a myriad of laws and regulations, observed and controlled by military police even when on leave from the base. I also felt suffocated by the incessant talk about politics and "the situation," the intensity of the collective experience, and the porous interpersonal boundaries imposed by the culture. So a couple of days after my "release"—the actual word used in Hebrew to denote the end of one's military service—I left for college in the United States.

I aimed as far away as California, but since this was my first time traveling overseas, I stopped in London for a few days. On my first morning there, as I was browsing in one of London's legendary bookstores, a local gentleman approached me. Assuming I was an employee, he showed me a small note and asked if I could help him find this book. I glanced at the note and couldn't believe my eyes. It read, *Twenty-Five Years of Social Research in Israel by Haya Gratch*. This extremely obscure academic title, with only a couple of hundred of copies in print, was edited by my mother, who worked as a secretary, translator, and editor for a small nonprofit academic institute in Jerusalem. Clearly one of those small-world coincidences, yet in retrospect I can't help but read into it some sort of foreshadowing. To close that circle, I heard nothing else about my mother's book in the next thirty-six years, but at the time of this writing I received an e-mail from an NYU doctoral student unknown to me. After googling my mother's last name, he was inquiring if I had in my possession an article referenced in her book, since the archive where these articles were kept in Israel had burned down.

But this was not my experience in Northern California. My relationship with Israel during my four years in San Francisco can be boiled down to a brief encounter I had while driving along and exploring scenic Highway 1 north of the city. When I stopped on a rocky beach to breathe in the ocean, I exchanged pleasantries with another lone visitor, who asked about my accent. Not only did he know nothing about Israel, but he also had no interest in war, geopolitical affairs, or politics—Israeli or for that matter American. I marveled at that carefree, uninhibited freedom, ever since intertwined in my mind with the Pacific Coast. During my college years in California I had no interest in my homeland whatsoever. I visited Israel only twice, read no Israeli newspapers or books, had no Jewish friends, and observed no Jewish holidays. Or at least that was the story line I told myself. The only exception suggesting otherwise was an Israeli friend with whom I went to the same kindergarten, grade school, and high school, and, now by complete coincidence, college. He was studying theater, and I, filmmaking, and in sophomore year we decided together to switch majors to psychology. He is now a practicing psychoanalyst in Jerusalem.

Then came graduate school in New York. On my first day, before my first class, I found myself chatting with a classmate, a Lebanese woman who had just come from Beirut. This was during the 1982 Israeli invasion of Lebanon, and since the Beirut airport was closed, to fly to New York she had to cross into Jordan. She literally escaped Beirut in a taxi as Israeli jets were circling and bombing the city from above. The two of us became so involved in a conversation about the Middle East that we were late to class with the program's director. We quickly became close friends and remain so today, to a large extent, we have always been aware, because we came from the same neighborhood.

During graduate school, while working on a doctorate in clinical psychology, I became interested in the psychology of groups and in conflict resolution. I also developed a curious and intense passion for American politics. I dated, got married, and started thinking about raising a family. My wife to be was Jewish—more so than I thought I was at the time—and so were most of the close friends I made in New York. I had little interest in religion, and contrary to everything I was taught growing up, I bought into the idea that one could be culturally Jewish yet have no significant attachment to Israel. In short, while Israel was where I came from, I was now just a New Yorker, or at most a secular American Jew.

But then came September 11 and all of a sudden the Middle East was back in my life. Three weeks before the terrorist attack that changed America, my brother Ariel—who had moved from Jerusalem to New York a few months before I started college—casually said to a friend while playing golf in New Jersey, "One of these days some terrorists will hijack a plane and fly it into the World Trade Center." In the aftermath of the attacks, when Americans were debating the merits of going to war with Iraq, Ariel was interviewed by *The New York Times* for an article discussing immigrants' feelings about the potential war. I hope the United States goes to war in Iraq, he said, because it will get so mired in the Middle East swamp that it will learn once and for all to stay out of it. Over the years, Ariel had remained far more connected to Israel than I. He had traveled there on business, his wife was Israeli, and unlike me he spoke Hebrew to his kids. But the basic Israeli sensibilities and ambivalence he possesses I share, and this I saw most clearly when we discussed America's involvement in the Middle East in the post-9/11 world. During this time I began to realize that, well, you can take the boy out of Jerusalem—though 9/11 seemed to have cast a doubt even on that—but you can't take Jerusalem out of the boy. Upon further reflection I came to see that since I'd left Israel, scarcely a day had gone by that I was not somehow, however vaguely, aware of my Israeli DNA. Around that time I began to entertain the idea of writing about the Israeli national character.

For a long time, however, I was torn. It was an intellectual minefield, I told myself. It posed too many methodological problems; too many theoretical questions; too many political ramifications. Indeed, one Israeli scholar I spoke to warned me that the very concept of a national character might be racist. There was truth to all these arguments, including that danger of a racist application of the concept. But these were not the real reasons I vacillated, nor did I understand why. But then, a couple of years ago, a friend from Israel visited. Not a psychologist herself, but rather a literary scholar whose work involves psychoanalytic interpretation of biblical narratives, she listened to my ideas as well as to my ambivalence. When I finished, she smiled wisely and said, "Perhaps you are afraid to get close to something you've kept at a distance all these years." This simple, if not obvious, formulation, which neither I nor my actual analyst had previously thought of, struck me, as they say in Hebrew, like thunder on a clear day. In a rare, Hollywood-fashion moment of therapeutic breakthrough, my ambivalence dissolved and my doubts metamorphosed into one of the most exhilarating decisions of my life: I would pursue this project not only as an intellectual endeavor to understand the Israeli mind, but also as an emotional journey to finally integrate my Israeli past with my American present. Along with my psychological skill set, I would bring to the task my unique insider-outsider perspective, striving to draw an objective and yet textured portrait.

Since that time I've reimmersed myself in everything Israeli. I have researched hundreds of academic papers in the fields of Israeli history, sociology, anthropology, psychology, political science, education, and literature. I have read and reviewed hundreds of secondary sources including books, newspaper articles, films, music, and artwork. I've taken more frequent and longer trips to Israel. I've met and interviewed leading Israeli psychologists, sociologists, historians, political scientists, journalists, artists, and businessmen. I've hired several Israeli research assistants to help me sift through decades of relevant empirical research, as well as to interview a good number of "average" Israelis from all walks of life. Last but not least, I've taken to watching Israeli television and listening to Israeli radio online daily.

Using my fieldwork in Israel, existing academic research, psychoanalytic theory, and my own professional and personal experience, I have attempted to forge a comprehensive, provocative, and accessible narrative about the Israeli mind. What follows is a road map to the journey, and an invitation to come along.

THE SABRA'S *DAVKA* AND WHY SHOULD WE CARE?

How representative is my family of the Israeli national character? By definition, the family's historical roots in Jerusalem are unique. Geographically speaking, its pre-Zionist experiences in Palestine and the impact they had on the family's culture are indeed singular. Having said that, as we shall see, many of the themes underlying and defining my family's way of being, including those established in its pre-Zionist days in the Holy Land, mirror the historical and cultural environments that gave birth to the Israeli national character as a whole. Certainly, the present-day descendants of the family, or at least their behavior during my son's bar mitzvah in New York, appear to be quintessentially Israeli.

To many Israelis this behavior would stand merely as a pale example of the "ugly Israeli," or on the positive side, the assertive, straightforward one. That behavior conforms to some of the widely held outside perceptions of the Israeli interpersonal style. Consider, for example, how American diplomats and political leaders describe their Israeli counterparts in their memoirs. Alluding to the personality of several Israeli prime ministers from both sides of the political map, Jimmy Carter, James Baker, and Bill Clinton, to cite just a few, resorted to the following descriptors: aggressive, arrogant, defensive, unyielding, intransigent, obstinate, argumentative, rigid, brusque, bullheaded, unreasonable, negative, mistrustful, obstructive, disruptive, and provocative. Here, too, each of these unpleasant adjectives can and should be complemented by its positive corollary. But regardless, if we were to apply the statistical technique of "factor analysis" to this list, we would surely reduce it to a small number of more meaningful and accurate descriptors. Even to the casual observer, *argumentative, negative, obstinate, unyielding,* and *intransigent* all obviously represent the same basic personality trait or attitude.

On the famous Rorschach inkblot test this interpersonal style would manifest in seeing images in the white, background space, rather than the more obvious black foreground. In the Israeli context, it is perhaps best captured by the unique Hebrew word *davka,* which translates into something in between "in spite" and "exactly so." "Why are you pulling a *davka* on me?" is what an Israeli child, or even an adult, would say to a friend appearing to be purposelessly oppositional. In short, it's a nay-saying tendency to disagree for the sake of disagreeing. I was once at a party in a stuffy Park Avenue duplex in Manhattan where the food was served buffet style. As I approached the buffet from the right, a woman was heading my way with her plate from the opposite direction. Seeing the line behind her and realizing I was going the wrong way in a one-way street, I jokingly said, "Excuse me, you are going in the wrong direction." I then added, "Just kidding, and how typical of an Israeli to be wrong and tell the other party *they* are in the wrong." The woman laughed and said, "That's really funny; my mom is an Israeli and that's what she has done to me my whole life!"

Now to the extent that this tendency is applicable to all or most Israelis, two questions arise. First, *why* are Israelis so oppositional? Could it be a defense mechanism, one developed over time in reaction to a particular set of environmental and historical conditions? Well, just as organisms, individuals, and organizations develop habitual modes of operating in a given environment, so do nations. These behaviors are considered a "defense" because they protect us from danger and help us to survive. Because they are necessary and useful in early, defining moments and/or for a long time, they become an integral part of our character and continue to operate even when they are no longer essential or are counterproductive.

A quick excursion into Zionist history would readily explain why the Israelis needed to develop this type of nay-saying defense mechanism. Consider what the Jews who immigrated to Palestine in the late nineteenth century and those who settled or were born there through the establishment of the Jewish state had to say no to. No to the parents and families they had left behind in their home countries; no to the age-old Jewish professions and lifestyle of moneylending, peddling, and Torah studying, derided and discarded by the pioneers in favor of working the land; no to the reality and self-image of the bookish, timid, and passive Diaspora Jew, ideologically rejected by the pioneers in order to create a new Jew, physical, assertive, and active; no to the Yiddish language and the multitude of other foreign languages and accents, all replaced by the fervently revived and modernized biblical Hebrew; no to the ethnic identities and cultural heritages from countries of origins, which were supposed to immediately dissolve in the new melting pot; no to religion as the organizing principle of the community, which was supposed to be replaced by socialism or urban modernity; no to the refined, class-oriented public discourse of the

European culture, which simply couldn't compete with the heat, the desert, local Oriental customs, and Arab hostilities; no to the home countries and societies that produced, or failed to protect the Jews from, anti-Semitism and the Holocaust; no to the British rule of Palestine when it began to curtail Jewish immigration and independence; no to the local Palestinians who didn't want them there; no to the Arab countries who vowed to drive them out of Palestine; no to depending on foreign governments and their police forces for protection, as the Jews did for a couple of millennia; no to "walking like lambs to the slaughterhouse," which was how the Israelis historically perceived the victims of the Holocaust; no to migration to a safer place, the traditional Jewish response to danger; no to decades of world pressure to accommodate the Palestinians; and no to the United Nations, pithily dismissed by Israelis as Oom Shmoom, or roughly the "United Nothings," for its historically anti-Israeli stand.

As evident in this history, becoming an Israeli meant rejecting both external and internal forces. But while, psychologically speaking, opposing external forces—the British, the Arabs, the world, etc.—is a relatively straightforward proposition, opposing parts of oneself is more complicated. After all, we are all attached to who we are. It is thus reasonable to hypothesize that notwithstanding their incredible determination, the Zionists were not wholly successful in ridding themselves of the old Jew within. Perhaps, goes this hypothesis, they've adopted a tough, new exterior that suppressed or repressed, but did not altogether eradicate, the timidity of the Diaspora. Perhaps there's truth to the old cliché that like the sabra—the cactus fruit native Israelis are named for—Israelis are prickly on the outside but sweet on the inside. But what lies beneath the tough Israeli exterior we have met so far—meekness, sweetness, or frankly, as we shall see, a more complex set of psychic structures—is precisely the subject matter of this book.

The second question concerning the oppositional bent of the Israeli national character is, why should we care? Well, for Israelis, it's a matter of natural curiosity, a fascination with their own psychological makeup. But it is also a matter of survival. If they fail to take a long, hard look in the mirror and make the necessary adjustments, they will simply not survive as a nation. However, the world as a whole also has a stake in getting to know the Israeli mind. Just over a hundred years ago, at a time when Arab violence against the still-tiny Zionist community in Palestine was quite rare, an Arab nationalist by the name of Najib Azuri published a book in which he predicted that the Arabs and the Jews will fight over Palestine until one of them is defeated, and that the fate of the entire world depends on the outcome of that war. This he somehow prophesied before the world was a global village with permeable boundaries, social media, and WMDs. Today the world is far more vulnerable, and after several wars, peace treaties, intifadas, and more wars, the Arab-Israeli conflict is anything but settled.

In the post-9/11 world it's all too easy to imagine how the amalgamation of such factors as the West's continued, if partial, dependence on Middle East oil, the proliferation of biological, chemical, and nuclear weapons, the explosion of suicide terrorism and the absence of a foolproof defense against it, the Arab Spring with its counterrevolutionary Islamist threats and Shia-Sunni wars, a nearly nuclear Iran, and an assertively nuclear Israel could trigger at any moment a number of global-crisis scenarios. America would be involved in any such crisis, but little Israel, too—in taking a preemptive military action, in forcefully overreacting to an attack, or in pursuing policies fueling Arab hatred toward America and the West. Granted, the Palestinians, along with the Arab and Muslim states, hold another key to global stability, and the radical elements within them, including organizations such as Hamas, that refuse to recognize Israel's right to exist as a Zionist state are a huge threat. But Israel's behavior is far from perfect, and the failure to understand, anticipate, and influence its actions could exacerbate, if not create, a crisis of unprecedented proportions. This is no news flash, which is why no matter how much they vow to stay away from its political quagmire, all American presidents and countless other Western diplomats eventually end up getting involved in the perpetually moribund Middle East peace process.

Thus, to the extent that the oppositional character of the Israeli mind drives or shapes Israeli actions, reactions, or policies, it is imperative, for Israel's as well as for the world's security, that we understand it and learn how to deal with it. If you doubt that such a nay-saying mind-set may play a role in international affairs, consider the testimony of former American secretary of state James Baker. Referring to Israeli prime minister Yitzhak Shamir as Dr. No, Baker concedes in his memoir that his famous 1990 statement to Congress—that the Israelis should call the White House at 1-202-456-1414 when they were serious about peace—was primarily motivated by his anger with Shamir and his colleagues.

But there is much more to the Israeli mind than nay-saying, and much of it lies unconsciously beneath this prickly surface. And let's be more specific about the threat. In at least two areas, it is no exaggeration to say that in the next couple of years the Israeli national character, with its conscious and unconscious components, might actually determine what kind of a world we'll all inhabit in the twenty-first century. At the time of my writing, no one knows if the West's negotiations with Iran will slow down or stop its apparent race to develop nuclear weapons. Israel has made its objections to these negotiations clear and vowed to keep its military options open. Thus, in the next year or two, whether or not a deal is reached, the whole world will be watching Israeli behavior.

Will it launch a preemptive attack? Will the United States be able to influence the timing of such an attack or hold Israel in check? If not, how will Israel respond if Iran actually converts and deploys these weapons?

Second, coinciding with this developing situation, the Israeli-

Palestinian peace process has returned to center stage. In the fall of 2013 with the relentless John Kerry, the American secretary of state, at the helm, the United States appeared ready to propose its own framework for a final peace treaty. This was a first, and by all news accounts, both parties were feeling the heat, with Israeli leaders in particular attacking John Kerry in public. Another first added to the mix that year was the European Union's decision to ban all economic cooperation with West Bank settlements and to explicitly exclude them from all future cooperation agreements with Israel. In spite of this overall diplomatic escalation, or perhaps because of it, in the spring of 2014 the process collapsed. With both parties reneging on existing agreements, the Palestinian Authority reconciled with Hamas, and Israel suspended the negotiations. If this results in a functional PLO-Hamas government or other unilateral steps on either side, or even merely in the final collapse of the peace process, it may well trigger the kind of violent crisis that followed Bill Clinton's failed push for peace in 2000, and/or slam the door on a two-state solution once and for all. A version of this scenario we have already seen in the bloody, fifty-day war between Israel and Hamas in the summer of 2014 and in the subsequent Palestinian decision to join the International Court of Justice in The Hague in order to bring war crime charges against Israel. But even if John Kerry or his successor is miraculously able to resuscitate the negotiations and reach a final agreement, violent radicals on both sides will come out of the woodwork, as was the case in the aftermath of the Oslo Accords. Their actions and counteractions are likely to further destabilize the region, threaten American interests, and dominate the news. Thus, in either scenario, the Israeli course of action would have fateful geopolitical consequences. While in many ways the Jewish state continues to thrive, it is also a fact that since 1967, its large-scale military confrontations with the Muslim world have grown more complicated and often less winnable.

If you doubt that psychology plays a crucial role in Israeli policy, consider historian Tom Segev's findings a few years back when he revisited the 1967 war. Reviewing newly released government documents, Segev's 2007 book, *1967: Israel, the War, and the Year That Transformed the Middle East,* shows that in deciding to go to war in 1967, the Israeli government broke its own series of well-debated strategic resolutions to the contrary. Concluding that in firing the first bullet the Israeli government acted primarily on emotion and impulse, Segev told me shortly after his book came out that the causes of the Six-Day War "were all about psychology."[1]

Needless to say, the Israeli mind is not all about war and peace. Indeed, in recent years Israelis seem to have become bored with, or more accurately exhausted and exasperated by, these hitherto unremitting preoccupations. I suspect the apathy many of them profess is a veneer, a barely disguised defense against the anxiety evoked by the geopolitical trajectory of the Jewish state. But regardless, this book will also account for the disproportional impact Israelis are having on the shape of our world in fields as diverse as art, business, medicine, literature, high tech, music, and science. In all these areas, the unique and complex idiom of the Israeli national character is clearly at play.

THE OLD BABY AND AN UNFORTUNATE EXCLUSION

At the heart of the Israeli national character lies a paradox, best captured by Israeli psychoanalyst Emanuel Berman, who described Israel as an old baby.[2] On the one hand, Israel embodies the continuation of Jewish history, indeed, the culmination of two thousand years of yearnings for resumed sovereignty in the biblical homeland. The Israeli character is clearly a product of this history. On the other hand, the Zionist movement rebelled against this very history and rejected the exile psychology it produced. Bringing extraordinary effort and resources to the task, it consciously set out to create a "new Jew," in many respects the polar opposite of his predecessor. By all accounts, the Zionist experience of the last 120 years, including the last six decades of Israeli sovereignty, has done just that. It also created a new type of Jewish environment that continues to reinforce the new creature. Israel is thus a young, growing society, uniquely weighted by centuries of collective memory. A leitmotif throughout *The Israeli Mind,* the effect of this paradox on the Israeli national character, will manifest in each of the book's chapters.

Lastly, there is the question of the Arab Israelis, who historically and psychologically stand outside this paradox. Caught in their own web of historical contradictions, and unquestionably deserving a psychological exploration of their own, they, too, have influenced and have been influenced by the Israeli mind. While this book will touch on their contribution, by and large they will be excluded from the narrative. This unfortunate exclusion is by no means to suggest that they are any less Israeli than their Jewish counterparts. Rather it is merely a reflection of the author's ignorance and limited capacity for research and analysis. Having said that, from a political standpoint it would hardly be unfair to accuse the author of a bias, in that he apparently views Israel as primarily a Jewish state. Well, this may not be consistent with democratic sentiments, but for now, the reality is that Israel is controlled by Jews, that this state of affairs was, and will always be, the essence of the Zionist enterprise, and that Israel's behavior as a state as well as its oversize influence abroad is driven predominantly by the psychological makeup of the Jewish Israeli. It is also the case that some of this psychology has been observed in Arab Israelis. Egyptian and Jordanian Arabs, for example, are said to liken Israeli Arabs to Israeli Jews along such negative stereotypes as rude, noisy, entitled, and supercilious.[3] To the extent that such influences persist—with positive dimensions undoubtedly also in the mix—it would be consistent with a more egalitarian political vision of Israel, of the kind proposed, for example, by political economist Bernard Avishai in his book *The Hebrew Republic*. Avishai would like to see an Israel that is secular, with a strict separation of church and state and full equality of rights to religious and ethnic minorities, and yet one that rests on the dominant tradition of European Jewish history. On the flip side, such an Israel would likely be even more receptive and susceptible to external cultural influences from its Arab neighbors, which in the long term may weaken the impact of the dominant, Western Jewish tradition on the Israeli mind. It certainly says something about the Israeli mind that you can't even discuss its psychology without descending into the quagmire of politics. Or in the words of novelist David Grossman when discussing his quintessential Israeli novel *To the End of the Land* with *The New York Times*, "Politics is like acid here. No matter how many protective coatings you put on yourself, it eats through them."[4]

ONE

WHO IS AN ISRAELI?

When I was nineteen, the Israeli Defense Forces sent me on a special mission. It was 1976, and I had just finished my basic training and a short tour in the Gaza Strip. Together with another soldier, a recent immigrant from Iran, I was assigned to manage a philanthropic "library" housed in an old Arab building in the Yafo section of Tel Aviv. The library was the brainchild of a seventy-year-old, retired army officer who, as he himself put it, "decided to continue to serve" as long as possible. Working as a volunteer, he provided all interested IDF units a free monthly delivery of books and magazines. Telling the world he was purchasing the publications, the old man—our boss—actually had an arrangement with a national distributor to pick up discarded foreign-language residuals at no cost. Thus, every month we would package and dispatch dozens of boxes containing a strange admixture of challenging European classics and bubbly American magazines: Nabokov's *Ada* and James Joyce's *Finnegans Wake*, along with *Woman's Day*, *Family Circle*, and *Good Housekeeping*.

But these were merely the cover—literally and figuratively—for what was at the heart of our highly popular book packages: *Playboy, Penthouse, Hustler,* and a couple of hard-core German publications, reserved for high officers and other favored visitors. When senior officers would drop by for a visit, the old man, who was also a veteran of the French resistance in World War II, would open a bottle of pinot noir before sending them off with their own personalized packages. There were also *Playgirl* magazines, but those our boss found too distasteful to distribute, so they just sat, collecting dust in a hidden back room. These were the butt of our jokes because, once a month, when we picked up the magazines from our supplier's warehouse, we would stop and chat with one of its employees, a young Arab man whose job was to go through all the *Playgirl* magazines and, page by page, blot out with a black marker all male genitalia. But one day we arrived at the warehouse to find that our buddy had lost his job, his services no longer needed. The distributor had lost a lawsuit brought on by the Israeli equivalent of NOW, which claimed that Israeli women were paying the full cover price for the magazine and were therefore entitled to the full product.

This improbable but true story captures a moment of great change in Israeli society. The decline in idealism and military heroism among the younger generations, the increasing influence of Western values and lifestyle, and the Israeli version of the feminist revolution are all here. All have been discussed by Israeli sociologists as the forces that radically transformed Israeli society in the 1970s. And the story's main characters—an idealistic yet corrupt European gentleman; an intellectualized, young, Ashkenazi sabra; a struggling, new immigrant; a self-effacing Arab; along with a supporting cast of testosterone-driven soldiers and officers, some religious, many from North African or a multitude of other ethnic backgrounds—tell the story of the particular fragmentation that characterized Israeli society at that time. Divided along cultural, religious, ethnic, class, and political fault lines, none of these people would normally affiliate with each other.

But the truly strange thing about this story is that it's not strange at all. Indeed, the twin themes of *change* and *fragmentation* have been a constant throughout Zionist history. Pick any decade and both will be there. The immigration of almost a million people from the former Soviet Union in the 1990s, for example, links both themes. That population shift would be the equivalent of the United States absorbing within several years some 35 million immigrants who speak no English and have a unique lifestyle, culture, and ethnic identity. Indeed, in a few short years, the Russian immigration drastically changed the face of Israel and added a new element to its fragmentation. American journalist Richard Ben Cramer described at least six distinct subgroups within the Israeli population: the Ashkenazi sabras, born in Israel from European families, the Sephardim who originally came from Arab countries, the Russians, the Ashkenazi ultraorthodox, the Sephardic ultraorthodox, and the West Bank settlers. These are further divided along socioeconomic, cultural, and, of course, political lines. As Cramer point out, some of these "tribes" generally don't talk to each other, and some even have their own language and media.[1]

"'Who is an Israeli?'" says sociologist Oz Almog, "is a very Israeli question." But, whereas for the political scientist or sociologist this question is about how Israel is changing, or about the characteristics of the various subgroups, the psychological inquiry is about the effect of change and fragmentation on individual—and national—character development.

WAR, PEACE, AND OTHER CYCLES OF CHANGE

Perhaps the best metaphor for change and how Israelis are affected by it was provided by the second Palestinian intifada (2000–2005), during certain periods of which suicide bombings took place almost daily deep inside Israel's population centers. In a typical sequence of events, a Palestinian bomber would detonate himself in a crowded Israeli café, shopping mall, or market; blood and pieces of human flash would splash across tables, clothing racks, or trees; emergency police and medical teams would arrive to evacuate the injured and dead; media vans with television cameras and journalists would appear; special, religious SWAT teams would collect body parts and tissue residues; cleaning crews would wash floors, walls, and furniture; and in a short time, sometimes within a day or two, the establishment would open its doors for business as usual as if nothing had ever happened.

Amplified, this dramatic sequence of change from ordinary, if boisterous, street life to terror, destruction, and death, and back again, is the story of war and peace in Israeli and Zionist history. The sense of today's Tel Aviv—vibrant, sophisticated, sensual, cultured, and securely self-indulgent, indeed, one of the top beach-city tourist destinations in the world—is vastly different from that of the frightening days of that last intifada, when hotels were deserted, their elevators shut down, and their walls covered with rust. Today's buoyant mood was nowhere to be seen amid the then-omnipresent feelings of dread and despair.

Of course, this was only one chain in the cycle of war and peace that has settled upon the Holy Land since the early decades of the twentieth century. Starting in the 1920s, with almost predictable intervals averaging in the single digits in number of years, a major, violent conflict erupted. Some wars dramatically changed the country's size and borders. Some exposed the average Israeli to whole new populations and cultures. Some ushered in an era of self-confidence and euphoria; others announced a time of self-doubt and annihilation anxiety. Some defined young Israeli soldiers as selfless, genuine heroes; others cast them as the oppressors of women and children. Some wars resulted in unity, others in division. Some were only seen on television; others exploded deep in the midst of civilian life. Some triggered political change; others entrenched incumbent powers. Likewise, each period of stability or peace brought its own change. Some saw the loss of land, others the expansion of settlements. Some triggered religious revivals; others allowed for the rise of secular liberalism. Some led to dramatic economic expansion, others to increased international isolation, economic stagnation, and social unrest. Some such periods were accompanied by negotiations, others by the pursuit of unilateralism. Some rekindled feelings of hope and held up the possibility of genuine reconciliation; others proved illusory, merely increasing mistrust of Arabs or the world at large.

A similar cycle of change has characterized the Zionist enterprise from the start in terms of population. The pre-Zionist immigrants to Palestine were mostly disciples of European rabbis and persecuted Jews motivated largely by religious zeal and messianic ideas. The Zionist immigration waves that started at the end of the nineteenth century consisted mostly of fiercely secularist Jews, many influenced by the socialist vision, who sought to work the land and establish agricultural communities. While each of these waves had a unique signature—one dominated by German professionals, others by able-bodied Russians who founded various paramilitary units—these were still mostly European Jews. But in the first few years after the declaration of independence, when the Israeli population more than doubled, a majority of the new immigrants were Sephardic Jews from Arab and North African countries. Most of these were poor, many were uneducated, and a large number had been persecuted and forced to leave their homelands. Once in Israel, most had to live in tent cities for years, integrating slowly into Israeli society. Subsequent immigration waves were from North America, Ethiopia, South Africa, and France. These were much smaller but were nevertheless significant in altering the human landscape in many parts of Israel. Most recently, as noted earlier, was the huge Russian immigration of the 1990s.

The cycles of arrival and absorption of such diverse groups of immigrants repeatedly exposed both the previous and new immigrants to foreign cultures, languages, lifestyles, and values. Other equally dramatic population shifts over the years were caused by border changes and variable birth rates. The percentages of Arab Israelis and orthodox Jews within the population have significantly increased. Israel's largest city, Jerusalem, for example, used to have a large, secular Jewish majority. At present, only about 40 percent of the population consider themselves secular Jews, 35 percent are Arabs, and over 20 percent are religious, mostly ultraorthodox Jews.

In Jerusalem and elsewhere, not only the human landscape has changed so radically. As Amnon Niv, a Jerusalem city engineer in the 1990s attests, starting in the early 1970s, in one generation Jerusalem underwent the kind of architectural and physical transformation that takes most cities decades or even centuries to achieve. And the pace of building and development in many parts of the country continues unabated. Other important changes taking place in a few short decades included the revival of biblical Hebrew and the transformation of a quasi-socialist, collectivist society into an individualistic, American-style, free-market economy. Last but not least, a tiny, poor, and existentially threatened country quickly became an economic and military regional power with the capacity to destroy its enemies at will.

So what happens when you grow up with, live in, or immigrate to a world of constant, dramatic change? On the positive side, you become an expert in adapting to, and creating, change. You learn how to learn new skills, how to navigate new rules, how to deal with people very different from yourself, how to improvise, how to manage uncertainty, how to start a new lifestyle, if not a new life. You understand that conventions, organizations, and landscapes are temporal. You become aware of your cognitive and emotional reactions to such extreme conditions as threat and vulnerability, and also triumph and power. In this respect, being an Israeli is like going through interminable basic training for the global information age, which is all about making change your friend. This is one of the reasons that every other young Israeli you meet in New York City is an aspiring, accomplished, or failing entrepreneur. It's one of the reasons that a country whose population size ranks 101st in the world has produced about 125 companies, almost all high-tech, that trade on the New York stock exchange. That's more than any other country in the world except the United States and Canada.

But all this agility has a downside. Israelis don't particularly value general norms of conduct. They have a basic disrespect for plans, rules, and procedures, which means the existing order cannot be taken for granted. Israeli history can count on one hand the number of prime ministers who completed a full term in office. Each new wave of immigration brings to the country a large group of displaced, shell-shocked individuals who for a long time try to decipher the erratic rules of a new land that often greets them with suspicion. The natives, recent immigrants themselves, often don't know whether to admire or pity the new arrivals, and how to relate to their culture and traditions. Similarly, each new wave of construction in the West Bank is met inside Israel proper with doubt and ambivalence: Are these the true heirs of our Zionist heroes of yesteryear or a band of lunatics, fanatics? And, of course, questions of basic identity are inner-, not outerbound. Are we a David or a Goliath? A small, powerless people struggling to outsmart the hostile powers surrounding us or a nation of aggressive warriors subjugating our helpless neighbors? Is this our permanent and only homeland, the one place where Jews can feel safe from persecution, or merely another brief and unsustainable episode of Jewish sovereignty? In other words, the negative flip side of adaptability is emotional and cognitive instability.

THE PROFESSOR AND THE TAXI DRIVER

A Hebrew University professor recalls how in a recent memorial service for a relative, a family member spoke of the deceased's love for the Bible. He cited the story of Ishmael, considered by Muslims their biblical ancestor, and how Abraham cast him away. It was a clear, liberal-left allusion to how the Israelis mistreat the Palestinians now. Soon thereafter, another family member stood up and countered with his own speech, about the deceased's love for the biblical sites of the Land of Israel. The same basic discourse, perhaps in a less rarefied form, is likely to take place every time you enter a taxi or board a bus anywhere in Israel. The radio will blast the latest news or perhaps music, but either way, the cabby or a fellow passenger will spew something to the effect of "These goddamn *yefey nefésh*" (essentially "bleeding-heart liberals") or "These frigging settlers."

In addition to the "tribal" fragmentation noted above, Israeli society is split along several other dimensions that overlap only to an extent with those subgroups. Chief among them in everyday Israeli consciousness is the political, left-right divide. While this type of split is commonplace in many democracies, in Israel, politics is intensely personal. Of course it is. Whereas in most countries the outcome of the political debate determines what kind of a state you get to live in, in Israel, it determines whether you get to live. Finally, Israel is a small place with an interpersonal culture of permeable boundaries—your business is everybody's business—so you simply can't escape the political. In a gossipy tidbit of conversation, an Israeli friend recently denounced a mutual acquaintance that he last saw many years ago as "literally the most despicable human being I've ever known." But he then added, "His only redeeming feature is his politics."

Another remarkable aspect of the Israeli political divide, one that is perhaps unparalleled among the nations, is that it's thousands of years old. Embedded in the social fabric of Jewish, Zionist, and Israeli history, it is breathed in from birth by every Israeli baby. As the eminent, late Israeli philosopher Hugo Bergman observed, Judaism has always had two competing trends: a loving, forgiving one, and a separatist, combative one; one seeking to please the gentiles and one hostile to them. In antiquity, the conflict was between those favoring accommodation with the neighboring imperial powers and those advocating full independence. In biblical narrative, for example, the prophets Isaiah and Jeremiah furiously denounced any foreign policy that failed to accommodate the regional superpowers, prophesying it would bring about national destruction. The book of Kings, on the other hand, condemned King Manasseh, who ruled Judea for almost half a century, for his sinful appeasement policy toward the Assyrian empire.

This division continued even after the destruction of the Second Temple and well into the history of the Jewish Diaspora. Many rabbis who lived after the anti-Roman Bar Kokhba rebellion of 132–35 CE, which resulted in the final extermination and exile of the Judean Jews, accused Bar Kokhba of being a false messiah. Other rabbis, as well as many of their followers, considered Bar Kokhba a hero of biblical proportions. The subsequent heated debate over the idea of a messianic return to national sovereignty in Jerusalem yielded the then-famous Talmudic Sanhedrin curse of "Blasted be the bones of those who calculate the date of the coming of the Messiah."[2] This debate continued through the Middle Ages and beyond, often focusing on how to respond to the humiliation and persecution of the Jews in the Diaspora. While a majority supported leaving matters in God's hands so as not to provoke the czar's wrath, some always called for more militant action. Some rabbis would speak of the glory of armed rebellions, going as far as sanctioning the use of arms on the holy Sabbath.

For most of the last two millennia, Diaspora Jews navigated this political divide from a position of powerlessness. This rendered the debate rather hypothetical. But as we now know, while vastly out-numbered by its enemies, the Yishuv, the Jewish community in pre-1948 Palestine, and certainly the Jewish state that emerged from it, were nothing if not powerful. In fact, Israel today is more like the Assyrian, Babylonian, or Egyptian empires of antiquity. In its regional hegemony, with its military, economic, and diplomatic resources it has dominated the lives of millions of its neighbors for the past four decades. In other words, once the Zionist dream materialized, the debate over how to exercise power became less hypothetical and more consequential. Therefore, it has become even more intense.

The Zionist story is punctuated by dramatic flashpoints that both highlighted, and hardened, the right-left political gulf embedded in the national consciousness. These confrontations included unresolved accusations, criminal charges, public investigations, political upheaval, academic papers, and never-ending press reports. Each generated multiple subplots often lasting for decades; some have continued to be referred to in the public discourse all along; others have been rediscovered by subsequent generations.

In the early 1930s, left-leaning leaders of the Yishuv negotiated complex "transfer" agreements with the Third Reich that would allow German Jews to emigrate to Palestine in exchange for increasing German exports to the area. The right-wing Revisionist opposition rejected any contact with the Nazis, and its press rebuked the Jewish Agency as "Hitler's allies." The leftist establishment counterattacked, with Chaim Weizmann, later Israel's first president, likening the Revisionists to "Hitlerism in its worst form," and David Ben-Gurion, later Israel's first prime minister, referring to Revisionist leader Ze'ev (born Vladimir) Jabotinsky as "Vladimir Hitler."

Among those condemned by the Revisionists was Haim Arlosoroff, head of the political department of the Jewish Agency, who had reportedly gone to Berlin to pursue a transfer agreement with the Germans. On the evening of June 16, 1933, Arlosoroff took a walk with his wife on a Tel Aviv beach, where he was confronted by two men who shone a flashlight on his face, pulled a gun, and shot him. The Labor Party accused the Revisionists of the murder, and the entire affair became a hot-button issue in Israeli society for many years. Forty-nine years after the murder, the right-of-center Begin government established an official commission of inquiry to determine the truth of the allegation. The commission uncovered no evidence, and the murder remains a mystery to this day.

In the 1940s, the Yishuv debated how to oppose British restrictions on Jewish immigration to Palestine and how to advance the cause of independence from British rule. The right advocated armed resistance, the left, negotiations. For a while, the left, represented by the establishment's security forces, the Haganah (Hebrew for "defense"), cooperated with the rightist underground, or, some would say, terrorist, organizations, Etzel and Lechi (National Military Organization and Israel Freedom Fighters, respectively). But after Lechi assassinated British minister Lord Moyne in 1944, the Haganah launched a full-scale attack on both Lechi and Etzel. The ensuing epoch, the Sezon—from the English *season,* referring to the hunting season in Britain—during which the Haganah turned over fellow Jews from the Etzel and Lechi to the British, has left indelible and personal scars in the minds of an entire generation of Israelis. To this day, right-wing politicians invoke the horror of the Sezon when they feel ganged up on by lefties.

The other momentous confrontation of that decade took place in the early days of the Jewish state and its War of Independence, when an Etzel ship, loaded with several hundred Jews of military age and large quantities of French weapons, arrived in Tel Aviv. While Etzel and Ben-Gurion negotiated over whether the underground organization would get to keep some of the weapons, a shooting broke out between their forces. As a result, the vessel, *Altalena,* burst into flames, killing scores of Etzel recruits and destroying some of the cargo. In the aftermath, Ben-Gurion abolished the Etzel and imposed unity on all the Jewish armed forces. But the *Altalena*'s huge, burnt shipwreck continued to protrude from the Mediterranean some thirty yards from the beach just outside Tel Aviv for many months, an undesignated, ugly, and ominous memorial. Even after it disappeared into the sea, the *Altalena* remained an open wound and a potent symbol in the minds of many Israelis. A cautionary tale about the danger of civil war for all, for the left, it represented a violent attempt to overthrow an elected government, while for the right, yet one more incident of Jews turning on their own.

In the 1950s, Israel was engulfed in a series of stormy debates over whether to accept financial restitution for the Holocaust from Germany. The Labor government was in favor, but the opposition from the right was fierce. While the bill was being debated in the Knesset, or parliament, opposition supporters attacked the building. They broke windows and threw stones into the chamber, injuring at least one member of parliament. Menachem Begin, head of the opposition, was said to have called on the demonstrators to "resist the Knesset," at which point Prime Minister Ben-Gurion called in the army. Ultimately, Ben-Gurion ordered the army to withhold fire even as demonstrators made their way into the building. Later in the day, he denounced the protest as an attempt to destroy democracy.

In the 1960s, Israelis were united by the fear of war and the euphoria of victory. The 1967 war, however, sowed the seeds for the great divide of the future. The land-for-peace versus the Greater Israel battle, which would dominate Israeli politics for decades to come, erupted only months after the war. In the 1970s, war once again briefly united the people. But together with rising socioeconomic and ethnic tensions, which the right successfully attributed to corruption among the Labor elite, the 1973 war brought about a political *mahapach* or revolution, which catapulted the right's long-standing leader, Menachem Begin, into the prime ministership. It was the first time in Zionist and Israeli history that the left-of-center Labor was out of power. Its supporters and other lefties, altogether about half of the people in the country, were stunned and fearful for many months.

The 1980s witnessed several national traumas that added more than their fair share to the discord. In 1982, as part of the peace treaty with Egypt, the government dismantled the Sinai settlement of Yamit. A small number of settlers refused to evacuate. They barricaded themselves on rooftops and for several weeks hurled burning tires and bricks at soldiers who had been their brethren and protectors. While the removal was ordered by the Begin government, many in his camp felt betrayed.

The left experienced its own traumatic moment less then a year later, during Israel's invasion of Lebanon. Following the Sabra and Shatila massacre, in which Lebanese Christians murdered hundreds of Palestinian refugees in an area under Israeli control, an official Israeli commission of inquiry strongly criticized Defense Minister Ariel Sharon for his conduct. On February 10, 1983, as the Begin government convened to discuss the commission's report, Peace Now mounted a demonstration calling for Sharon's resignation. A crowd hostile to the demonstrators gathered and heckled them. This not atypical confrontation took a tragic turn when one of the counterdemonstrators threw a hand grenade into the Peace Now group, killing one of its members and wounding several others.

The young man killed, Emile Grunzweig, was a graduate student in political science. In his master's thesis, submitted three days before his death, Grunzweig quoted philosopher Karl Popper's statement that "the great tradition of Western rationalism is to fight our wars by means of words not swords." Grunzweig then noted,

"This sentence expresses the faith that without universal standards for rational choice among competing propositions, the speaker becomes the only source of authority for his own proposition, and a resolution of the conflict can be achieved only by annihilating or silencing adversary spokesmen." For the Israeli left, Grunzweig instantaneously became a heartbreaking example and an icon of the right's proclivity to fight with swords rather than words.

The Lebanon war, conceived officially as a limited offensive against the PLO north of the border, escalated into a complex and lengthy engagement, lasting for eighteen years. Considered by the left as Israel's first clear war of choice and its own Vietnam, it continued to divide Israelis for many years.

In the late 1980s, the first Palestinian intifada pitted young Israeli soldiers against mass, sometimes violent, often even younger, Palestinian demonstrators. Civil disobedience, rock throwing, stabbing, and one case of lynching by the Palestinians were met with beatings, tear gas, and live ammunition from the Israeli side. Watching daily on television and hearing about these personal clashes between their sons, brothers, or grandchildren and the civilian Palestinian population in the West Bank and Gaza tore Israelis apart along the historical political fault lines. Things got even worse in the early 1990s as a new Labor government, headed by Yitzhak Rabin, revealed it was secretly and illegally negotiating with the PLO—an anathema to most Israelis at that time. These negotiations led to the signing of the Oslo Accords, which set in motion a process that was supposed to culminate in the establishment of a Palestinian state in the West Bank and Gaza. The right condemned, protested, and raged. When Palestinians opposed to the agreement carried out a series of suicide bombings across the country—at the time, a shockingly novel type of terrorism for Israelis and the Western world—all hell broke loose. Agitated, incendiary rhetoric was followed by a virulent and now reciprocal cycle of blame.

But the pain and drama of these confrontations paled in comparison to what transpired on the evening of November 4, 1995, at a peace rally in Tel Aviv and in its aftermath. At the end of the rally, a slender, yarmulke-wearing young man—a brilliant law student and a zealous opponent of the Oslo Accords—approached the poorly protected soldier-turned-peacemaker Rabin and fired three shots at his back from close range. The confirmation of the prime minister's death shortly thereafter touched off an unprecedented wave of grief along with unparalleled levels of rancor and polarization in Israeli society. The assassination cost Labor the government, and as pointed out by, among others, American president Bill Clinton, quite likely put an end to the peace process. A full decade after the assassination, the Israeli high court—in a decision that impressed many as emotionally driven—ruled that the murderer, unlike other dangerous prisoners serving a life sentence, would not be allowed to consummate his relationship with his fiancée.

The next major confrontation took place prior to, and during, Israel's unilateral withdrawal from Gaza in 2005. The usual large demonstrations came this time from the right. There were also political complications, such as the loss of a majority for the government in the Knesset. But these failed to stop Prime Minister Sharon from executing the withdrawal, and for several long days during the heat of August, the entire country was transfixed by television images of Jewish soldiers forcibly evicting Jewish settlers and dismantling their homes. These scenes showed troops dragging screaming settlers from houses and synagogues, and other settlers blocking roads and setting fires. One West Bank settler set herself on fire near a Gaza checkpoint, and some settlers reportedly had their children leave their homes wearing the Star of David, to associate the actions of the government with Nazi Germany.

Watching all this on television, left-leaning political scientist Yaron Ezrahi told me at the time that the settlers' resistance to the

Gaza evacuation was merely a reality-television show, enacted as a preview and a warning for what would happen if and when Israel decided to withdraw from the West Bank. Indeed, should this come to be, the confrontation between the military and the fifty thousand or so far-right settlers, who appear to be committed to violent resistance, and their growing support within the military command structure, might well reach a new peak in this long, ancient story of fraternal strife and divisiveness.

In light of this history, it is hardly surprising that many Israelis on both sides of the political map agree on only one thing, which is that they have nothing in common with each other. But paradoxically, because both groups have emerged from the same polarized environment, they do, in fact, have a great deal in common in their psychological makeup. To grow up or even just reside in such a divided society means to strongly identify with one side, usually the one you are most exposed to through such role models as parental figures and peers. This identification starts with emotions, not thoughts, as we all tend to imitate, stay close to, and cast our emotional lot with those we depend on, biologically and socially. In a society such as Israel's, it is further reinforced when, to counter the fundamental uncertainty they live with, Israelis on both sides of the divide endow their political positions with just the opposite, a sense of unquestioned certainty. The fight-flight, or anger-and-fear, response set is reactivated with every new war or terror attack. It's no longer right and left or even right and wrong; it's all-good and all-bad. In psychological terms, this is the defense mechanism of splitting and projection: you protect yourself from internal conflict by attributing one part of it to your opponent. So if going to war might protect your country from the risk of a first strike by the enemy, but may risk the lives of its young soldiers, you internalize the latter risk, project the former onto your opponent, and declare him a paranoid, warmongering sociopath; you, of course are a rational, peace-seeking defender of humanity. Or, you internalize the former risk, project the latter onto your opponent, and judge him to be a naïve, quivering, girlie man, and yourself, a realist, a security-minded tough guy. From here, it's a short road to a you-are-either-with-us-or-against-us psychic typography and a more generalized black-and-white view of the world.

On top of this emotional blueprint, cognitions, or thoughts, are tacked on. In the case of the Israeli mind, this means building a strong, logical argument to support your already passionate predisposition, populating it with classic, historical sound bites, conveniently selected to fit your narrative and destroy your opponent's. When the two sides then meet once and again in the no-exit vortex of opinions and facts otherwise known as the national debate, the unremitting intensity of their confrontations only further sharpens their hearts and minds, rendering the typical Israeli an expert, a true believer, a spokesperson, and spinner-in-chief on all matters right and left.

Another way to account for this polarization is by means of Freud's concept of reaction formation. Whereas the splitting and projection mechanism is more common in group psychology, reaction formation, a developmentally more sophisticated defense, belongs to the psychology of the individual. With this defense mechanism, you so desperately wish to submit to the enemy's demands so as to arrive at safety and tranquillity that you are fearful of your own desire and must assume the opposite stance. You thus become a hypervigilant security hawk. The right is thus conceptualized as the bully who is fearful of his inner wimp. Or, you are so eager to wipe out your enemy from the face of the earth so as to achieve safety and tranquillity, you are terrified of your own aggression and must escape into the opposite, antiwar mentality. This defense is akin to the yin/yang element of classical Chinese philosophy, according to which the whole is divided into two opposing but equal forces, and stability depends on the balance between the two. Indeed, like a husband and a wife who complain about each other's deficiencies but compensate for and thereby enable them, the relentless juxtaposition of the opposing views merely serves to reinforce them, as each side reacts in backlash to the other. We will return to this momentarily, but note that, in this formulation, these two opposites contain and mirror each other as a wish and as a fear. The right would like nothing more than peace but is afraid to trust that desire, and the left would like nothing more than strength but is afraid of its own belligerence.

Regardless of how you conceptualize this, it should be clear that as a result of this historical and chronic polarization, the right and the left do have a great deal in common. Both sides clearly share a passionate and principled conviction in their own cause along with the capacity to advocate for it. Or viewed negatively, they share a rigid emotional stance, a narrow-mindedness of thought, and a lack of appreciation for nuance and complexity. Also, in a country where, in the words of *New York Times* correspondent Steven Erlanger, "everybody argues about everything," this divided identity is not limited to political polarization. While each of the religious, ethnic, cultural, and geographic divisions mentioned before possesses its own unique dynamic, all share, create, reinforce, and multiply the same dialectic of opposites, which is indeed evident wherever you cast a stone in the Holy Land.

CROSSING CHANGE AND FRAGMENTATION

So if constant change produces a highly adaptable but unstable identity, and ongoing fragmentation yields a passionate yet rigid one, what happens when you are exposed to both? Do you end up being adaptable and passionate, or rigid and unstable? Or perhaps another, more muddled mixture of both dimensions? Let's consider a couple of iconic examples, starting with a very Israeli Israeli, the late former prime minister Ariel Sharon. Depending on how you connect the dots, Sharon can clearly be seen as the quintessential *adaptable-passionate* Israeli. Sharon's passion for his muscular national-security and political philosophy jumps off the pages of any of his biographies. He led highly effective military campaigns as a general and defense minister, pushed the government to dramatically increase the buildup of settlements in the occupied territories, and vocally advocated for his vision of Greater Israel within and without the country. Undoubtedly, his accomplishments in these areas are attributable, in part, to the strength of his convictions and his single-minded dedication to the cause. Sharon's facility in creating, and adapting to, change was also legendary. In the 1973 war, he famously outmaneuvered the Egyptian army in a bold offensive, snatching victory from the jaws of defeat. In his postmilitary life, he created a new political party, merged it with an old one, only to found yet a new one years later, and in one of several major policy reversals, he oversaw the dismantling of the Sinai settlements once peace with Egypt was obtained. And after spending years in political exile, to which he was cast away by a shameful dismissal from the Defense Ministry post in the aftermath of the Sabra and Shatila massacre, he bounced back to become one of Israel's most powerful and popular prime ministers. In his personal life, too, he coped with several tragic losses only to rebound with new engagements time and again.

But a counternarrative to all this would be just as illustrative of the *rigid-unstable* identity formation. Sharon's narrow-minded, black-and-white view of the Israeli-Palestinian conflict played a role in the killings of countless Palestinian civilians, in violation of international law, in Jordan, Lebanon, and Gaza. In 1982, he led the Israeli government into a military adventure in Lebanon that ultimately proved to be a costly, tragic mistake. His West Bank settlements project, also pursued in contravention of international law, may yet prove to have irreversibly sabotaged a two-state solution, now the official policy goals of both the Israeli and

Palestinian establishments. All this exemplifies, hand in glove, the dark side of passion—fanaticism, rigidity, and extremism.

The unstable dimension in this narrative is best denoted by Sharon's attitude toward Gaza. For more than three decades, he had advocated holding on to and settling Gaza at any and all cost. Indeed, as late as 2004, he articulated this position by alluding to Netzarim, the tiniest, most remote, and most isolated Jewish settlement in Gaza. Like the rest of Gaza, Netzarim had none of the historical and religious significance of the West Bank. "The fate of Netzarim," Sharon declared, "is the same as Tel Aviv." Yet barely a year later, he withdrew from Gaza and dismantled all the settlements. The hasty, unilateral retreat resulted in a Hamas takeover and a radicalization of the Palestinian population, undermining both Israel's security and the prospects for peace.

So which is the real Sharon, the passionate-adaptable Israeli or the rigid-unstable one? Let's take another famous Israeli archetype, this time from the business, rather than political, world. At the age of thirty-nine, Shai Agassi was next in line for the position of CEO at SAP, the world's largest business-software company. While he had previously aspired to the top position, he left to pursue a fantastic vision described by Deutsche Bank analysts as having the potential to massively disrupt the auto industry and altogether eliminate the gasoline engine. In three years, during the worst economic downturn since the Great Depression, Agassi raised $700 million and sold the governments of Israel, Denmark, Australia, Hawaii, and California's Bay Area, among others, on a previously nonexistent business model for electric cars. Developed as a joint venture with the Renault-Nissan car-manufacturer alliance, Agassi's concept was based on the cell-phone service model. Consumers would own their own cars, but would have a service contract for the energy to fuel them, which required Agassi's venture to design and build not only the new electric cars but also thousands of automated battery-switch stations around the globe.

Had this grand project succeeded, it would surely have provided a brilliant display of the adaptable-passionate twin Israeli mind-set. By anticipating, recognizing, and adapting to transformative changes in the energy market and the geopolitical arena, Agassi concocted a far-fetched yet credible business concept. Through the strength of his convictions, his fervor, and his persistence, he convinced a few big-time business and government players to go along for the ride. At the time of this writing, however, it appears that the project has failed, so the annals of business might well judge Agassi's departure from SAP, where he was slated for the top job, to be the action of a less-than-steady individual. And his venture into the electric-car market may ultimately be viewed as the action of a fanatical, blind believer, a fixated builder of castles in the sky. In other words, the real Sharon, like Agassi, is both passionate and rigid, both adaptable and unstable. Whether the outcome of these dimensions is positive or negative, and in what combination, is a matter of interpretation, as well as a host of other variables such as personality, external circumstances, and luck. To one extent or another, this is true for all Israelis, including those not destined for such grand designs or accomplishments.

A personal example, certainly not a grand one, comes to mind from my early college days in America, a year or so after I arrived from Israel at the age of twenty-one. I had just found a part-time job as a doorman in a fancy San Francisco condominium and drove in on my first day on the job in my old, beat-up Ford Impala, which I had bought for $200. I entered the building garage but could not find a parking spot except for one under the security camera and the sign NO PARKING, TOW AWAY ZONE. Rationalizing that I would be manning the security monitor, I figured my car would be fine there, parked, and reported to the job. After a couple of hours of on-the-job training, my boss, the superintendent, noticed the car on the monitor in front of us. "Is this your car?" He pointed to the screen. Fearful of the consequences, I reflexively replied in the negative, only to quiver when the super told me to call the tow-away company and watched over me as I made the call, ordering the car to be towed away. So here we have an everyday example of the unstable, rule-breaking Israeli engaging in erratic, potentially self-defeating behavior. My adaptable side came into the picture when I finished the call and the super left, instructing me to alert him when the tow truck arrived. Improvisationally inspirated, I called an American friend who was on a lunch break from his job a few blocks away: "Come to the front desk in the lobby. Don't ask any questions, just pick up my car keys, go to the underground garage, and drive it away." Which he did—as I pushed the button to open the security gate for him and anxiously watched his hurriedly approaching figure in close-up on the monitor— literally seconds before the tow truck arrived. I then informed the super that the car had mysteriously disappeared, saving my job, if not my credibility.

In another car story, three years later, when I started graduate school in New York, I landed a part-time job in one of the Israeli companies dominating the airport car-service business in Manhattan. On my first trip as a limo driver, I took a couple from the city's wealthy Upper East Side to the airport. I had visited New York twice before and had never driven there, but embarked on this pre-GPS journey without a map and with only the vaguest of notions of how to get to JFK, one of the busiest airports in the world. After picking up the couple at their residence—late, because I first drove to the wrong address, going to 82 East Sixty-Fourth Street instead of 64 East Eighty-Second Street or something to that effect—I took a left turn, knowing I needed to head north. "Aren't you going to take York Avenue?" the man politely inquired. Before I had a chance to consider my response, he added, "Oh, I see what you're doing, never mind." That was helpful, and apparently my route was at least as good as his! I somehow found my way to JFK, but not before almost exiting at the wrong airport, a disaster averted by another gentle assist from my passenger. Once again, no Shai Agassi, but both unstable *and* adaptable even in the minor league of limo drivers.

As for the passionate-rigid dimension, a relative, an otherwise cultivated woman in her eighties, provides a telling example. Called on the eve of a national election by the office of the Chief Rabbinate to solicit her vote for the religious party of the chief rabbi's choice, she told the caller, "Tell the rabbi he can kiss my *tuchis!*" and hung up. Rudeness aside, if, like many Israelis, you consider the Chief Rabbinate an antidemocratic institution in charge of implementing and cementing the enforcement of religious law on secular Jews, this was merely an impassioned advocacy for freedom, a bold response against the oppressive forces of darkness. From a different perspective, however, *biased, closed-minded, intemperate,* or *fanatic* could be some of the choice words to describe her behavior.

The bottom line on Israeli identity is that it's extremely fluid. Israelis are bold, opinionated change-makers one day, spineless and unbalanced respondents the next. This is hardly surprising given the internal contradiction between the continuity of Jewish history and the revolutionary nature of Zionism. Nor is it surprising that this dialectic is not yet settled, for in the historical time frame of national development, Israel is merely an adolescent.

This fluidity highlights a larger question challenging the premise of this book: Is there such a thing as a national character in the first place? As anthropologist Clyde Kluckhohn and social psychologist Henry A. Murray put it, "A group can no more have a 'common character' than they can have a common pair of legs."[3] On the other hand, as pointed out by anthropologist Raphael Patai, even though there are only individual bodies, scientists study "the human body" and are able to make true and useful observations about it.[4] Thus, while struggling with this issue, many scholars agree that individuals from a cultural group can share a set of specific features—if not a group mind—which they have learned by being members of that group. Israeli political scientist Yaron Ezrahi offers a more subtle formulation: "National character is a spectrum phenomenon, consisting of shared memories and experiences, as well as a range of potential behaviors. The specific behavior displayed at a given moment is a function of the interaction between this spectrum and the external situation."[5]

This formulation can explain, among other things, the similarities between some national characters as well as what happens when they interact with one another. Remember the ridiculous, caught-on-camera power struggle between Israeli prime minister Ehud Barak and the Palestinian Authority president Yasser Arafat at the opening of the 2000 Camp David Summit, whose failure set the stage for the extreme violence of the second Palestinian uprising? With both men insisting "after you," refusing to budge, and literally pushing each other to enter the guesthouse first, they literally wouldn't move until President Clinton ultimately shoved them jointly through the doorway. If they even argued over a matter of courtesy, was it any surprise they didn't reach an agreement on Jerusalem and the refugees?

When you watch the occasional Israeli spokesperson debate his or her Palestinian counterpart on American television, they may or may not look alike, but they often act alike. Argumentative, combative, and self-righteous, they mirror each other in articulate but furious attempts to seize and occupy each other's and the viewer's ears. To the extent that these interpersonal interactions represent an aspect of the Israeli-Palestinian conflict as a whole, Ezrahi's definition is instructive in two important ways. First, the similarity between the two national characters is based only on one of the many behaviors in their respective spectrums.

And second, this potential behavior materializes only in certain circumstances, in this case, when confronting an opponent who shares the same potential behavior in his or her own national character. Ezrahi's definition also allows for the reality of opposite or contradictory traits within the same national character, which is critical to the understanding of the Israeli mind.

SPEAKING OF CONTRADICTIONS

Over the last decade or two, the rapid population growth among the ultraorthodox sector of Israeli Jews has dramatically sharpened the secular-religious split within Israeli society. "We hate the religious people," my then young, secular, American kids were shocked to hear from secular Israeli visitors who were explaining why they didn't want a rabbi to officiate their upcoming wedding. This fraternal hatred is often reciprocal, leading some scholars to ask whether Israel, by definition and inspiration both a Jewish and a democratic state, is getting the worst of both worlds. From a national character perspective, however, this hatred, like the other tribal rifts dividing the Israeli social landscape, merely disguises the similarities between the two camps. Indeed, as in the case of the political left and right with which they overlap to a significant extent, these camps produce and share the same identity dimensions discussed above. However, the fundamental incompatibility between democracy and state religion casts an even darker shadow on the Israeli psyche, and this contradiction goes to the heart of the question of who is an Israeli.

At first glance, it seems that both the religious and the secular tribes are blessed with an abundance of passion and rigidity but come up short on the adaptability and instability side of the equation—at least in relation to each other. Both have remained locked into their worldview, lifestyle, and geography and, if anything, have only become more polarized since the establishment of the Jewish state. Having said that, their relationship is profoundly symbiotic. The secular Israelis subsidize and protect their ultraorthodox brethren, who, by and large, do not work or serve in the military. They not only allow them to pursue religious studies or an ultraorthodox lifestyle, but also tether them to reality. The ultraorthodox, on the other hand, provide the secularists with a historical mirror, a reflection of their singular, ancient identity, without which there is little rationale for a Jewish state. The notion that Israel is a Jewish state is sacrosanct for the vast majority of secular Israeli Jews.

While this symbiosis serves to intensify both sides' resentments, over time it has also generated osmotic phenomena suggestive of a hopeful, if unusual, integration of the two extremes. For instance, in the days between Rosh Hashanah and Yom Kippur, when religious ritual requires daily repentance, praying between midnight and dawn, the mostly Arab Old City of Jerusalem is a staging ground for one of the most surreal Israeli encounters of the night. Starting at about 4:00 a.m., thousands of throbbing, singing, religious Jews stream down the narrow streets on their way to the Western Wall, while hundreds of secular Jews watch them from above as they partake in guided tours of the city's sixteenth-century walls and roofs. Meanwhile, merely thirty miles to the west, in the more secular city of Tel Aviv, Israeli families celebrate Yom Kippur with their own derivative of the religious prohibition on driving during the holiday. Over the years, they have turned the Day of Atonement into a festival of bicycle riding for children.

As improbable as these signs of religious-secular integration are, they reside at the core of the Israeli national character and are ubiquitous everywhere in Israel. For those social scientists who are skeptical of the concept of national character, this aspect of Israeli society offers a one-of-a-kind case study, at least in Western civilization. National character is formed not only by the internalization of child-rearing practices, moral values, norms of behavior, and lessons from social institutions and educational systems, all of which tend to share significant commonality for most individuals within a society, but also by the story a nation tells itself about itself. This includes the collective memory of historical events that precede the life of the individual, or more accurately, the collective interpretation of the collective memory of such events, which was interpretative from the start.

Now, unlike many other people, Israelis learn about their story, first, second, and third, from their book of books, the Bible. That book chronicles their presumed origins following the creation of the world. For virtually all Israelis, the study of the Bible commences before kindergarten, when it is taught through tales and songs of magic and miracles. From there it goes all the way through twelfth grade with a gradual evolution of perspective, and merging of geography, history, literature, and ultimately ethics, theology, and philosophy. Also, from the start, and at all levels of this academic journey, Israelis learn and talk about their story in the same ancient language that their book of books tells them about it. The dream of an integrated curriculum—an elusive goal for many American educators—is a reality, by means of compulsory Bible studies, in all Israeli, even Arab-Israeli, schools. And just in case students don't pay attention in the classroom, it all gets reinforced in an endless series of *tiyulim*, or school trips, to various biblical sites, some truly ancient, many merely named as such. Even if you are homeschooled, you can't quite avoid the official state holidays, the street, village, and town names, many of which, like the Hebrew calendar, are steeped in biblical etymology.

It is said that the fish is the last to know anything about water, and many secular Israelis don't appreciate—apart from what they

perceive as the external assault on their freedoms by state religion—
the depth of the religious waters they are born into and swim in.
Interestingly, a large 2009 public-opinion survey found that Jewish
Israelis hold what would appear to be a series of contradictory,
though sometimes integrated, views about the role of religion in
their lives: 80 percent believe in God, 51 percent say *Jew* best describes their identity, 41 percent say *Israeli* best describes their identity, 61 percent feel public life should be in accordance with Jewish
religious tradition, 68 percent say cafés and restaurants should
be open on Shabbat; and finally, 44 percent support preserving
democracy over Jewish law when there is a conflict, 20 percent think
Jewish law must always be followed, and 36 percent think sometimes one, sometimes the other should prevail.[6]

Notwithstanding, the extreme polarization of the ultraorthodox
and the secular tribes represents the ultimate existential threat to
the state of Israel, and no air strikes, special operations, computer
worms, or two-state solution can fix it. Because the lines between
the camps are so hard drawn, Israelis are particularly fascinated
by the occasional secular celebrity who embraces religious orthodoxy, or the lonesome son of a famed rabbi who converts to secularism. The words used by Israelis to describe the two phenomena,
khozer bet-shuva and *youtze be-she-ela*, respectively, reveal once
again the paradox embedded in the Israeli national character. The
former, literally meaning "returning to the answer," refers to coming back to God; the latter, the exact opposite, "leaving with a
question," refers to abandoning faith. Not coincidentally, both exist only in relation to God or religion, and the one who leaves it
has no answer, only a question. While posing questions is hardly
a less valid way of life than finding answers, in the Israeli case,
this questioning stands intrinsically in reactive relation to the
Jewish past, all of whose roads lead to God.

Israelis love to witness this phenomenon, and not only because it is often accompanied by celebrity scandals or painful family dramas. First, whichever side they are on, they feel validated when an opponent deserts the front lines and joins their forces. But on a less conscious level, it resonates with what they know but don't really want to think about, i.e., that deep inside, they, too, contain their own opposite.

This takes us back to Freud's concept of reaction formation and the Chinese yin/yang. Deep in his soul, the extreme secularist wants to believe, while the ultraorthodox wants to stray. But fearful of such desires, each resorts to fortifying his own extremism by attacking the other's, which in turn further reinforces his own. Nonetheless, like an authoritarian regime, extremism is unstable and can become its own opposite at any time—wholly consistent with the unstable dimension of the Israeli identity. But whereas with the religious divide the whole of this yin/yang is in fact rather stable, and the potential for a flip into the opposite is largely symbolic, the same cannot be said about the political divide. In response to Anwar Sadat's 1977 peace overture, Menachem Begin, one of the original security hawks and propagators of Greater Israel, agreed, virtually overnight, to dismantle settlements and return the entire Sinai to Egypt—all in exchange for "a piece of paper," which was how he had previously characterized the idea of a peace treaty. We already discussed Ariel Sharon's flip-flop, but now can also include that of Ehud Olmert, a decades-long Likudnik who had been to the right of Begin and voted in the Knesset against the 1978 Camp David peace accords with Egypt. Days before leaving the prime minister's office in 2008, Olmert offered the Palestinian president a deal that included Israeli withdrawal from the vast majority of the West Bank and additional land from within Israel proper, the dismantling of settlements, and a partial internationalization of East Jerusalem. And let's not forget that it was a left-leaning, semi-socialist government that in the aftermath of the

1967 war gave birth to the Jewish settlements in the West Bank and Gaza, in contravention of its own policies. More recently, it appears that the strong convictions of the Israeli left have been decimated by the second intifada, the relentless firings of rockets from Gaza, and the aftermath of the Arab Spring.

In all these cases, people with long-held, passionately felt dogmas converted to their opposites when confronted by a dramatic, external event—a genuine peace gesture, sustained violence, a threat of indictment, a victory at war, or a radicalization within the enemy's rank. At present, it appears that whereas Israel's official adoption of a two-state solution policy is a historical victory for the left, Israeli society as a whole has moved to the right—once again a telling paradox. But no matter how right wing and ideological it is perceived to be, any Israeli government, current or future, may well end up turning into its own opposite.

An Israeli friend recently recalled shopping at a small clothing store in an isolated village nestled deep in the French Alps. As he examined some of the country-style shirts on the shelves, two young Israelis passed by him speaking Hebrew. "Someone is actually buying these disgusting shirts," one of them sneered, failing to imagine a third Israeli could be in that spot. Well, he should have known better, because if nothing else, Israelis are big travelers, with Hebrew readily competing with German, Japanese, or Chinese as a language heard loudly everywhere you go. Whether a cultural remnant of Jewish displacement and the ancient, biblical journeys of Abraham, Jacob, and Moses, a reincarnation of the medieval concept of the wandering Jew, or merely the expression of the need to get away from their suffocating present-day environment, Israelis are always on the go. In the past two decades, many young Israelis have taken an extended overseas trip after finishing their military service. One psychological study reports that these youth are seeking not an external adventure but

rather an internal exploration. This is why they often choose remote Far Eastern and South American, so-called spiritual, destinations. Like these young "identity seekers," Israelis in general are
forever searching for the answer to the question of who is an Israeli. Given the fractured nature of Israeli society and its age—the
baby part of the old baby—this question shall remain unanswered
for a long time to come. The very search for identity is thus a central property of the Israeli mind. While the divided, fragmented
nature of Israeli society is of sufficient magnitude to generate such
a questioning of one's identity, several long-term, historical cross-
currents have additionally contributed to the confusion. For one
thing, in the last thirtysome years, Israel has been gradually
transformed from a backwater socialist country with an intensely
collectivist culture to an aggressively free-market one, with uninhibited individualistic leanings. Also, the European flavors imported to Palestine by the early Zionists have slowly but surely
been challenged if not replaced by the growing influence of all
things American. Last but not least, in the last two decades, the
number of Israelis viewing themselves, some for religious and
others for political reasons, as non- or post-Zionists has grown
significantly.

Israelis live in a small country where everyone is subjected to
the same dramatic swings of history and its molding influences.
In this highly interconnected society, only one or two degrees of
separation exist between you and everyone else. On top of that, Israelis are extremely interactive by nature. They are addicted to all
forms of communication and are among the highest per capita us-
ers of cell phones and computers in the world. Indeed, their country is the birthplace of many instant-messaging technologies. In
what must be a one-of-a-kind news story, a few years ago an Israeli driver was arrested for driving while talking on two cell
phones, holding the steering wheel, as it were, with his elbows. All

this is to say that even the greatest skeptics must concede that if national character, born out of a nation's history and how its people share it, did in fact exist, the Israeli mind would be a case in point.

TWO

IT'S EASIER TO CHANGE A SONG
THAN A CITY

T he Israeli mind is layered with two types of narcissism, at once complementary and clashing: the old, religious chosen-people variant embedded in Jewish psychology throughout history, and the new, miracle-in-the-desert Zionist variant, which has taken root in the Israeli mind in the more recent past. Both play a role in how Israelis interpret the world. To a large extent they are also responsible for Israelis' extraordinary record of achievements, as well as their failures and their persistent, potentially tragic denial of certain Middle Eastern realities. Finally, they are essential ingredients in the intense attachment Israelis have to their land.

The concept of the chosen people is sometimes advanced to describe or even explain the disproportional influence of Jewish thought and Jews throughout history. In truth, from their presumed inauguration of monotheism in Mesopotamia, through their cultural contributions during the Golden Age of Muslim rule in Iberia, to their list of individual game changers in every aspect of modern Western history, their outsize accomplishments do make you wonder. With such names as Einstein, Freud, Kafka, Disraeli, Mendelssohn, Spinoza, Mahler, George Soros, Jacques Derrida, Steven Spielberg, Billy Wilder, Henry Kissinger, Heinz Kohut, Milton Friedman, Karl Marx, Trotsky, Wittgenstein, Martin Buber, Robert Oppenheimer, Jonas Salk, Michael Bloomberg, Bruno Kreisky, Woody Allen, Arthur Miller, Ayn Rand, Rothschild, and of course Jesus, the full list is way too long and diverse to detail here, and these few do not even begin to be instructive as to the magnitude of the phenomenon.

Having said that, the notion of the chosen people is religious and historical, not sociological or demographic in origin. It is based on the biblical idea that because the Jews were the only people to have received the revelation of a universal God, the Jewish people and their land were at the center of world history. But as pointed out by Judaic scholar David Biale, the reality of biblical times was quite different. Judea was a provincial backwater whose destiny was controlled by the great superpowers and cultures to the north, east, and south. Had the Jews of biblical times had real power, they would have been challenged by those superpowers rather than have been left alone and would likely have followed the fate of the Assyrians and Babylonians. On the other hand, had they not developed a belief in their own greatness, they would have vanished like many other small nations. So as Biale put it, "Relative lack of power combined with a myth of power was perhaps one of the keys to Jewish survival in antiquity."[1] Along the same lines, economists Maristella Botticini and Zvi Eckstein trace Jewish success in the Diaspora to their very loss of sovereignty and the destruction of their holy Temple in the year 70 CE. According to this theory, when the high priests of Jerusalem were no longer able to read and study the written Torah in the Temple, in order to survive as a religion, the dispersing Jewish masses had to become literate. Using historical evidence, Botticini and Eckstein show that, over the centuries, becoming literate in a largely illiterate world allowed the Jews who did not convert to other religions to transition from rural farming to the professional and educational occupations of the towns and cites.[2] As implied by this analysis, the concept of the chosen people was compensatory in nature. This is sometimes acknowledged within the Jewish tradition, for instance, in the famous midrash—a rabbinical interpretation of a Torah portion—according to which the Jews were chosen after all other nations turned God down. That the Jews, when emancipated, have been overrepresented on so many measures of success can thus be seen not as testament to their having been chosen, but rather as a result of their immense compensatory drive to deny their insignificance and to take advantage of what they've learned from wheeling, dealing, and surviving in the margins of society. From a psychological perspective, this formulation fits neatly into our general understanding of narcissism, both healthy and pathological. Contrary to popular belief, the ambitious pursuit of success and status, the large dose of vision or grandiosity, and the well-developed sense of entitlement that characterize the high-achieving narcissist are not the consequences of excessive self-love. If anything, along with the self-confidence, exuberance, or even arrogance that accompany them, they are motivated by a relentless internal pressure to elevate one's low self-esteem and to gain acceptance and recognition from others. In that sense, narcissism is more about self-hate than self-love.

This compensatory model of the self applies not only to the historical Jewish notion of the chosen people but also to the basic Zionist premise of building the Jews a home of their own in their ancient homeland. Undisputedly, in less then one hundred years the Zionist movement transformed both a people and a land, building a vibrant and assertive first-world democracy in the middle of a hostile and challenged neighborhood. Today, relative to its size, Israel continues to boast many extraordinary accomplishments in fields as diverse as military, music, high tech, architecture, medicine, mathematics, literature, science, entertainment, and fine arts.

On the political front, the main pro-Israeli lobby in Washington—the capital of the West's sole remaining superpower—is one of the most powerful organizations of its kind in the world.

Yet, as every Israeli child is taught in grade school, the Zionist movement was born only after the Jews realized that they would never be fully accepted by European society. Indeed, Theodor Herzl, the founder of political Zionism, initially supported a complete assimilation of European Jews through conversion to Christianity and intermarriage. Only after he covered the Dreyfus Affair and the related anti-Semitic outbreaks in France as a journalist did he change his mind. This was the prototypical path to Zionism, and as pointed out by Israeli scholar Benjamin Beit-Hallahmi, it was reactive and defensive. In a sense, it didn't reflect a choice, or at least not a first choice. This was also the case for most of the Jews emigrating to Palestine and Israel in subsequent decades—by and large they ended up there because they escaped persecution or were rejected or expelled.[3]

The original Zionist vision was both grand and grandiose, and both the land in which the early Zionists started their enterprise and many of the trailblazers themselves did not always exude unalloyed promise. Referring to the idea of a Jewish state in Palestine, Herzl famously said, "If you will it, it is no dream." But even though most Jews at the time didn't seem to oppose Zionism, they remained indifferent to it, viewing it as fantastic and impractical. Whenever they felt they had a choice, the vast majority of Jews preferred to stay in the Diaspora rather than move to the ancient homeland. It was therefore hardly surprising that when Herzl presented his ideas to fellow Jewish journalist and Zionist-to-be Max Nordau, he reportedly asked Nordau to assess his sanity. According to some sources, at the end of the conversation, Nordau responded, "You may be mad, but if you are, I am as mad as you."[4]

Now if Herzl was a madman—or a visionary, to use the positive flip side of the word—what were the men and women who put his ideas into action? Who were the people who uprooted themselves from their European homes, families, and communities and moved to a desert-hot, swamp-filled, Arab-populated sliver of land, in order to create a state for the Jews there, practically out of nothing? While many were simple Eastern and Central European Jews fleeing persecution or poverty, history books depict a multitude of driven, colorful, and totally out-of-the-box leaders and trendsetters. Some rebelled against their parents and ran away from home to Palestine, and some sought to shed their Jewish identity and embrace a new Zionist one; some were swept away by socialist ideals and communist fervor; some sought spiritual redemption in the Holy Land; and some were looking for business opportunities in an undeveloped land.

There was A. D. Gordon, a white-bearded, Tolstoy-like farmer-preacher, who spread the gospel of manual labor and a return to nature in Galilee, and who became one of the founders of the labor movement; there was Manya Wilbushewitz, a young, spiritually tormented Russian woman, who galloped over the Galilee hills dressed in Arab garb, and who was one of the founders of a communal farm, an early version of the kibbutz; and there was Alter Levine, an insurance agent from America, who settled near Tel Aviv but traveled around the Middle East, setting up a chain of brothels where intelligence information desired by the approaching British army was obtained from clients through extortion.

As historian Tom Segev sees it, the people drawn to Palestine at the end of the nineteenth century "created a magical brew of prophecy and illusion, entrepreneurship, pioneerism and adventurism." Segev goes on to say, "The line separating fantasy and deed was often blurred—there were charlatans and eccentrics of all nationalities—but for the most part this period was marked by drive and daring, the audacity to do things for the first time. For a while, the new arrivals were intoxicated by a collective delusion that everything was possible."[5]

So these were the *Mayflower* immigrants of Israel, the people who by virtue of their character and culture shaped the values of the Israeli elite for several generations to come. For better *and* for worse what these pioneers had in common was the willingness to follow their own grand design, regardless of the obstacles presented by reality. Psychologically speaking, what united these early Zionists was a large dose of narcissism, which manifested in an all-consuming quest for the heroic, the exceptional, or the just-enough special. Many of these early arrivals were unusually gifted and keenly aware of that. This was perhaps best illustrated by the bizarre story of William Flinders Petrie, an Englishman considered by some the father of modern archaeology. Drawn to Jerusalem after excavating in Egypt and Palestine, he settled there in his old age. After he died, his widow had his head severed from his body, placed in a jar with formaldehyde, and shipped to London for a pathological examination intended to discover the secret of the dead man's genius.

But like the old Jewish narcissism, the early Zionists' drive for excellence had a strong compensatory flavor. In fighting to create a Jewish state, they sought to transform not only their external reality, but also their inner world. Psychologically, they wanted nothing more than to escape the self-image of the timid Diaspora Jew, which they had internalized during their formative years in the old European homelands. So intense was their drive for transformation that they had to ignore the obstacles presented by the reality on the ground. When this type of effort is successful, we call it vision, or positive thinking; when it fails, it's denial. On the fine line demarcating the two now rests Israel's fate, for this psychological defense mechanism, largely responsible for her success thus far, is also at the core of one of the most intractable aspects of the Arab-Israeli conflict.

In 1843, many years before the Zionists began to settle Palestine, an American preacher by the name of David Millard, who visited Palestine, wrote:

> Should the time ever take place when the Jews shall again possess the land of their fathers, a very important overturn must first take place with the nations and tribes that surround it. The land is at present inhabited by the native Arabs who till the soil and mainly people the towns and villages. The question arises, how are these inhabitants to be dispossessed of the land? Is a purchase contemplated? Who or what power is to enforce such a purchase, and where would the present inhabitants emigrate to? Or is it contemplated that they are to be driven out by the sword? This, I am convinced, is the only means by which the land can be cleared of its present population. But in this case, the native inhabitants would, of course, be driven back upon Arabia, which bends like a crescent round the south and east of the Holy Land. The present inhabitants would not thus be driven out without obstinacy and bloodshed, carrying with them at the same time, the most malignant inveteracy. From Arabia, aided by other tribes, they would sally from time to time, to ravage and lay waste the whole land.[6]

From where we stand now, this bitter prophecy cannot fail to amaze us. Yet, it should have been obvious to anyone with the scantest knowledge of Palestine at the beginning of the Zionist enterprise. In fact, the early Zionists did know that many Arabs lived in Palestine, but they denied its significance. For example, in 1918, Ben-Gurion and Ben-Zvi, later Israel's first prime minister and second president, respectively, published a book in which they acknowledged that more than a million Arabs lived in Palestine. They rationalized, however, that these natives did not feel at home there and showed no signs of connection to the land.[7] In a way, they continued to believe in the earlier Zionist slogan of bringing the "people without land to the land without people." Consistent with this notion, the very name the Zionists picked for their settlement, the Hebrew word *yishuv,* meant not only a settlement, but also the opposite of wasteland. And as if to blindly stare reality down, as early as the 1920s, Zionist leaders insisted on giving Hebrew names to exclusively Arab villages and towns.

While some view this as a cynical Orwellian or public-relations ploy mobilized to disguise Zionism's colonial intentions, from a psychological perspective a different problem is at work here. The Israeli mind's historical denial of Palestinian demographics and nationality is a manifestation of its general tendency to subjugate external reality to internal fantasy. One of the most poignant examples of this can be found in the story of Israel's all-time top-of-the-chart song, the beautiful, if sentimental, "Jerusalem of Gold." Written on the eve of the Six-Day War by legendary Israeli songwriter Naomi Shemer, the lyrics wistfully mourn the loss of the Old City of Jerusalem, captured by Jordan in 1948. The song's second verse laments the Old City's empty marketplace and dried up cisterns. It longingly notes that no one visits the Temple Mount or travels down to the Dead Sea through Jericho.[8]

The song sent shivers down every Israeli spine in the tense days of the "waiting period" that preceded the war. A fourth grader at the time, I was moved to write my own Jerusalem poem for the school newspaper. However, the lyrics of "Jerusalem of Gold" dispensed with the prosaic reality that the marketplace was not at all empty but rather densely populated with Palestinians. And that these inhabitants *were* drinking from the cisterns, praying in the Temple Mount, and traveling to the Dead Sea via Jericho. After the war, which saw the Old City falling into Israeli hands, the song-writer added a new verse to the original lyrics, celebrating the return to those places. In reality, to physically return to the marketplace, the Israelis had to displace Palestinians, which to some extent they did—for instance, by demolishing scores of Palestinian houses to create a large public square in front of the Western Wall. As Naomi Shemer herself said years later, it's easier to change a song than a city. Or put another way, it's easier to live in fantasy than in reality. Indeed, "Jerusalem of Gold" evinced no awareness of the bitter irony concealed in its title: the only piece of gold to be found in the stony Jerusalem skyline is on the Dome of the Rock mosque.

It's tempting to think this is all but a poet's prerogative to stretch the truth. However, the vast majority of Israelis who lived through the birth of this song actually bought into the denial, if not the fantasy, it embodied. I spent my first eighteen years on earth literally a couple of miles from "the marketplace" and it never occurred to me that Arabs were there. Not even when the Old City was "liberated," nor when "houses were demolished" near the Western Wall, did the people living there truly enter my consciousness. Furthermore, while some of my friends' families in Jewish West Jerusalem lived in beautiful, old Arab houses, no one ever mentioned that merely twenty years earlier these magnificent homes were inhabited or owned by Arabs who were now in refugee camps.

I was not alone in my obliviousness. Indeed, for more than four decades Israelis have known that if they continue to hold on to the West Bank and Gaza, the huge birthrate differential between Arabs and Jews will eventually catapult the large Arab minority into a majority. But they ignored this reality and launched a massive settlement movement, which slowly but surely put more than half a million Jews in Arab East Jerusalem and the West Bank. Perhaps the most dramatic illustration of the denial underlying that movement were the two crucial decisions taken by the Israeli government in the immediate aftermath of the 1967 war. Though warned by experts that the inclusion of the Muslim holy sites in the area to be annexed to Israel would sow the seeds for a future jihad, and that the Christian world would never accept the inclusion of the holy Christian places, after only a two-hour debate the government decided to go ahead with the plan. In retrospect it appears that this decision greatly contributed to the infusion of religious hostilities into what was previously largely a political conflict. In the 2000 Camp David summit, it proved to be one of the major issues, if not the main issue, blocking a potential political solution.

The second decision was reached a few days later, likewise with little deliberation. Rejecting a proposal to reunite Jerusalem by annexing East Jerusalem as defined by the previous occupier, Jordan—an area of merely seven square kilometers—the government chose to include sixty-four square kilometers, incorporating twenty-eight West Bank villages into the city and tripling its size. Once again ignoring warnings, government officials concluded that by building tens of thousands of housing units they would be able to stem the demographic tide and actually increase the Jewish majority in Jerusalem. But a high Arab birthrate and the Arab labor needed for all the new construction trumped their fantasy. Within forty years, the proportion of Arabs in the city went up from 18 percent prior to the annexation to 34 percent. And based on current birthrates, it is likely to reach 50 percent of the population within fifteen years.[9]

Over the years, the same vision, resistant to reality as it was, has spurred the settlement of the West Bank. Though not officially annexed to Israel, the facts on the ground created in the Palestinian heartland made its return to Palestinian control politically implausible, which was indeed part of the whole idea. But here, too, reality didn't quite bend to accommodate fantasy. Years of Palestinian resistance and violence, originating from Gaza and the West

Bank, ultimately brought home to the Israeli mind the ticking clock of the demographic differential. At present, most Jewish Israelis are beginning to realize that pretty soon they will have to choose between losing their government to an Arab majority and losing their imperfect democracy to an Apartheid-like system. According to Hebrew University expert Sergio DellaPergola, based on current demographic trends, by 2020 the population living between the Mediterranean and the Jordan river will have more Arabs than Jews.[10] Many Israelis, however, still rationalize it away or simply avoid thinking about it, unable, so it seems, to acknowledge the limited power of mind over matter.

Of course, there have always been exceptions: the Hebrew author who warned as early as 1913 that the vast Arab majority already ruled the land and that mutual hatred was all but inevitable; the government minister who opposed the decisions over Jerusalem, warning that an anticolonial twentieth-century world would never accept such an expansion; a journalist who reported on third-generation Palestinian refugees who had never stepped foot in Yafo but were just as attached to it as Israelis were to Tel Aviv or Kinneret; and the usual smorgasbord of leftists, pacifists, and radicals who objected to the occupation principally on moral grounds. But these were largely the exceptions that proved the rule. Even now, when many more Israelis acknowledge the "demographic problem," the denial persists, manifested by the politicians' lack of urgency with respect to the peace process, and symbolized perhaps best by the notion that a ten-foot-tall wall of separation can protect the Jewish state from the demographic reality knocking on its door.

Tellingly, this denial also extends to the reality of the Israeli Arabs, who by 2013 constituted about 20 percent of the total population. Though they are Israeli citizens and enjoy a higher standard of living and far more freedom than many of their counterparts in the Arab countries or the Palestinian Authority, they are nonetheless subjected to both official and unofficial discrimination. By design, they are unable to feel at home in the Jewish state, as evidenced most profoundly by their exclusion from the national anthem, which celebrates the yearning of the Jewish soul for its homeland. More concretely, as noted by British journalist Martin Fletcher, while Israel has been one big construction site since its inception, not a single Arab town has been built in all these years.[11] Without question, government policies have consistently restricted Israeli Arabs' access to economic opportunities and denied them full civil integration. Coupled with the growing resistance of their Palestinian brethren in the occupied territories, and the global march toward democratization and equality, over time this legacy has greatly radicalized this population. Indeed, in the aftermath of the 2014 war in Gaza, there were significant anti-Israeli riots in the Arab Israeli towns as well as terrorist activities initiated by Israeli Arabs from East Jerusalem. Given the rebellions and revolutions that spread across the Middle East in 2011 and 2012, it is now more likely than ever that Israeli Arabs will one way or another join the resistance to Israel, and in this case from well within the Jewish state. Yet, Israelis show no sign of comprehending or internalizing the potential impact of such a revolt. While some cities have mixed populations, many Israeli Jews, even in these towns, have little to do with Arabs. Most typically, they know them as school janitors, construction workers, drivers, and perhaps nurses, if at all. Thus, out of sight, out of mind.

As alluded to earlier, denial is not always a bad thing. The denial of death at various points in life, when not extreme, is what keeps us from descending into meaninglessness and hopelessness, what allows us to transcend some of our physical limitations and do extraordinary things. All of which is generally true about Israelis. Denying the apparent limits of reality and seeking to transcend it can have a profoundly positive psychological effect. A classic illustration of this principle in Israeli history is provided by Tel Aviv literary and film scholar Nurit Gertz. Analyzing a host of fiction and nonfiction Hebrew texts from much of the twentieth century, Gertz shows how at times the denial of military defeat was used to motivate and strengthen Jewish morale in the early days of the state. During the 1948 war, the fall of the Old City of Jerusalem to Jordanian hands was described by one newspaper as a moral victory for the Jews who fought in the battle, while the Arab conquest of the city was said to have been an ostensible victory that accomplished nothing. Another newspaper, reporting on the famous battle for kibbutz Yad Mordechai in the south, first described how the Egyptian armed battalion withdrew in shame and humiliation, fearful of the Israeli boys who repelled them merely with their bodies and their rage. Only then did it deliver the real news of the battle, i.e., that the Israeli fighters subsequently withdrew and abandoned the kibbutz to the enemy. The latter part of the report was brief and devoid of emotion.[12]

Even more important, denying reality's limitations can actually transform it, something the Israelis have done again and again. In 2007 Israel started developing the Iron Dome, a missile defense system, which just a few years earlier many considered unrealistic, akin perhaps to Ronald Reagan's much ridiculed Star Wars. The Iron Dome became operational so quickly that by 2014 it changed the nature of Israel's war with Hamas, likely saving thousands of lives on both sides.

Israel's attitude toward its Arab minority and the Palestinians in the territories reveals another facet of Israeli narcissism, namely the Israeli mind's paucity of empathy, or the capacity to identify with and understand the other's situation and experience. In recent years, as Israel and Hamas have clashed in repeated cycles of asymmetrical military conflicts, it has become common for the Israeli media to report something to the effect of "Today, seventeen Palestinians, including women and children, were killed in Gaza while there were four anxiety casualties on our side." *Anxiety casualty* is the term used in Israel to identify a panic attack, which may or may not trigger more lasting symptoms such as post-traumatic stress disorder. Or one paragraph in a newspaper might report, "Nine Palestinians were killed in an IDF attack on houses belonging to Hamas militants," and "a rocket from Gaza caused extensive damage to a greenhouse [or a shed] in Ashdod."

This narcissistic overvaluing of one's feelings and perspective compared to the other's characterizes the Israeli interpersonal style not only in relation to Arabs, but also to fellow Jews. It is one of the things that makes driving, shopping, dining, or doing anything requiring superficial social interaction in Israel quite maddening. An Israeli friend, a soft-spoken academician, recalls returning from an overseas trip with his three-year-old son. "We were waiting by the baggage-claim belt, my kid all excited with anticipation as the luggage started coming in, when all of a sudden a Hasidic man in his seventies or eighties pushed us aside to get to his bag, knocking my son down. In a second I found myself lunging forward, pushing this elderly man to the ground on my way to rescue my son." Though most times it doesn't come to blows, this clash of narcissistic entitlements is omnipresent in Israeli daily life. It is often aggravating, sometimes comical. On a radio talk show in which the host advises the speaker he has three or four minutes to make his point, the two may spend half the time arguing whether three or four minutes are called for, given the generous time allotted to the previous caller. During their training in El Al, flight attendants are told that when Israelis purchase an airline ticket, they believe they buy not only the ticket but also the plane, the pilot, and the flight attendants. Or as Martin Fletcher put it in his book about hiking the length of Israel's Mediterranean coast, "Where else would ten friends sit together for coffee on Friday, all talk at the same time, and afterward have not the foggiest idea what anybody else said?"[13] Sometimes, however, it is disturbing.

On a recent shivah call in Jerusalem I was struck by how

much of the conversation—or, really, the multiple, competing monologues—was about the visitors' worldly accomplishments, and how little about the dead man or his family. Fighting for airtime, one man spoke about his Los Angeles real estate projects, another about his close ties to the government, a third about his grandchildren at Harvard and Stanford, and a fourth about his grandchild at Google. Vociferous and argumentative, the visitors showed little concern for, or sensitivity to, the frightened and exhausted elderly widow.

In 1938, a short time after Kristallnacht, Ben-Gurion, then head of the Yishuv, spoke about the rescue of Jewish children in Germany. If he could save all the children in Germany by transporting them to England, he said, but only half by bringing them to Palestine, he would have chosen the latter. Nothing was more important than saving the Hebrew nation in its land, he explained. Consistent with this ideology, as described by, among others, Tom Segev in *One Palestine, Complete,* the Zionist leadership tended to view the Jews of Europe as "human material" needed to build the state, rather than seeing the state as a means to save the Jews. Ben-Gurion himself asserted he preferred young to old immigrants, and workers to children. During the 1930s only 20 percent of immigration permits were issued to women, and while a small number of permits were assigned to children, no children with mental retardation were allowed.[14] Such policies were justified on the grounds of what was good for the collective, but the underlying disregard or outright disdain for the "weak" and the defenseless has remained a hallmark of Israeli society to this day. From the casual derision of young men who do not perform combat duty in the military to the historically low sentencing standards for violent crimes, especially those committed against women, children, and Arabs, Israeli culture has never enjoyed a surplus of empathy.

Understandably, Israelis are particularly indifferent to Palestinian sufferings. In part this is due to the state of war between the two peoples and the history of Palestinian atrocities, but to a large extent it can be accounted for by narcissistic projections. Israelis have often viewed Palestinians as passive, submissive, craven, pathetic, and conniving, pretty much the historical portrayal of the Diaspora Jews by the gentiles, and therefore the internalized, repressed, or denied negative self-image of their Israeli offspring. A common Israeli refrain with respect to Arabs is that they *only understand force.* But arguably, as demonstrated by Israel's conciliatory responses to the 1973 war and the two Palestinian intifadas—returning the Sinai to Egypt, recognizing the PLO, and retreating from Gaza, respectively—this, too, looks like a narcissistic projection. I observed another example on a recent guided walk in the Old City of Jerusalem, where the Israeli guide explained to the group that the mosque's tall minaret demonstrates the Muslims' desire to dominate. The truth, related, among other things, to early Christian influence, is more complicated, but when asked how this was different from the oversize Jewish houses dominating parts of the Old City, or the hilltop settlements in the West Bank, which, fortresslike, tower over the small dwellings of the nearby Arab villages, he simply denied the facts. "Jewish buildings are not big," he said, just as we stumbled upon a huge synagogue, at the end of a narrow, Muslim-quarter lane with tiny Arab houses on both sides. In any case, attributing negative aspects of the self to Palestinians is a common Israeli pastime that heightens the emotional distance between the two nations and deepens Israelis' hatred and contempt toward their fellow Palestinian Semites.

To further complicate matters, a more specific projection has been ascribed to Arab Jews, widely known in Israel as Oriental Jews, perhaps, as suggested by Israeli psychologist Avner Falk, because the word *Arab* in Israel is so negatively loaded. As proposed by Falk, compared to their Ashkenazi counterparts, Israelis with origins in Arab countries have additional reasons, both external and internal, to project negative aspects of the self onto the Palestinians and other Arabs. It is joked that the iconic, Zionist Hebrew poet Hayim Nahman Bialik, who immigrated to Palestine in 1924, hated the Arabs because they resembled the Oriental Jews. So both because they have been discriminated against due to their Arab culture by the Ashkenazi Israelis and because they needed to distance themselves from that part of their identity so as to elevate their self-esteem, the Oriental Jews have adopted far more hostile feelings toward the Palestinians than have Israelis of Western origins. Public opinions polls consistently show that Oriental Jews hate Arabs more than their Jewish counterparts of Western origins.[15]

The Israeli mind's failures at empathy, its lack of regard for reality, and its relentless drive for success, all produce a predilection for cutting corners, bluffing, and lying. Seated in an upscale coffee shop in central Jerusalem, I witnessed a typical flirting or pickup encounter between a male graduate student and a young, female high school teacher. The teacher was working jointly with a colleague, preparing lessons for the upcoming week. Teasing her, the young man said, "Working together? This is cheating! What would you do when you catch a student cheating on a test?"

"Well," she countered, "if I caught a student cheating, I wouldn't view it as a negative. I would see it as an indication that he wants to succeed. He is motivated."

Everyone laughed, and a conversation about cutting corners ensued. This brought to mind an Israeli patient who had previously seen an American psychoanalyst for a number of years. "In some ways, she didn't get me," he complained. "One time I said, 'You can't just play by the book if you want to do well in life.' 'Why should you be exempt from playing by the book?' she asked. How American!" A more sociopathic version of this mind-set: A New York–based Israeli locksmith describes how he makes a living. When called at night by a customer who had locked himself out, he fiddles with the lock as if to gain entry. He then "inadvertently" breaks it, which leaves the customer with the options of spending the night in an unlocked home or having a new lock installed on the spot for double the normal cost. Perhaps this is no more appalling than the personal and political corruption that has plagued the Israeli body politics for decades. When an American politician transgresses, it is often about sex; in Israel, it is more likely to be about money. In recent years, the penetrating transparency of Israeli society has repeatedly exposed financial and ethical wrongdoing at the very top of the establishment, with criminal investigations, indictments, or convictions in the cases of ministers, prime ministers, and a president.

An Israeli businessman residing in Europe ambivalently acknowledges how his European associates perceive the Israelis they work with in an apparent amalgam of honest observation and good old anti-Semitism: liars, thieves, and untrustworthy manipulators. When negotiating with fellow Israelis, this businessman warns them at the outset not to start the process unless they are willing to walk away from the deal. Illustrating the underpinning dynamic of a narcissistic projection he explains that since Israelis always bluff—even if unconsciously—they never believe the *no* of others. They think everything is negotiable, and unless they themselves are willing to say no and mean it, he says, they'll be wasting his time in endless negotiations. Arguably, this is why Israeli governments are eager to forever negotiate without preconditions with the Palestinians: they believe that one day they will convince the Palestinians to, say, give up on East Jerusalem. It is also how the Israelis deal with their allies in the international community. In December 2014, for example, Israeli Defense Minister Moshe Yaalon found a way to expand West Bank settlements under the radar so as to defy the West without incurring criticism. Using a law that allows the IDF to seize land in the West Bank for military use, he moved military bases near existing settlements to other locations, enabling the settlements to expand into the empty bases without a formal government decision. The daily ramifications of this attitude in Israeli life are evident to anyone trying to get anything done requiring cooperation, agreement, permission, or license—from driving a car to renting an apartment. As a veteran Tel Aviv architect told British journalist Martin Fletcher, "The trouble in Tel Aviv, as everywhere in Israel, is that nobody takes no for an answer. A negative response from the city planner is not the final word, but just another obstacle to overcome."[16]

Related to all this nay-saying and monkey business are two other patterns embedded in the Israeli mind. First, there's a fundamental disrespect for authority, originating perhaps from the legitimate distrust of persecuted people toward Diaspora governments they couldn't rely on for protection, along with the struggle to survive in the margins of business life. In the Zionist narrative, however, it joined forces with the more active, aggressive ideal of the new Jew. Some psychologists and writers have suggested that the Zionist story is one of oedipal rebellion against, and competition with, the hapless father of the exile. The historical Jewish man of the Diaspora, so goes this theory, was stuck in negative oedipal territory, that is, identification with the mother and submission to the father.[17] This dynamic the early Zionists clearly rejected, and perhaps it can account for the fascination of their intellectual establishment with Freud, though his theories were incompatible with those of another of their heroes, Karl Marx. Both Freud and Marx were revolutionaries, which, oedipal or not, is the point. Freud is still more popular in Israeli psychoanalytic circles than in those of many other countries, and so is the explicit and assertive questioning of authority. A couple of years ago I attended an after-school Holocaust Memorial Day *pe-ulah,* or activity, in an Israeli high school for American kids. This *pe-ulah* was fashioned after the traditional Israeli Boy Scouts pack meeting, and the leader gave a couple of kids a needle each and instructed them to start popping some of the dozens of balloons that filled a large room as an apparent decoration for a party the next day. Within seconds other kids followed, and in a minute or two the entire pack was jumping up and down popping balloons all over the place. When subsequently asked by the leader why they popped the balloons, the kids unself-consciously explained they did so because everyone else did. What was surprising about this activity, the only one in that Holocaust Memorial Day pack meeting, was that it had nothing to do with loss, heroism, or anti-Semitism. Rather, the lesson of the activity was all about not being a follower. Challenge authority and do your own thing was the message. A related concept, *don't be a frier,* or, roughly, a sucker, is probably the most common social imperative in Israel, with the vernacular *frier* referring to someone who is following the rules, gullibly or passively, to his own disadvantage. To be taken for a fool is one of the gravest psychic injuries for an Israeli.

But the central narcissistic aspect of this resistance to authority comes from the defensive arrogance of the presumed centrality and superiority of the Israeli self. A typical incident is described by an Israeli lawyer who travels internationally most of the year. While flying El Al's business class with serious back pain, he pulled on the seat in front of him to help him get up to go to the bathroom. The passenger occupying this seat, a fellow Israeli, with a barely disguised smirk on his face said, "Tell me something, you don't fly much, do you?"

"Why are you asking?" the lawyer played along.

"Because people who fly know you don't lean on the seat in front of you" was the predictable response.

"Any other civilized person would have said something to the effect of 'Excuse me, would you mind not doing this when you get up?'" explains the lawyer. "But for a typical Israeli, it's an opportunity to put you down, to demonstrate his superiority."

To use a term coined by one of Freud's more controversial followers, Wilhelm Reich, this facet of the Israeli mind is not unlike that of the *phallic-narcissistic character*. Armed with bold, self-confident, and boastful surface defenses—all designed to deny any hint of passivity—this character is more suited to lead and dominate than to follow or be subordinated. Donald Trump with his towers is perhaps the quintessential caricature of this personality type.

The second pattern related to the Israeli proclivity to push the envelope, by hook or by crook, is the culture's permeable attitude toward boundaries. An extreme example is provided by an Israeli woman who was, in the 1970s associated with a radical leftist political organization that was tracked by the government security apparatus. While a university student, she started a relationship with a man who told her he was trailing her as part of his job for the Shabak, or Israel Security Agency, which did not deter either of them from pursuing their affair. While this is not unheard of in other cultures, nonetheless the audacity, the almost nonchalant manner in which they disregarded professional and personal boundaries, reflects something particularly Israeli. On a more ordinary, cultural level, compared to Americans, say, Israelis are far more open with respect to their innermost thoughts: sex, money, family troubles. They'll be the first to tell you what you should do about such personal matters, what you should think, or what you *do* think but don't seem to know. The charm of this is greater intimacy, warmth, and spontaneity; the downside, violation and suffocation. Many young Israelis who travel overseas or leave the country to study or work abroad cite the need to get way from this smothering, claustrophobic environment, which they also love like no other. When personal boundaries are so permeable, little respect is shown for your separateness as a person, your needs, or your words. If we are all one, what's yours is mine, and I might as well con you before you con me.

Looked at from the outside, this permeability of personal boundaries makes for great drama, a terrific illustration of which was offered by the highly successful 2005–8 Israeli television series *BeTipul,* adapted later in America by HBO with the literal translation of *In Treatment.* Following the weekly appointment schedule of a psychologist with several of his patients and his own therapist, the riveting psychological drama within the natural confines of each session featured an almost routine violation of every clinical boundary possible. No session started or ended on time; the personal life of the therapist intruded on some, family members of the patient on others; provocative gifts dominated other sessions; and ultimately a sexual relationship between therapist and patient materialized. In the Israeli series, all this felt credible; in the American version, it seemed like a contrived ploy intended to bring action into a sophisticated show laced with too much verbiage. In reality, most Israeli psychologists are unlikely to break so many boundaries; however, an Israeli patient of mine reported on his treatment in Israel as a nineteen-year-old. His psychologist once told him, as he struggled with sexual insecurity, that if he didn't have sex with a girl he was friendly with by the following session, he shouldn't bother coming back. The patient discussed it with the girl in question, and with her cooperation he did obey the authority, perhaps because the therapist herself seemed like a rebel. After all, everyone knows a therapist should not assign such homework, especially to an impressionable or vulnerable youngster.

MAN IS BUT AN IMPRINT OF HIS NATIVE LANDSCAPE

With few exceptions, the Israelis who leave Israel take it with them wherever they go. Not only do they associate with other Israelis and retain many of their cultural rituals and preferences—in food, language, music, art, and politics—but they also forever plan or fantasize a return. My brother who recently returned to Israel after living in New York for more than thirty years says the question is not why he returned to Israel, but rather why he was never able to leave it. In my own case, there weren't many return plans or fantasies. For one thing, my wife, and later my kids, were unequivocally American. Not wishing to inhabit two different worlds, I consciously chose not to speak Hebrew to my children when they were growing up. Nonetheless, when they were little and I would sing them a lullaby at bedtime, I somehow resorted to the beautiful "Kinneret Sheli." The song, composed to the poem of the early Zionist poet Rachel, so idealizes the object of her longings, the Sea of Galilee, that it questions whether it only existed in a dream. As the sole freshwater lake in the country, the Sea of Galilee was one of a handful of vacation destinations for my family, and thus, in my child's mind, both real and indeed magical. But the poem, along with the brilliantly sentimental melody to which it was put, amplified the latter. In reality, the lake is nicely situated, but with the exception of a magnificent little church on its northern shore is nothing to write home about. The same is true of Israel's physical landscape as a whole. Like most countries, Israel has several truly beautiful spots, but it is mostly arid, flat, perhaps rocky-hilly here and there, mostly yellowish, with bits of green in some areas. Other than the Sea of Galilee, water-wise it has about three large creeks—all referred to as rivers in Hebrew—and a Dead Sea. It has a few dusty-dry, sparse forests, and three or four mountains in the pre-1967 borders. It has several delightfully ancient town centers and religious sites, a few Mediterranean-beach treasures, and a smattering of attractively modern and contemporary buildings and villas. And it has many fascinating archaeological sites. But it houses no Alps, hilltop medieval villages, Renaissance palaces, Black Forests, Salzburgs, nor the English countryside, the Grand Canyon, or San Francisco. On the whole, its towns and cities are poorly designed, cluttered, polluted, and architecturally challenged. But despite all this, or, I would suggest, because of it, Israelis' attachment to the physicality of their land is as deep as it gets.

Man is but the imprint of his native landscape; however one interprets that statement, it is hardly a coincidence that this famous line was written by a Hebrew, Zionist poet. Russian-born physician and poet Shaul Tchernichovsky, who died in Jerusalem in 1943, penned it in a poem about how the underdeveloped young mind determines his person's life—a basic psychoanalytic concept. Whether universally true or not, by virtue of a past that, to paraphrase William Faulkner, is never really past, and a relentless reworking of its psychic deposits through the popular culture of *tiyulim*—an emotionally laden Israeli version of nature hikes, which permeate grade- and high-school field trips, family outings, and military foot excursions—the connection between the Old Baby and his land seeps into every Israeli mind from early childhood onward. In addition, as discussed by Israeli scholars Eyal Ben-Ari and Yoram Bilu, the early Zionists, as well as many of the West Bank settlers of present days, have transformed themselves by transforming the landscape, further linking their psychological development to that of the land.[18] It is thus hardly a surprise that from pop and rock music, to literature and poetry, creative Israeli narratives are full of longings to the geography of Israel, which are also generalized in the Israeli mind to the very idea of landscape, wherever it might be. More so than other tourists, Israelis traveling overseas are obsessed with finding the best "view" in popular, as well as off-the-beaten track, tourist attractions. While their admiration of foreign landscapes is invested with the emotional energy associated with the idealization of their own land, they also envy the treasures of other countries and disparage what they ultimately know to be the truth about their own geography.

The Israelis' connection to Eretz Israel is not an Israeli invention. Rather, as evident everywhere within the internal world of the

Israeli national character, it is a paradoxical reinvention, a rejecting embrace of two thousand years of Jewish ties to the Holy Land. Indeed, though the Jews have been deterritorialized since the destruction of the Second Temple in 70 CE, one of the most distinctive features of the Jewish religion is its territorial claim to a singular, divinely promised strip of real estate. Israeli literary historian Sidra DeKoven Ezrahi argues that the Jewish claim to Jerusalem is more the product than the cause of the city's rich historical representation in Jewish poetic imagination. From the beginning, she points out, the biblical vision of the city had an elasticity, later reflected in the extension of the term *Zion,* one of the biblical names of Jerusalem, to the land of Israel as a whole. Since the destruction of the Second Temple the material city has had little Jewish political reality—no temple, republic, or any other type of territorial sovereignty. As DeKoven Ezrahi sees it, into that absence, and far away from the ruined shrine itself, stepped a succession of Jewish poets and writers who, from the days of antiquity, through the Middle Ages, and all the way to modern Zionism, preserved Jerusalem as a symbol. They did so in part, as DeKoven Ezrahi, A. B. Yehoshua, and others have shown, through the personification of Jerusalem and Eretz Israel as a woman—a mother, a wife, or a lover. Consistent with the oedipal rebellion hypothesis mentioned above, Zionist literary and poetic narratives are full of erotic male claims to the land. The narcissistic thread suggested by this analysis lies in the valuation of symbols and ideas over reality.[19]

As discussed in detail by Israeli psychologist Avner Falk, from a post-Freudian psychoanalytic perspective, this literary history reflects the notion that the narcissistic overvaluation of Jerusalem is underlined by the inability to mourn its loss. According to this theory, the humiliation brought upon the chosen people by their loss of sovereignty in the Promised Land was too much to bear.[20] Coupled with the denigration, rejection, and persecution they subsequently suffered in the Diaspora, it created a powerful cognitive dissonance: How can all this happen to *us*? The answer came in prayer books and religious texts with such rationalizations as *it's a punishment from our God* or *it's only a test, God does not abandon his favorite children*, and *one day, our God, the only God, will bring us back home*, and ultimately, *it didn't really happen, because Jerusalem is a spiritual, not a geographical, place, which will forever stay in our heart*. Rather than accept and mourn the loss, generations upon generations of Jews repeated such mantras and prayers, trying to escape feelings of humiliation and worthlessness by clinging to fantastical, compartmentalized notions of a glorious past and a future return. Then, when a combination of historical forces made the Zionist dream a reality, this pocket of narcissistic omnipotence, a version of what psychoanalyst Heinz Kohut called *the grandiose self*, exploded on the ground in Palestine. Seized by this unconscious residue of the early childhood hubris we all bring into adulthood, the early Zionists sought to erase the Jewish history of loss and humiliation and to replace it with a view of themselves as the heirs of ancient Jewish heroes.

Now, lest we conclude that the early, or for that matter current, Zionist vision is inherently pathological, it should be noted that Kohut, one of the most influential analysts of the twentieth century, believed that narcissism is fundamentally a healthy developmental dimension, turning pathological only at the extremes. And in truth, this defense mechanism has been a huge success story, especially when the Yishuv and, later on, the young state of Israel was a tiny and poorly armed community fighting bravely and brilliantly for its survival. But in its inception, the Zionist project was indeed an outlier. Less than 2 percent of the Eastern European Jews who emigrated in the late-nineteenth and early-twentieth centuries chose Palestine as their destination, and of those, many did not stay. The vast majority, some 2.5 million people, made the more obvious choice of the United States.[21]

In the past few decades many Israelis have tried to get away from all this, or from what DeKoven Ezrahi calls the poetics of return to Jerusalem. In her words regarding one of Israel's most well-known and loved poets:

"In the poems of Yehuda Amichai, covering the second half of the twentieth century, we find some of the answers to the questions that survive our season of longing: not how to pine for but how to live in this city; how to relinquish some of the love of the city for love in the city."[22]

But try as they may, for most Israelis, the idea of Jerusalem and the land of Israel as a whole still trumps reality; and the loving still permeates, if not altogether supplants, the living. A direct line connects Yehuda Halevy's medieval poetic longings to a land whose sand is more pleasant to the mouth than honey, Bialik's celebration of a land that spring eternally adorns, and Israeli government decisions driven by an emotional attachment to Eretz Israel rather than by policy or even political considerations. The most obvious example was the impulsive decision to conquer the Old City of Jerusalem in 1967, taken, as documented by Tom Segev, without proper process and debate. The almost manic intoxication associated with that decision was evident in the later writings of Mordechai Gur, the general who led the assault. Describing his feelings upon first entering the Temple Mount, where the Dome of the Rock mosque dominated the presumed site of the ancient temple, Gur wrote, "I feel at home here. The object of our longing. The Temple Mount! Mount Moriah. Abraham and Isaac. The Temple. The Zealots, the Maccabees, Bar Kokhba, the Romans and the Greeks. They all tumbled together in my mind."[23]

While of lesser intensity elsewhere, such euphoria was not limited to Jerusalem or other areas with significant religious sites. During that war, Prime Minister Eshkol is reported to have said, "I have great passion for Gaza, perhaps because of Samson and Delilah."[24] A passion for an arid strip of land, densely populated with poor Palestinian refugees and open sewers; a passion apparently based on the appeal of a biblical superhero and the lover who destroyed his power by cutting his hair! One of my own favorite spots in Israel is also linked to, biblically speaking, a bad hair day. Nestling in an Arab village just outside the walled city of Jerusalem is Yad Avshalom, a grand tomb erroneously assumed to be the burial place of King David's beloved son, Avshalom. A handsome prince with long hair, Avshalom had led a failed mutiny against his father, and as he fled on a donkey, his hair was caught in the boughs of a large tree. He was thus suspended in midair only to be killed by his father's commander in violation of the king's order to "spare the boy." As secular as such attachments might be, emotionally speaking they are not all that different from those of the hard-core religious settlers, who vow to never abandon their towns and villages, located at the heart of biblical Judea and Samaria, otherwise known as the West Bank.

Falk's analysis regarding the Jews' inability to mourn makes sense, but it's not the whole story. One of my earliest arguments with my wife—who grew up in a traditional Jewish American family, celebrated the holidays, and even visited Israel when she was eighteen—erupted when she stated that as a Jew she had no emotional connection to Israel. She further claimed that this was unremarkable for an American Jew. I simply couldn't fathom it, even though by that time I have been living in the States close to a decade. Could it be that, from an emotional standpoint, the Eretz Israel of the prayers, the holidays stories, and Jewish history had nothing to do with the actual place? In retrospect, I realize she was not off-the-wall, and perhaps like my reaction, Falk's analysis is a bit Israel-centric. To a great extent, Jewish national identity was formed outside the longed-for geographical homeland. In biblical narrative, the Jews received the Torah and became a people in Sinai, on their way to the promised land. The first Jew, Abraham, per God's command, left his homeland not once but twice, including the one promised to him by God. And his grandson Jacob and his offspring left for Egypt, never to return. As for history, merely forty years after the destruction of the First Temple, when the king of Persia called upon the Jews to return to Judea and rebuild their temple, many did not heed him, preferring to stay in their newly adopted communities. Furthermore, contrary to popular belief, in the aftermath of the destruction of the Second Temple, the Romans never exiled the Jews. Rather, the estimated 2 million Jews who lived in Eretz Israel at the time left gradually on their own volition, mostly after the failed Bar Kokhba revolt. Nor were the Jews prevented from returning for about fifteen hundred years following the collapse of the Roman Empire. In the Israeli version of that Jewish wanderlust, standing in paradoxical connection to their idealized attachment to their land, at present upward of 750,000 Jewish Israelis, at least 10 percent of the current Jewish population of Israel, reside overseas.[25]

THE STATE COMPTROLLER MOTHERBOARD

Much of the Israeli mind is preoccupied with regulating its own self-esteem. For the outside observer it is hard to imagine that underneath or alongside the assertive, brash Israeli there's a self-doubting and self-critical person of equal proportion. To the external world Israelis often come across as insufferably aware of their own feelings of superiority. Among themselves, too, Israelis devalue all others: Americans are naïve, Europeans are hypocritical, Chinese are worker ants, and Arabs are just animals. They think of Israel as possessing the best hospitals, the best high-tech companies, and the best and most moral military in the world. They also believe that their occupation of the Palestinian territories is the most enlightened in world history. A comprehensive 2009 public opinion poll found that 70 percent of Israelis believe the Jews are the chosen people.[26] But scratch the surface, or listen to other conversations among Israelis, and you will hear them disparage themselves or fellow Israelis as rude and obnoxious, liars, cheats, and incompetents. "Oh, no," thinks the typical Israeli when he gets into a taxi in New York or Berlin only to realize that the driver is Israeli. An Israeli American friend, who is a political scientist and an expert on international law, articulates the positive side of such self-criticism. Israel, he explains, is a very critical society, even from a legal standpoint. It has, for example, an exceptionally powerful State Ombudsman that investigates and criticizes the executive aggressively. In addition, as a testament to the social importance of and deference held toward this institution, its annual reports receive a great deal of media attention and are kept on the record for many years. "Come to think of it," says my friend, "the Israeli State Ombudsman reminds me of my mother." Perhaps he is right; perhaps the Israeli version of the Jewish mother is tinged with a harshly critical accent.

Call it self-confidence or arrogance, self-criticism or self-hate, the constant vacillation between the two extremes is evidenced when a great Israeli innovation succeeds on the world market one day, and the floor of a poorly built catering hall collapses and swallows a wedding party and scores of guests with it the next. It is also evident in the perpetual swings between the brilliant successes and dumb failures, real or perceived, of the Israeli military and intelligence operations in the Middle East and beyond. These mood swings resemble those of the bipolar or manic-depressive individual, except that in the Israeli case it's not about chemical imbalance. The highs, like that following the 1967 war, are an expression of defensively high self-esteem, and the lows, such as the national depression that followed the second intifada, are about the death of an illusion. In a doubly ironic bit of narcissistic projection, back in 1943 David Ben-Gurion commented that the German Jews who emigrated to Israel in those years had both a superiority and an inferiority complex, stemming from their German education—Kant, Beethoven, and the like—on the one hand, and their realization that the Eastern European Zionists who had preceded them had actually built something of significance in Palestine. It takes one to know one, or, as the saying goes, *you spot it, you got it.*[27]

This duality is a hallmark of the narcissistic character, representing his struggle to accept and love himself in spite of his limitations. The corollary, certainly in the Israeli case, is that the narcissistic person forever longs for acceptance, validation, and love from others. This is one of the reasons the Israeli public and government responded to Anwar Sadat's 1977 visit to Israel so positively, giving him practically everything he wanted, with the exception of meaningful self-determination for the Palestinians. In going to Jerusalem, a city not recognized as Israel's capital by the vast majority of the international community, and personally addressing the ultimate Zionist sovereign, the Israeli legislature, and by demonstrating an effusive, loving interpersonal style in his interactions with Israeli leaders, Sadat reached directly at the heart of the narcissistic wound inhabiting the Israeli national character: the notion that Israel would never be accepted as a legitimate national presence in the historical homeland of the Jews. Sadat's visit was a major psychological breakthrough, but similar moments have occurred over the years, albeit less dramatic. In 1997, three years after Jordan and Israel signed their own peace accord, a Jordanian soldier killed seven Israeli girls who were on a school trip near the border. In the aftermath, King Hussein took the unusual step of visiting the family home of each of the victims to express his condolences. The emotional and empathic expression of sorrow he displayed preempted the formation of a national narcissistic rage on top of the personal feelings of loss and anger experienced by the victims' families. The victims' families themselves were deeply touched, so much so that upon Hussein's death they released a statement to the effect that he was a king, but also a human being. One of the families went as far as naming their newborn Yarden ("Jordan" in Hebrew) to honor the king. To oversimplify, Heinz Kohut's cure for pathological narcissism is a massive and sustained administration of empathy, a treatment that unfortunately is often in short supply in the Middle East. Indeed, the absence of such validation and empathy compels Israelis to reject many peace proposals and to react with rage when they perceive that their very legitimacy is questioned.

A final complication is that in his desperation, the narcissist often behaves in such ways that all but assure he will receive the opposite of what he needs. A curious anecdote illustrative of this conundrum involves legendary Israeli general and statesman Moshe Dayan. In a conversation with a Palestinian poet in the aftermath of the 1967 war, he reportedly compared Israel's relationship with the Palestinians to that of a bedouin man who kidnaps a girl to be his wife. For their children, he said, the initial kidnapping will be meaningless, and they will accept both the man and the woman as their parents. So not unlike the loquacious, self-adulating politician who sends photos of himself bare-chested to young women over Twitter, the Israeli desire for conquest and domination is motivated, in part, by a search for acceptance, a need to be seen and loved for one's real and imagined greatness. This conquest mentality bespeaks the discontinuity between the Diaspora and Zionism, but the underlying psychology is wholly consistent with the historical, compensatory fantasy of the chosen people.

THREE

THE WHOLE WORLD IS AGAINST US
AND THE WORLD IS SILENT

I t is easy enough to see how the long, unremitting history of hostilities toward the chosen people—the deep, bigoted hatred and atrocities in the Christian West, and the more variable mixture of disdain, scorn, and discrimination in the lands of Islam—has been internalized by the Jews. Reinforced by the historical refusal of the Arabs to accept Israel's legitimacy, this internalization produced a mental structure ranging from a healthy skepticism about the intentions of others to an outright mistrust and paranoia. In the Israeli mind, these ancient feelings of insecurity clash with the more recent reality of Israel, its being the most powerful and advanced country in its neighborhood. Indeed, more than their Jewish counterparts overseas, a number of Israeli authors, psychologists, and even politicians, precisely because they are members of the dominant Jewish majority in their own country, have long felt secure enough to observe that both the Jewish and Israeli stories of victimization are more complicated than they appear.

Bernard Susser and Charles Liebman, political scientists at Bar

Ilan University—a respected institution of higher education combining a Jewish religious identity with modern academics—described this element of Jewish psychology as the "ideology of affliction." Reinterpreted and applied in our context, their analysis draws a straight line between the Chosen People and the Persecuted People, or narcissism and paranoia. As they see it, without an ethnic-religious ideology that would explain Jewish persecution, Jewish history would be nothing but a meaningless tale of impotence and humiliation. Therefore, the orthodox rabbis that led the Jewish communal existence in the Diaspora for close to two millennia vindicated Jewish suffering with the concept of the Chosen People, whose enemies are merely agents of Israel's God as he punishes his people for their sins. In the end, the messiah will return the Jews to the land of Israel, at which time the gentiles will recognize the singular mission of the people of Israel and accept their God as their own. The uniqueness of the Jewish people is thus embodied in their victimization and self-aggrandizement, with a chicken-and-egg causal relationship between the two: because they were persecuted, the Jews decided they were chosen, and because they acted as if they were chosen, they were persecuted.[1]

A more poignant, less academic rendering of this story is drawn by novelist David Grossman in *To the End of the Land,* where the protagonist, Ora, relates an anecdote about her young, sensitive son from one of the family's Passover seders:

> Suddenly [he] starts crying that he doesn't want to be Jewish anymore, because they always kill us and always hate us, and he knows this because all the holidays are about it. And the adults look at one another, and a brother-in-law mumbles that it is kind of difficult to argue with that, and his wife says, "Don't be paranoid," and he quotes *"that in every generation, they rise up against us to destroy*

us" and she replies that it's not exactly scientific
fact, and that maybe we should examine our own
role in the whole *"rising up against us business,"*
and the familiar argument ensues, and Ora, as
usual, flees to the kitchen to help with the dishes.[2]

Ora's son, who grew up to become a tight-lipped, tough young
man and a combat IDF soldier, represents what was supposed to
be the revolutionary transition from the Diaspora to the Israeli Jew.
After all, the point of Zionism was not only to end Jewish affliction, but also its ideology. And to a large extent, on the healthier
end of the continuum, the Israeli version of mistrusting the gentiles yielded much success. Journalist Thomas Friedman suggested
that the historical Jewish attitude toward the gentiles and the absence of such sentiments among Arabs was one of the reasons the
Jews have a state and the Palestinians don't. Whereas in the Arab
world today's enemy could be tomorrow's friend, Friedman observed, the Eastern European Jews who built Israel came out of a
"culture of sharp edges and right angles," where today's enemy was
tomorrow's enemy.[3]

More concretely, as reported by historian Tom Segev, while the
British military and government were preparing to exit Palestine
in 1948, the Jewish Agency assumed that they would depart in a
sudden panic, leaving chaos behind. One of the agency's intelligence agents predicted the British would depart with a scorched-
earth policy. The British, however, had no such intention. Their
mentality as a ruler was to secure a functional continuity of the government infrastructure, which they had worked hard to create for
twenty-five years. But unlike the Arabs, and as a consequence of
their distrustful assessment of the situation, the Jews made sure to
have a government-in-waiting, so before leaving, the British had
no one else to turn over the administration to.[4] Many other instances, particularly in the military arena, can be counted here to

illustrate the survival value of this Israeli reinterpretation of the old biblical trope: *remember that which Amalek did to you.* Most famously, in 1967 Israel initiated what it perceived to be a preemptive strike against Egypt, destroying its air force within hours and defeating the armies of four Arab countries. By the war's end six days later, Israel had expanded its territory by a factor of three. This military campaign was remarkable by any measure, though one admittedly waged against countries with then-subpar, if large, armies. The 1973 war, by contrast, was the exception that proved the rule, as Israel was caught unprepared, insufficiently paranoid as it were, in the aftermath of its extraordinary, previous victory.

But then again, as several Israeli scholars have noted, the intended Zionist transformation of the ideology of affliction in Palestine, and later Israel, has never been an unalloyed success. For one thing, the narcissistic-paranoid link appears to have survived the revolution. As pointed out by Segev in his discussion of Jewish and Arab labor markets in Palestine, starting in the 1920s the Zionists would often call the employment of Arabs by Jews *avoda zara.* The use of this phrase, which translates literally to "foreign labor" but is actually the historical, religious term for idolatry, reveals both the contempt for, and fear of, the gentile world. That it also meant a huge differential in salaries—as if the Arabs were illegal immigrants rather than the natives—goes without saying. In trying to capture the sense of the 1920s in Jerusalem, Segev quoted from, among many sources, the letters of a Jewish university student to his parents overseas. Commenting on a rare earthquake that apparently damaged one of the mosques on the Temple Mount, but not the adjacent Western Wall, the young man noted it was "the hand of God."[5] Some years later, and far away from Jerusalem, an ethnic storm erupted in Safed when Arab children started coming to play in a new, Jewish school playground. The Jewish parents objected, and the head of Safed's Jewish community and the town's mayor supported them. Among other things, he insisted that Jewish children must be educated in the spirit of the Torah and Jewish ethics and should be kept away from "bad company." The Arab children, he wrote, had a corrupt character from the beginning of childhood: "Even in the ages between zero and ten not only are their mouths always full of filthy and rude language, but they are also capable of perverted acts."[6] These attitudes did not solely target the Arabs or Islam. For instance, after it was revealed that Hans Herzl, the son of the founder of Zionism, had converted to Christianity, the editor of one of the Yishuv's daily newspapers commented that at least, unlike Jesus, he was not a bastard.

The real conflict in Palestine, however, was not religious, but rather demographic and national, as the Zionists were forced to deal with the reality of an overwhelming and increasingly hostile Arab majority. Israeli scholar Nurith Gertz, who surveyed nonfiction texts in literary publications during the 1930s, notes that many of the writings discussing the ostensibly inexplicable nature of the Arab attacks on Jewish settlements attributed such attacks to anti-Semitism. *Nothing changed from the days of the second and first temples, the same hostility to the industrious Jew,* she describes a typical newspaper article.[7] Tom Segev provides a glaring example of the gap between such interpretation and reality in the case of the infamous 1929 Hebron massacre. David Ben-Gurion compared the massacre to a pogrom and later alluded to a Hebron without Jews by using the Nazi term *Judenrein*. Other leaders and writers also referred to it as a pogrom, with Rehavam Ze'evi writing that the vast majority of Hebron's Arabs took part in the killings and that "pogroms, slaughters and massacres have been part of our nation's history in their Diaspora and now this horrifying spectacle has been repeated in the Land of Israel."[8] The reality, however, was that unlike in the pogroms of Eastern Europe, the authorities did not initiate or condone the riots. Additionally, over two-thirds of Hebron's Jews were saved by Arab families who took them into their homes. Also, even though sixty-seven Jews were killed and several dozens injured, by historical standards, this could not compare with the pogroms of Eastern Europe, where in some cases hundreds or thousands of Jews were killed. Finally, as pointed out by Segev, the reasons for the Hebron massacre were different, ranging from fear of religious violation and of being dispossessed by Zionism, to hatred of foreigners and socioeconomic class warfare. Many of the classic European and Russian pogroms, on the other hand, were triggered by a local, violent incident for which the Jews were unjustly blamed.

Sociologist Oz Almog observed that the language used by the Jewish press to describe Arab hostilities starting in the 1920s and 1930s also created an image of the Arabs as a version of Amalek, a biblical enemy of the Hebrews who sought to destroy them, and an often-used simile for any anti-Semite or enemies of the Jews or Israel. Almog draws our attention to the myth of *the few facing the many* as another way in which the New Jew failed to replace the old one. The themes of those inferior in numbers but superior in courage, faith, craftiness, or moral values is everywhere in Jewish history, biblical narrative, and Jewish prayer. The drowning of pharaoh's army at sea, the victory over Amalek at Refidim, the conquests of Joshua, the Maccabees' rebellion against the Greeks, and Bar Kokhba's rebellion against the Romans are but a few examples. The same theme is most evident in the way the Jewish holidays, for example, Hanukkah and Lag b'Omer, have been interpreted by the establishment. In secular, modern Zionism the superiority of the few is said to manifest in the notion of quality over quantity, with intelligence, initiative, heroism, and morale compensating for numerical inferiority.[9]

While these comparisons with the Arab states obviously had an element of truth—by and large the Zionists were, and still are, far more educated, productive, and accomplished—this self-defined superiority did not earn them any sympathy in the neighborhood. As demonstrated by Gertz, during the 1948 war, both the Jewish press and fiction writers depicted the Zionists as active, powerful, heroic, rooted, and normal. The Palestinian Arabs they described as weak, frightened, passive, and alienated. Generalizing beyond such narcissistic projections, Israeli psychologist Ofer Grosbard likens Israel, the country, to the psychotherapy patient who insists in the initial consultation that nothing is wrong with him. The problem, he tells the therapist, is that he is so talented, so exceptional, and so successful that everyone else is simply envious and hateful toward him.[10]

Consistent with such defensiveness, nowadays many of those who criticize Israeli government policies with regard to the Palestinians are met with the accusation that something is wrong with *them*, not government policies—they are anti-Semitic. Sometimes this is a conscious gambit to shoot the messenger, but more often it originates from a deeper conviction, and not a new one. For example, during the British mandate in Palestine, the British foreign secretary objected to the settling of Holocaust survivors in Palestine. The Yishuv widely condemned him as an anti-Semite, even though his rationale was that it was Europe's moral responsibility to repatriate the Jews and he emphatically objected to racism of any kind. He may have been anti-Zionist, but not anti-Semitic. Contemporary examples of some American Jews, but even more so Israelis, equating criticizing Israel with anti-Semitism are too numerous to list. When the critic is Jewish himself, he is often viewed as a self-hating Jew. That each round of Israeli-Palestinian conflict seems to awaken some old-world anti-Semitism does not mean that no distinction exists between a strong critique of Israeli policies and anti-Semitism. This was apparent during the 2014 Israel-Gaza war, when the same governments that criticized Israeli conduct in the war harshly condemned the frightening increase in anti-Semitic incidents in their societies. To make things more complicated, however, during that conflict, for a number of reasons, including the radicalization of Muslim communities in Europe and the nature of the war, an ugly fusion of anti-Israeli and anti-Semitic sentiments did appear to materialize around the world.

The dangerous nature of the link between the narcissistic compensatory drive of the Chosen People and the paranoid element of the Persecuted People was highlighted, in slightly different terms, by Israeli philosopher Moshe Halbertal. Discussing the Scroll of Esther, the biblical book traditionally read by Jews on the Purim holiday, Halbertal points out that it ends with the Jews taking revenge upon all their enemies. According to Halbertal and Ezrahi, Jewish fantasies of such divine retribution were common in Jewish thought, designed to cope with the fear and humiliation that characterized life in the Diaspora. As Halbertal sees it, now that Israel has significant military power, to give such fantasies a literal interpretation can lead to the kind of actions taken by Baruch Goldstein, who, on Purim of 1994, massacred 29 and wounded more than 125 Muslim worshippers in Hebron's Cave of the Patriarchs.[11] In a more recent, and far more perilous, twist of this link—though one that is arguably closer to the healthy end of the paranoid continuum—when meeting with President Obama in the spring of 2011 to discuss Israel's threat to strike Iranian nuclear facilities, Israeli prime minister Bibi Netanyahu presented him with the Scroll of Esther as a gift. Not only does Esther's story end with a grand retribution upon the enemy, but it starts with nothing other than a Persian plot to annihilate the Jewish people.

IF I FORGET THEE, O EXILE

Perhaps the most dangerous point along the skeptical-paranoid spectrum inhabiting the Israeli psyche comes into focus when you consider the common, and in the Israeli case clearly applicable, refrain that even paranoids have real enemies. The truth is, paranoids are guaranteed to have real enemies because, well, they create them. The paranoid person cannot tolerate and is unaware of his own hostility and therefore projects it onto others, feeling they are out to get him. Naturally, this accusation is perceived by the others as an attack, to which they react by counterattacking, providing the paranoid the proof that they are in fact out to get him. So while Israel has plenty of external reasons, many historical, some current, to feel threatened, some of its existential insecurity is the result of just such a "projective-introjective" cycle. As documented by Nurith Gertz, this paranoid projection, alongside its narcissistic cousin, was a common feature of Jewish perception of the native Arabs during the Zionist settlement of Palestine. The Zionists considered themselves a model of the civilized, benevolent West, attacked and murdered for no apparent reason by the intrinsically violent desert people who lived in their vicinity. They failed to see any hint of hostility or aggression in themselves, in their settling of a land already settled. Israeli psychologist Benjamin Beit-Hallahmi attributes the failure of modern-day Israelis to acknowledge what he calls *the original sin*—that in addition to helping many Jews, Zionism was also a colonialist movement—to the terrifying expectation that if they admit any guilt, they would be punished in a magnitude devastatingly proportional to the crime.[12] Another way of thinking about it is that the Israelis must project their own aggression onto the Palestinians because they cannot tolerate the feelings of guilt associated with it.

Whereas Israel has internalized the historical threat of anti-Semitism and the unconditional hostility of the Arab states in the first three or four decades of its independence, it has not yet fully internalized the reality of its own strength, its greater acceptance by some of the Arab states, and the relative powerlessness of the Palestinians. Thinking they act in self-defense, the Israelis overreact to perceived threats and use overwhelming force, which only re-creates the enemies of the past—as if there weren't enough of them in the present—and reinforces Israel's deep annihilation anxiety. It is not merely the result of anti-Semitism that since Israel occupied the West Bank and Gaza in 1967, much of the world has become critical of Israeli aggression. Up until then, because it was a tiny state, born out of the ashes of Europe's Jewry and surrounded by hostile Arab countries, Israel was viewed, certainly in the West, more as a victim than a victimizer.

But whether or not Israel is now more of an aggressor than a victim, in the Israeli mind the distinction between the two is often lost, drowned by recurring, tsunami-like waves of abandonment and annihilation anxiety. Israel's existential insecurity was perhaps most palpable on the eve of the 1967 war. In the weeks before the war, expecting tens of thousands of casualties—the equivalent of several millions in America—officials from the Tel Aviv Religious Council were surveying vacant lots, parks, and basketball courts and sanctifying them as cemeteries. A few days before the war, Prime Minister Eshkol stumbled on his words in a live radio address, triggering severe public anxiety, which then forced him to revamp his cabinet and establish Israel's first national-unity government. The emotions of that period were movingly captured by Ari Shavit in the opening lines of his 2013 book, *My Promised Land: The Triumph and Tragedy of Israel.* Will the Arabs win? he asked his father as a nine-year-old boy. Will his beloved homeland be overwhelmed by enormous Arab masses or mighty Islamic forces, becoming another Atlantis lost in the depths of the sea?

In reality, the Israeli army was far superior to the combined military forces of several Arab countries and defeated them in just a few days. The anxiety subsided or, more accurately, just went underground, in the heady, euphoric months of the war's aftermath. But it never went away and returned with great vengeance after the surprise attack and early defeats of the 1973 war. In subsequent military campaigns, even when Israel mobilized overwhelming and superior forces, paranoid anxieties persisted. For instance, during the 1982 Israeli invasion of Lebanon, when then Defense Minister Ariel Sharon declared that Israel could behave as the greatest power in the Middle East that it was, his prime minister, Menachem Begin, compared the level of threat posed by PLO forces in Lebanon to that of Nazi Germany in World War II. It was not insignificant that Sharon focused on Israeli power, and Begin, on Israeli vulnerability. Sharon, a sabra, came out of the Labor Zionist tradition that aspired to break with the Diaspora psychology of weakness; Begin was born in Poland and had lost his family in the Holocaust. Begin was never able to buy into the new philosophy. For him, the Jewish state was more of a continuation of the Jewish experience, defined by the hostility of the non-Jewish world. In that respect, the 1977 election of Begin—a largely irrelevant minority opposition figure for some twenty-nine years before—to prime minister can be seen, in psychoanalytic terms, as the "return of the repressed." What had been denied or repressed before had now returned to the surface. This is one way to understand the Israeli overreaction—and therefore public-relations disaster—to the Turkish flotilla of 2010 and subsequent attempts by peace activists to break Israel's naval embargo on Gaza. In the Israeli mind these were not merely minor or illegal protests against the Israeli policy toward impoverished, if radicalized, Gaza, but rather "an armada of hate and violence," as well as attacks on Israel's sovereignty and legitimacy.[13] On the less paranoid end of the spectrum, much of Israel's present existential anxiety is focused on Iran—as observed, even paranoids have real enemies. Hamas and its offshoots in Gaza are also real enemies, contaminated with their own brand of anti-Semitism. As of 2014, however, they were militarily and politically weak, representing no existential threat to Israel.

In the 1980s, a strangely upbeat song, "The Whole World Is Against Us," hit Israel's airwaves and made it to the top of the charts. Commenting on the Israeli outlook at the time, Israeli artist Yair Garbuz reportedly juxtaposed the song with the common Israeli accusation that "the world was silent" during the Holocaust: "The whole world is against us and the world is silent."[14] Garbuz's observation remains as true as it is sarcastic today, placing Israel's present international isolation in the historical context of Jewish persecution. Garbuz's paradox also holds a deep psychological beauty, for it depicts the Israelis as surprised or resentful that the "world" is not protecting them from itself. Whereas the early Zionists focused on "what can *we* do to build a country," subsequent generations have increasingly focused on "what *others* can do to destroy us." In this respect, paranoia is not about trusting others but rather trusting them too much, or correspondingly, not trusting oneself enough. It's about attributing too much power to others and not enough to oneself, and therefore having to strike first. It is no coincidence that the Hebrew word for security, *bitahon,* shares the same root for the word *livto-ah,* to trust, because it is only through trusting, of self and others, that we can attain a real sense of security. Not heeding their own language, but instead clinging to the historical persecution of the Jewish people, over the past two or three decades the Israelis have greeted with fundamental mistrust several peace initiatives, even those originating from their biggest supporter, the United States. They often referred to proposed negotiation terms as "a Munich appeasement" and to the borders associated with a potential peace deal as the "Auschwitz borders." This rhetoric may become a self-fulfilling prophecy, by which Israel dooms itself to repeat the experience of the ghetto as a pariah among the nations and confirms its preexisting narrative about the "Jewish fate," known to every Israeli preschooler as *ha-goral ha-yehudi.*

One feature of this "fate" has been that because the Jews did not or could not trust the gentile population around them, they tended to establish direct relationships with the kings, princes, popes, and bishops—the highest central authorities in the Diaspora. They have thus developed relationships of dependency, hoping against hope and much historical evidence that these powerful figures would be their protectors. In reality, this only further alienated the local populations, and the authorities of the states often betrayed the Jews anyway. As American writer Leon Wieseltier posited during the Arab Spring of 2011, Israel, too, seems to resort to this type of "vertical alliance," relying on such dictators and monarchs as Mubarak and Abdullah to secure regional stability, rather than working to develop a "horizontal alliance" with the Arab populations. If, as a consequence of the Arab Spring, the Arab countries become more democratic or are instead run by even more autocratic or populist regimes as appears to be the case at the time of this writing, this strategy, too—again, one based both on justified and self-inflicted premises of suspicion and mistrust—could prove to be catastrophic. That Egypt and other regressive Arab states have turned out to be Israel's closest allies in its 2014 war with Hamas will do little in the long term to foster a "horizontal alliance" between Israelis and Arabs. The same logic of paranoia and dependency is evident in Israel's relationship with the United States, both in developing a grave military and economic dependency on one superpower, and in embracing one American president over another, say, George W. Bush over Barack Obama. A better strategy would have been to diversify its dependencies by striving for good relations with many countries and to reestablish a wider range of support among the American people at large, including secular, modern Jews and the nonevangelical segments of the general population.

In his memoir, *A Tale of Love and Darkness,* Amos Oz relates a childhood experience familiar to many Israelis of his generation. Before the telephone was common in households in Israel, you'd have to visit the neighborhood pharmacy and place a preplanned call to the other party, which was waiting at the appointed time at the pharmacy of their choice. Oz recalls one such call his parents made from Jerusalem to his aunt and uncle in Tel Aviv as follows:

> "Hello, Tzvi?"
> "Speaking."
> "It's Arieh here, in Jerusalem."
> "Yes, Arieh, hello, it's Tzvi here, how are you?"
> "Everything is fine here. We're speaking from the pharmacy."
> "So are we. What's new?"
> "Nothing new here. How about at your end, Tzvi? Tell us how it's going."
> "Everything is OK. Nothing special to report. We're all well."
> "No news is good news. There's no news here either. We're all fine. How about you?"
> "We're fine, too."

And then Oz's mother and later, Amos himself would get on the phone and repeat the entire sequence. And they would agree to write to set a time for the next call.

Reflecting on the memory, Oz writes:

> But it was no joke: our lives hung by a thread. I realize now that they were not at all sure they would really talk again, this might be the last time, who knows what would happen, there could be riots, a pogrom, a blood bath, the Arabs might rise up and slaughter the lot of us, there might be a war, a terrible disaster, after all Hitler's tanks had almost reached our doorstep from two directions, North Africa and the Caucasus, who knew what else

awaited us? This empty conversation was not really empty, it was just awkward.[15]

Later Oz adds that these conversations also revealed how people in his parents' generation were unable to express private feelings. They had no trouble expressing communal feelings, talking excitedly for hours on end about Nietzsche, Stalin, Freud, Jabotinsky, nationalism, colonialism, anti-Semitism, justice, and so on, but private feelings were a different matter. Today's Israelis still like to converse about communal matters, intellectually and emotionally, but they have no trouble articulating their innermost thoughts to anyone who will listen. Not only is much of Israelis' communal discourse underlied by the same sense of insecurity, their mistrust is also a characteristic of their casual interactions with other individuals. Consistent with the low self-esteem, the permeable boundaries, and the narcissistic projections that power their negative views of fellow Israelis, the Israeli mind has a suspicious, paranoid social core. Amos Oz beautifully traces this back to the Diaspora, when the Jews had to live with the terror that, heaven forbid, they would make a bad impression on the gentiles, who would get mad and "do things to us too dreadful to think about."[16] As Oz's aunt Sonia, an Eastern European–born Jew, saw it, because this was hammered into the head of every Jewish child a thousand times, it distorted Jewish dignity and integrity, making the Jews "dishonest and full of tricks as a cat."[17] "I dislike cats intensely," Sonia says. "I don't like dogs much either, but if I had to choose, I prefer a dog. A dog is like a Gentile, you can see at once what it's thinking or feeling. Diaspora Jews became cats, in the bad sense, if you know what I mean."[18] Sociologist Oz Almog traces this further back in history, well into biblical days. "For by deceptions thou shalt make thy war," the book of Proverbs advises.[19]

Unlike the Diaspora Jews, the Israelis care precious little about making a good impression on the gentiles. In this respect, the Zionist revolution succeeded beyond its wildest dreams. But at the center of the Jew within, fear and mistrust live on and continue to eat away at Israeli integrity and honesty. On the outside, however, the Israeli Jew is more like a dog than a cat, the kind of dog that barks and bites out of fear as much as out of aggression. Amos Oz sheds light on this, too. This time he puts it in the voice of one of the founding fathers of the kibbutz to which he escaped from the suffocation of Jerusalem and his family at age fifteen. Speaking of then opposition leader Menachem Begin, he told Oz:

> Basically he is a good man, that Begin . . . A sort of lapsed *yeshiva bocher,* who believes that if we Jews start shouting at the top of our voices that we are not the way Jews used to be, we're not sheep for the slaughter, we're not pale weaklings but the opposite, we're dangerous now, we're terrifying wolves now, then all the real beasts of prey will be scared of us and give us everything we want, they'll let us have the whole land . . . They, Begin and his chums, talk from morning to evening about power, but they haven't the first idea what power is, what it's made of, what the weaknesses of power are."[20]

This relationship between Israeli anxiety and aggression has been noted for both its positive and negative consequences by several Israeli psychologists. A 1994 study by Erel Shalit concluded that fear of annihilation in the aftermath of the Holocaust was converted into aggressive energy when the Israelis fought their war of independence against the invading Arab armies.[21] Ofer Grosbard described how Israelis struggle with their repressed or denied feeling that their existence is "a bluff," that they live on borrowed time. Unable to contain such anxieties and stress, he explains, they turn it toward others in the form of aggression.[22] Perhaps more convincing is Avner Falk's account, written during the second Palestinian intifada and tying it all together:

> The Palestinian Arab terrorists have added external fears to our inner anxieties. The ever-present danger of a suicide bombing makes us live in a constant state of vigilance and fear for our lives. We express our anxiety through aggressive, even violent behavior in the streets, in the stores, in the banks, offices, on the road, everywhere. Tellingly, Israel has a very high rate of road accidents per capita."[23]

That fear, externally justified and internally contrived, leads not only to loss of integrity and aggression. It also guides many Israelis to formulate personal decisions regarding their and their children's lives trajectories. Israeli couples who spend time overseas often discuss giving birth to a child abroad, to provide him or her with a second citizenship, "just in case." A relative in her thirties with a Polish-born grandmother was planning to pursue a Polish citizenship for her kids. "Polish?" I asked with some surprise. "It's part of the European Union," she said, laughing. But as Oz would put it, it is no joke. A 2011 Bar Ilan University study revealed that about one hundred thousand Israelis already hold a German passport, with seven thousand more Israelis joining them every year, a singular phenomenon among first-world nations.[24] With such survival ploys in mind, many Israelis, if not Israel as a whole, will survive, no matter what the future brings.

Furthermore, the survival value of reality-based fear, or even paranoia, when it compensates for others' complacency is a true and tested principle. In personal, professional, and international relations, hypervigilance propels us to demonstrate strength, and when calibrated correctly, it deters bullies. In the case of Iran, for example, it is still possible that a good-cop/bad-cop strategy will work. Whether explicitly or implicitly coordinated, or simply a by-product of cultural-psychological differences between the United States and Israel, the combined impact of American-promised carrots and Israeli-threatened sticks could theoretically persuade Iran to reach a deal on nuclear energy with the P5+1 group of powers—the five United Nations Security Council permanent members plus Germany—with which it has been negotiating. At the time of this writing, this strategy seems to have worked at least temporarily, as Iran agreed to freeze its nuclear program during the extended negotiations. There is also something to be said for the useful role paranoia plays in the subjective, creative space we call art. As universal an author as Franz Kafka was, to cite an obvious example, it can hardly be denied that many of his masterpieces— from the novels *The Castle* and *The Trial* to his shorter works *The Metamorphosis* and "The Judgment"—are colored by distinctively Jewish paranoid sensibilities. Contemporary Israeli author Etgar Keret, who cites Kafka as the most important literary influence on his work, is perhaps the Israeli version of that Jew. Like Kafka's, the world he has created is both particular and universal, sharing many of the same imaginative, surreal, and sometimes paranoid sensibilities. His work is not as dark as Kafka's, though, and if anything, it underscores the light side of paranoia as a feature of the human imagination.

Nonetheless, the paranoid element within the Israeli psyche does pose a real threat to Israel. In his memoir of the 1948 war, Israeli author Yoram Kaniuk recalls how his generation of Jewish teen-agers in Palestine was taught to rebel against the "Jewish fate" of the Diaspora. With that in mind, during the last Hanukkah holi-day before the war, he and his high school peers climbed Masada. When they summited, just before dawn, they "said something" about how the Germans exterminated the Jews, and they carved on a stone, "If I forget thee, o exile."[25] In a purposeful and ironic reversal of the classic Psalm expression of longing for Zion, they armed themselves with additional motivation for fighting in the war to come. But doubly ironic and potentially tragic, they, like the Israeli mind itself, have recommitted to remember the Diaspora, which in the paradoxical core of its mission Zionism was all too eager to forget.

It is no coincidence that slowly but surely, as I draw this chapter to a close, the Holocaust is creeping its way into the discourse. Nor is it an oversight that this historical event of unparalleled persecutory dimensions was not explored in this chapter. The impact of the Holocaust—the ultimate, nightmarish culmination of anti-Semitism and therefore a major cause of Jewish and Israeli annihilation and abandonment anxieties—on the Israeli mind was of such magnitude and complexity that it requires a chapter of its own.

FOUR

CRYING WHILE SHOOTING

SILENCE AND HALLUCINATIONS

My "aunt" Clara was an enchanting, slightly eccentric, distant relative. When I was growing up in Jerusalem, she was the only person I knew who had something to do with the Holocaust. Not that I knew what it was—it was never mentioned even though she lived only two blocks away and would come over for coffee and cake every Wednesday afternoon, like a German clock. And I never thought about the Holocaust when bumping, almost daily, into the elderly, childless German couple that lived in our five-story building across the short hall from our apartment. Not even as a teenager, when Mr. Gottlieb knocked on our door, not to complain about the loud music I was playing, but rather to compliment me on my taste and give me a recording of Richard Strauss's *Der Rosenkavalier* to add to my budding opera collection.

This was odd, considering I lived in a country where, until the massive immigration of Jews from Arab and North African countries in the 1950s, almost one out of every three persons was a

Holocaust survivor. A country that poured tremendous resources into commemorating the Holocaust, that would send all school-children as well as foreign diplomats and visiting dignitaries to the Yad Vashem Holocaust Museum before allowing them to attend to other important business, and a country whose children would argue with each other while playing soccer in the street about whether the richest guy in the neighborhood was a traitor because he drove a Mercedes.

I've always attributed this detachment to my family's never having been directly touched by the Holocaust. While there was certainly truth to that, many years later I came to see that my own peculiarly dual relation to the Holocaust—my emotional denial of it even as it was staring me in the face—was merely a version of the general Holocaust-related dichotomy that resided in every Israeli at the time. This duality, of an intrusive presence and a dissociated absence, offers a window with which to view much of the psychological legacy of the Holocaust for the survivors themselves and, at one remove, for all Israelis during the early decades of the Jewish state.

Perhaps the most illuminating example of this dual relationship with the Holocaust lies in the life story of one of Israel's most famous Holocaust survivors, the author internationally known by the pen name Ka-Tzetnik. Born in Poland in 1909, Yehiel Feiner was an aspiring young writer and musician when he was sent to Auschwitz, where he lost his entire family. After the war, while recovering in a British army camp in Italy, he spent two and a half weeks writing down everything he had seen and experienced in the concentration camp. When he finished, he handed over the manuscript to a British soldier and asked him to send it to Palestine. The soldier looked at the manuscript. He saw the title *Salamandra* but noticed that the author's name was missing. He bent down to the weakened, emaciated youth and whispered, "You forgot to write the name of the author." "The name of the author?"

cried Feiner. "They who went to the crematories wrote this book! Write their name: Ka-Tzetnik." That name came from the German acronym *KZ* (*ka tzet*) for "concentration camp," where the inmates were referred to as *Ka-Tzetniks*, along with the number assigned to them. Yehiel Feiner had been *Ka-Tzetnik* 135633.[1]

Once he followed his manuscript to Israel, Feiner changed his last name to De-Nur, which means "from fire." His *Salamandra* was one of the first books about the Holocaust to be published in Israel. Like all his subsequent books, most famously *House of Dolls*, it was an autobiographical novel detailing the horrifying and disturbing events of the daily routine at Auschwitz. But as he revealed many years later, putting this in writing did nothing to relieve his sufferings. For years he continued to experience the Holocaust in his sleep, waking up nightly from nightmares feverish, dripping sweat, and sobbing.

Whereas in his books and dreams—both of which are a form of fiction—he told the story of the Holocaust, in his daily life he went to great lengths to distance himself from it. Like many other survivors he was intensely introverted. He never told his wife his prewar name. Though he became a household name in Israel and his books were translated into many languages, he forbade his publishers to print his photograph. He refused all requests for interviews and never spoke in public. For thirty-five years he did not own a short-sleeve shirt so as not to expose the blue, six-digit number branded on his arm and known to every Israeli as an ID from "there." He later wrote that he didn't even know his concentration-camp number by heart, and that furthermore, as a result of this identity trauma, his mind could never retain numbers.

Only once during these long years was Ka-Tzetnik's anonymity punctured. In 1961, Israel captured and put on trial Hitler's right-hand man and head of the Department of Jewish Affairs in the Gestapo, Adolf Eichmann. Ka-Tzetnik was a witness for the prosecution. When he took the stand, he spoke in a haunted, prophetic style, describing Auschwitz as a far-away planet whose inhabitants lived and died by the laws of another nature. They had no names, no parents, and no children. They were dressed differently and they adhered to a different time cycle. It was as if he were reading from one of his books, noted the author Haim Guri, who was covering the trial for a newspaper. When the prosecutor and judge tried to bring Ka-Tzetnik back to the task at hand, he suddenly fainted and collapsed to the floor. This was the most dramatic moment during Eichmann's trial, and perhaps one of the most symbolically loaded moments in Israeli history. Many years later Ka-Tzetnik told historian Tom Segev that he had fainted, because, testifying as Mr. De-Nur, he was asked for the first time in his life to admit that he was Ka-Tzetnik.[2]

After the trial, Ka-Tzetnik did everything in his power to wipe out the connection between De-Nur and Ka-Tzetnik. The one time he agreed to appear in public—to take part in an award ceremony named after him, or rather his pen name, for literary works on the Holocaust—he changed his mind on the way to the ceremony at the presidential palace and never showed up.

Ka-Tzetnik was thus compelled to reexperience the trauma of the Holocaust through creative representation, while at the same time distancing or dissociating from it in his day-to-day life. In principle, this was the case for the survivors as a whole: they could never forget or ignore the Holocaust, yet they could never accept or digest it. To use a common Hebrew refrain, it was something you could neither swallow nor throw up. To cope with this anguish, survivors sometimes "divided" it into two separate and therefore more manageable parts. Mental-health professionals who work with adult children of survivors often discover that these patients grew up in one of two, seemingly opposite types of homes. In one, the surviving parent never stopped talking about the Holocaust. His or her sufferings and loss could not be contained, and the family was flooded with detailed stories of the experience or, alternatively, with pedantic lectures about the lessons of the Holocaust for the younger generation and the Jewish people. Either way, the child in such a family was directly exposed to the horror and the grief, as well as the overwhelming nature, of the Holocaust. To protect himself, this child gradually learned to turn off and check out when the stories or lectures came pouring out. As an adult, he might well end up not wanting to know or think much about his parents' past nor the Holocaust itself.

In the other family type, the surviving parent never spoke about what happened to him or her. The sufferings and loss were not to be brought into the new life, the Holocaust experiences suppressed or repressed (the former, conscious; the latter, unconscious). A child raised in this kind of a family is burdened by the unspoken. He can't help but sense the parents' ongoing struggle to ward off the potential intrusion of a frightening past. He thus grows up with anxiety, insecurity, and fearful curiosity. In adulthood, many such people are driven to uncover the disavowed story of the parent and to find out as much as possible about the Holocaust. Sometimes this is promoted by other people in their lives who cannot tolerate their unnamed anxiety or emotional absence.

The duality of the trauma—the conflict between the need to re-experience it and the wish to escape it—is plainly evident in both of these homes. In both cases, one side of the conflict is projected onto, and is subsequently played out by, the second generation. In the former type, by dwelling on the past, the parent unconsciously sets up the child to escape it, or to do what the parent himself wished but was unable to do. In the latter type, by totally avoiding the past, the parent unconsciously sets up the child to want to know more about it, or to experience it *for* him, obviously in a far more tolerable fashion.

These two types of survivors' reactions are consistent with the two principal versions of post-traumatic stress disorder as it manifests in postcombat veterans or other individuals who have been through an equivalent trauma. In one version, the victim continues to reexperience the traumatic event in nightmares, flashbacks, anxiety, the startle response, and so on, while in the other, he numbs himself to any feelings and withdraws from people in order to avoid being emotionally triggered and overwhelmed. In therapy, the goal is to integrate these two syndromes, helping one patient to contain the anxiety and move away from the trauma, and the other, to confront the trauma and let in some anxiety. Many individuals with PTSD are somewhere in between the two extremes, vacillating from one to the other in an effort to find a resting place.

Ka-Tzetnik had, it appears, struggled mightily to integrate these two positions. We know that after years of suffering silently through his nightmares, his wife finally pleaded with him to seek help. He refused for a long time, explaining that nobody, not even those who had been to Auschwitz, could ever understand him. When his wife heard about a new form of treatment, developed by Dutch physician Jan Bastiaans, at the Center for War Injuries in Leiden, Holland, she again begged Ka-Tzetnik to try it. At last he gave in. He was just about sixty when he arrived in Holland for what he knew was a highly controversial treatment. Bastiaans's therapy rested on the reasonable-enough assumption that in becoming introverted many survivors created an internal concentration camp, walling themselves off from the healing touch of other people. The more questionable element in his approach was his use of LSD to break down these defenses. Unlike drugs with soothing or numbing effects, LSD tends to sharpen perceptions. It usually precipitates powerful flashbacks from significant events in the past. Bastiaans injected his patients with several rounds of LSD, recorded or videotaped their reactions, and then analyzed them. The idea was to force the patient to reexperience and confront his trauma directly, under supportive medical supervision. Bastiaans received permission to administer his treatment in the 1960s only after several Dutch Holocaust survivors sent a petition to the queen.

During his LSD-induced trances, Ka-Tzetnik experienced the most horrific hallucinations. He saw his mother standing naked with other women on line to the crematorium and then going up in smoke. He saw his sister among the camp prostitutes. He saw a friend from the barracks being beaten to death on his naked buttocks. He saw starving prisoners attacking one of their own after his face was covered with jelly by the guards. Within seconds, a thousand prisoners were licking and biting each other, and when it was all over, Ka-Tzetnik saw the bloody, eaten-away corpse of a friend, surrounded by laughing German guards. And he saw an SS soldier murdering a boy whom he had sexually abused. The soldier then grilled the boy's body on a skewer and ate it piece by piece.

During a break between trances, Ka-Tzetnik was able for the first time in his life to expose the number on his arm—to a group of German tourists when he was taking a walk on the beach. He later wrote that when one of these tourists, who had strange, elaborate tattoos on his chest and arms, approached Ka-Tzetnik on the beach to examine his simple and therefore more unique tattoo, Ka-Tzetnik suddenly panicked. "A crazed beast was awakening inside me, ready to plunge its fangs into the throat of this creature standing over me. I jumped to my feet, shouting curses, and ran."[3]

In a subsequent trance, Ka-Tzetnik saw himself in an SS uniform, wearing a hat with the skull insignia. He then came to what he considered the major discovery of his treatment: *Auschwitz was man-made, and in different circumstances he himself could have been the Nazi murderer, and the Germans, his victims.* This insight triggered a horrible sense of guilt and a desperate plea to God: "O Lord, merciful and compassionate Lord, am I the one, the one who created Auschwitz?"[4] This new awareness also apparently cured Ka-Tzetnik of his nightmares—strangely, though logically, by creating a new problem for him. While letting go of his nighttime dreams about the past, he now developed daytime fears about the future. If the Holocaust was indeed man-made, what could man do now when he had the atom bomb at his disposal? He thus began to have tormenting visions about a nuclear holocaust. "Wherever there is humankind, there is Auschwitz," he later explained.[5] He had gone to Holland demanding an explanation for Auschwitz of the night, he wrote, but where might he go now for an explanation of Auschwitz of the day?

Whatever one makes of this type of treatment, in broad conceptual terms it bears some similarity to contemporary psychoanalytic therapy. Both seek not to eliminate symptoms but rather to replace them with more authentic sufferings, which is what Ka-Tzetnik's outcome appears to have been. Indeed, as part of the horrific realization that under certain circumstances he, too, could have been a Nazi, Ka-Tzetnik came to see that Auschwitz was not another planet after all. It was very much man's creation and should therefore not be walled off or delegated to dreams and other works of fiction. It had to be—it was—part of everyday reality. Thus, Ka-Tzetnik and De-Nur were one and the same, not of two different worlds, and with this resolution Ka-Tzetnik terminated his therapy. Dramatically, Ka-Tzetnik's LSD-induced hallucinations allowed him to leave the "other planet" behind, in Holland, or more accurately, to bring it back into his reality in Israel. He continued to struggle with integrating the two, and it was ten years before he was able to write the story of his treatment, which further reinforced this integrative process. When that book finally came out, Ka-Tzetnik did something that was unthinkable for him before: he gave Israeli television an extended interview.

THEY KNEW WHAT WAS COMING

With one important exception, which we will soon visit in some depth, Ka-Tzetnik's personal journey paralleled that of Israeli society as a whole over the past sixty to seventy years. For a long time, starting with the early days of the state, the Holocaust was omnipresent in symbolic, creative forms everywhere in the country, yet generally absent from the real, person-to-person lives of most Israelis. Poems were read, movies shown, and history told, all in commemoration ceremonies, museums, and schools. Blustery political and ethical debates took place, full of theatrical accusations and, at times, violence. Did some labor leaders negotiate with Hitler's top echelon to save their own relatives and a few, privileged others? Should Israel accept financial restitution from, and have diplomatic relations with, Germany? Constant public vows were made to never forget, with the often-expressed exclamation of *never again*. But on the rare occasions when private emotions came to the foreground, the general rule was "Whoever wishes to make history is obligated to forget history."[6] This quote, from French political theorist Ernest Renan, was actually used by an Israeli diplomat to support negotiations with the Germans on the grounds that "policy is not a matter of emotions."[7]

Certainly until the Eichmann trial, some fifteen years after the end of World War II, and to a great extent for a number of years afterward, the real personal pain and sufferings of actual survivors remained unspoken. During all those years I never asked my parents what Aunt Clara's story was. When I finally did, sometime in the 1980s, I found out she had survived by jumping off a train going to Auschwitz. In a more recent conversation my mother added that over the years she had twice asked Clara about it. But all Clara said was that her mother, who was on the train with her, had urged her to jump, and that after she did, she was taken in by a farmer. She then raised her hand to signal "no more." She said nothing further about her mother, or about what happened to her at the farmer's house, leading my mother to speculate that she had been raped there.

Clara's silence was nothing if not typical. As noted by historian Hanna Yablonka, up until the Eichmann trial, Israeli survivors lived behind a fragile though tangible wall, defensively built to help them function in their daily lives.[8] Struggling to contain their sufferings and fearful of burdening others with their pain, they forwent emotional expression in their interactions with other people, at least insofar as it could trigger emotions related to the "other planet." This reserve was unusual in a country so intimate, where everybody's business was everybody else's, and where nonsurvivors hardly contained their own feelings about the Holocaust. When on May 23, 1960, Prime Minister Ben-Gurion announced in the Knesset that Israeli security forces had captured Adolf Eichmann, the country was overcome with emotion. For several days, newspapers focused on the emotional reactions of the public as well as of the journalists themselves. According to Yablonka, people reacted with a mixture of shock, pride, gratification, feelings of vengeance, and heightened anticipation. Holocaust survivors, however, about 25 percent of the population at that time, expressed no more than guarded satisfaction. They knew what was coming: center stage, exposure, and the opening of barely patched wounds. Here once again we see the dual essence of the trauma, divided, in this case, among not survivors and their offspring, but rather two population groups. It was safe for nonsurvivors to articulate emotions, yet the same prospect left survivors disturbed and silent.

But the survivors' reluctance to expose their wounds was not merely a severe version of a typical post-traumatic reaction. It was also the result of how they were treated by the early Israelis. Even before the Holocaust, when German Jews started emigrating to Palestine after Hitler's ascent to power, the Yishuv didn't exactly embrace the Yekkes, as they were referred to, often derisively. While the Jewish Agency wanted to create a Jewish majority in Palestine, it advocated selective immigration. The labor Zionists who dominated the agency envisioned a new, agriculturally based society and therefore preferred young, single, and physically fit immigrants. They were unhappy that many of the German immigrants were businessmen with families and, worse, social-welfare cases. They complained that the "human material" coming out of Germany was poor. Henrietta Szold, who headed the Jewish Agency's division of social work, periodically demanded that sick or needy immigrants be returned to Nazi Germany so that they would not burden the Yishuv.[9]

The Yishuv also condemned the Yekkes for their difficulties with, or unwillingness to learn, Hebrew. In Tel Aviv, Israeli youths vandalized the Rivoli café because its German owners did not speak Hebrew. Sometime later, the Tel Aviv municipality itself sent letters to German-speaking residents advising them that holding private parties in the German language at their homes ran counter to the spirit of the city and could not be tolerated. In addition, the immigrants were widely ridiculed for what was perceived to be their excessive obedience to authority, their pedantic concern with rules and regulations, and their longing for German culture. In a meeting with German immigrants, Ben-Gurion, at the time head of the Yishuv, repeated many of these stereotypes. He joked that in Germany if you wanted to have a revolution, you had to get a permit. He explained that the German character trait of obedience had made it possible for Hitler to gain power. Meanwhile, in Jerusalem, the press reported that a fourteen-year-old immigrant was told by a fellow student to "go back to Hitler." German-born writers complained that the vitriolic language used against the Yekkes was reminiscent of the language of the anti-Semites in Europe, perhaps even of the Nazis.

Clearly, much of the hostility toward the Yekkes was colored by the early Zionists' rejection of what they viewed as Jewish weakness, passivity, and dependency. In the Yekkes, the Zionists detected and detested the "exile mentality" of yesteryear, against which they had fought their entire lives. Tragically, the Holocaust, or certainly the Zionist interpretation of the Holocaust, only reinforced this attitude, which in turn compounded and exacerbated the silent alienation of the survivors who made it to Israel. When I think further about my own detached, even cavalier attitude toward the Holocaust as a teenager in the 1960s and 1970s, I must admit it had a somewhat hostile edge. In part, it was no doubt a function of my personal immaturity and lack of empathy at that age. However, in my mind's eye, I can easily summon up rows of other bored and irritated teenagers, all struggling to sit through the annual Holocaust and Heroism Day school assembly, making sarcastic comments about the program and mocking the movies of mass graves and piles of skeletons, shoes, gold teeth, and clothes. This was not merely disagreeable teenage behavior, but rather a symptom of a general tendency within Israeli society at the time.

At the end of World War II, mindful as always of its mission to expand the Jewish population of Palestine, the Yishuv was eager to absorb as many survivors as possible. Notwithstanding, the early reports from its envoys to the displaced-persons refugee camps in Europe described the survivors in such harsh, judgmental terms as "human debris" and "a community of beggars."[10] One envoy, later a general in the IDF and an ambassador, wrote a report suggesting that those who survived were "egoists" who looked out for themselves first. Others criticized the refugees for their petty thievery, for getting married too quickly out of despair, and for having sex in front of their children.

About this time, a charismatic partisan resistance fighter, who later became famous for leading a group of Holocaust survivors in a plan to poison the drinking water of 6 million Germans, wrote that the Jews "should not go like lambs to the slaughter."[11] This phrase was subsequently appropriated by the Israeli establishment and general public and, perhaps more than anything else, came to represent the disparaging stance of Israelis toward the victims and survivors. Consciously, the Israelis could neither comprehend nor tolerate the lack of significant resistance among the Jews who were sent to the death camps. As noted by Segev, this was the reason the word *heroism* became affixed like a twin to the word *Holocaust* in official commemoration language.[12] In a particularly twisted form of moral judgment, unofficial, popular language often referred to German survivors and their offspring as *sabonim,* or soaps—an allusion to the widespread if unfounded notion that the Nazis used the bodies of murdered Jews to produce soap. The singular *sabon* later became a general, derogatory vernacular equivalent to the English *square* or *goody two-shoes.*

On a less conscious level, the survivors represented an internal psychological threat to the national ego's ideal of the sabra. As Segev observed, during that period the sabras themselves were still struggling to ward off their own "exile mentality." After all, most Israelis then had previously been Diaspora Jews themselves. The disdain for the survivors, therefore, reflected the sabras' need to distance themselves from the historical mirror thrust in their midst in the aftermath of the war. The more the survivors resisted the new national ideal or failed to measure up to it, the more they reminded the sabras of the gap between reality and the ideal, and of their failure to close it. Israeli novelist Aharon Appelfeld commented on this in a story about a boy arriving from Poland and trying to get a suntan like his sabra peers so that they would accept him. When he fails, the sabra boys beat him because the paleness of his skin forces them to confront the Diaspora and the Holocaust.

This type of projection and scapegoating is universal, as attested to by comedian Yakov Smirnoff's joke that as soon as he was sworn in as an American citizen, he looked around at the crowd of immigrants sworn in with him and said to himself, "God damn all these immigrants." But the uniquely Israeli version of this goes beyond the issue of immigration and acculturation, right to the core of the Israeli national character, with its paradoxical search to reinvent, not merely put behind, the past. Thus, for the first two to three decades after the Holocaust, survivors were fearful not only of their own pain, but also of being judged for their supposed weakness. Their neighbors and friends, on the other hand, were fearful of pain and weakness by association.

NOT ONE OF US WILL LEAVE HERE
AS HE WAS BEFORE

The trial of Adolf Eichmann has been described as the beginning of Israel's national therapy for the wounds of the Holocaust. But a genuine therapy of this type is long and complex. It is often unpredictable and sometimes downright dangerous. As with Ka-Tzetnik, the dredging up of memories and the searchlight of self-examination can be extremely painful. The result is rarely a Hollywood-style happy ending. Sometimes the outcome looks worse than the presenting problem, at least for a while, as the patient unravels and appears unable to put himself back together.

Israeli academics have studied in some depth both the short- and long-term impact of the Eichmann trial on Israeli society. Israel had no television in 1961, but the trial was carried live on radio and received daily newspaper coverage for nine months. People listened to it at home, in coffee shops, in restaurants, and in stores. Over 60 percent of Israelis over the age of fourteen listened to at least a part of the trial, and to many it became an important life event. As Holocaust survivors, representing different countries, ages, religious orientations, and types of torture and losses suffered, stood up in endless succession and described for the first time in public their experiences in the camps, the entire country convulsed in cathartic identification and empathy. Witnesses related in excruciating details the horrific atrocities they had seen and experienced, including mass shootings, sexual abuse, sterilization, naked bodies of dead parents or children, starvation, and the eating of human liver. Every once in a while someone in the courtroom audience would faint and be taken out by first-aid workers. Gideon Hausner, the state prosecutor handling the case, later wrote, "Listening was torture. I felt almost as if I was breathing the gasses and the stench of the burnt flesh."[13]

Reporting from the courtroom, Haim Guri famously wrote, "Not one of us will leave here as he was before."[14] Most researchers in the field agree that the effects of the trial were profound and long lasting, extending far beyond the courtroom and those who participated. Historian Hanna Yablonka concluded that the survivors' testimony has settled deep in the minds of young Israelis, effectuating a far greater understanding and acceptance of the survivors' burdens. In the aftermath of the trial—which produced the only state execution in Israeli history—survivors began to feel more comfortable telling their stories. Yablonka called this "the privatization of the Holocaust." It was no longer about the generic "six millions," but rather about the individual reclaiming his or her personal anguish. The change was gradual but dramatic, and with time it proved to be all-encompassing.[15]

In the immediate decade after the trial, authors born or raised in Israel started writing for the first time about the Holocaust, treating it as an intimate protagonist in their novels and stories. In the past, these authors wrote solemn, heroic, and above all national, commemorative poetry. Now they were weaving the horror of the Holocaust into the psychological narrative of their characters. A classic example was Yoram Kaniuk's 1969 novel, *Adam Ben Kelev,* in which a man is admitted to a psychiatric hospital after attempting to strangle a woman. The man had been a clown in a German circus and used his talent to survive a concentration camp by becoming a German officer's toy pet. At the German's demand, he learned how to bark, walk on all fours, and eat from a dog bowl. Eventually he moved in with the officer as his dog. Tragically, this masochistic survival strategy remained part of his personality even after the war, and he couldn't rid himself of it. In the end, unlike the many other tormented survivors in the hospital, the man does heal—chiefly through a cathartic dialogue with a schizophrenic boy who also believes he is a dog.

But once they migrated from the courtroom, the sufferings of the survivors did not stay on the bookshelf. Coinciding with the growing influence of Western, and especially American, individualism, the stories of individual survivors began to appear everywhere. Yom Hashoa Vehagvura, until then a formal, national memorial to the Six Millions and the heroism of the partisans, gradually transformed into a personal show-and-tell. State programs shifted away from familiarizing the public with the facts of the Holocaust to bringing the experience closer to home. High schools, once content to take students on the obligatory day trip to the Jerusalem Holocaust museum, Yad Vashem, now began to fly them over for a weeklong tour of Auschwitz and other concentration camps in Poland. These overseas trips, a common practice by the 1990s, eventually became a highly emotional and sometime traumatic rite of passage for many Israeli youth. Typically, the trips are preceded by months of intellectual and psychological preparation, which are integrated into the school curriculum. Tom Segev joined one of those trips. Prior to the journey, he later reported, some students expressed the fear that they would feel nothing in the camps. But this turned out to be an unfounded concern: sooner or later on the trip, each and every student broke down, and most more than once. Commenting on these students' pilgrimages to "discover their 'roots,'" author David Grossman wrote, "For non-religious young Jews, the Holocaust often becomes the central element in their national identity."[16] Cognizant of the powerful impact of these heritage trips on the young Israeli mind, in 2011 the Israeli Ministry of Education announced a plan to subsidize the trip for those high school students who could not afford it.

In the early 2000s Yad Vashem itself underwent a transformation. After a ten-year, $56 million renovation, the museum is more than three times larger than before. Gone are the document-driven, didactic exhibition halls telling the story of the collective 6 million. In their place is a largely underground structure, architecturally designed to enhance the experience of descending into a dehumanized abyss, where the personal stories of about one hundred victims are told through artifacts, photographs, diaries, and testimonials. In reviewing the renovated museum, Steven Erlanger of *The New York Times* started with a profound, if simple, statement: "The Holocaust is the cornerstone of the Israeli state, and Yad Vashem is its guardian."[17] Yad Vashem is also the ultimate symbol of the Holocaust trauma pervading the Israeli mind from top to bottom. Due to the language barrier and the general intensity and vitality of life in Israel, foreign observers and visitors often fail to appreciate the magnitude of this phenomenon. But Israelis, too, can be blind to it, in part because Holocaust-related references, images, and sensibilities are so embedded in daily life that they are hardly noticeable. So even now, some seventy years after the Holocaust, as the survivors are bidding farewell to this planet, their psychology, at least in Israel, is not leaving with them. Consider a story reported a few years ago by veteran Israeli journalist Yaron London in a leading Israeli tabloid. London was traveling in southern Israel to the town of Dimona with a younger friend, a second-generation sabra who had no personal connection to the Holocaust. They drove by a modern outdoor sculpture boasting tall, colorful ceramic posts. A happy sculpture alluding to a roaring elephant's tusks, London thought.

"Auschwitz," uttered his friend.

"What are you talking about?" asked London.

"Well, we are on the way to Dimona, the site of our nuclear arms, which is the answer to the Holocaust, and these chimneys make me think of Auschwitz."[18]

Alluding to the Holocaust in his memoir of the 1948 War of Independence, author Yoram Kaniuk put it this way: "Israel is in fact a state of the dead. It was founded for the dead. It is a reminder that maybe they didn't have to die, had we founded it fifty years earlier. How can a Jewish state live with the historical glue of a God who in cold blood murdered a third of its people?" Tel Aviv–born Kaniuk notes that most of his friends' parents lost the families they had left behind in Europe "They eagerly sent us to create a state for their lost families," he explains, "to found a state for their dead, not knowing that this state would be a kind of an insane asylum in the desert, seeded all over with the bone dust of the Jews who didn't make it alive."[19]

Several historians, most famously Hannah Arendt, pointed out that the Eichmann trial was not conducted in accordance with the general principles of legal practice in Israel.[20] Most of the survivors' testimony, according to this view, was presented not to build the case against the accused, but rather to advance the Zionist narrative that the Holocaust was another chapter in a history of Jewish persecution, which goes all the way back to the slavery of ancient Egypt. During the trial, the judges tried to rein in the prosecution and the witnesses, but most historians agree that the state used the trial for extrajudicial purposes. While some opine this to have been a legitimate educational enterprise, others characterize it as a cynical political ploy. Either way, the trial undeniably reintroduced to Israeli consciousness the notion of "the whole world is against us and the world is silent." Under the surface, the "contribution" of the Holocaust to this historical orientation was in evidence even before the trial. Indeed, as proposed by a number of historians, Israeli awareness of the near-total annihilation of European Jewry played a significant role in the country's drive to acquire nuclear technology in the 1950s. Upon retiring as chairman of Israel's Atomic Energy Commission in 1966, Ernst David Bergmann justified Israel's nuclear project by warning that various other countries might one day reach nuclear capability. "I cannot forget," wrote Bergmann, "that the Holocaust came on the

Jewish people as a surprise. The Jewish people cannot allow them-selves such an illusion for a second time."[21] Yet for obvious strate-gic reasons, and perhaps also for the same psychological reasons that the survivors' personal memories remained hidden for so many years, Israel's nuclear project and its rationale were a top state secret until uncovered in a 1960 *Time* magazine scoop.

Generally speaking, however, prior to the Eichmann trial Holocaust-related anxieties rarely broke to the surface of public consciousness. A notable exception occurred on the eve of the 1956 war—in which Israel, together with France and England, invaded Egypt's Sinai—when Israeli leaders described Egyptian president Nasser as a fascist dictator surrounded by Nazi emissaries. One Is-raeli newspaper ran a full-page story about a former SS officer whom it depicted as the man behind Nasser. It turned out this man was most likely also an undercover Israeli agent. After the war, claiming self-defense, Ben-Gurion wrote to an American general, "You know as well as I do what they did to us fifteen years ago."[22] But just as the trial released the survivors' personal stories, it un-leashed the collective annihilation anxiety previously suppressed in the forward-looking mind-set of the founding generation. When asked during the trial why they didn't resist the Nazis, witnesses repeatedly said that up to the last minute they did not believe they were going to be killed. Witnessing the witnesses' denial, Israelis vowed never to make the same mistake. Unfortunately, this very oath, combined with the historical burden of Jewish persecution, predisposed them to make the opposite mistake. Since the Eich-mann trial, Holocaust-related existential anxiety has played a role in every foreign-policy and security decision made by the coun-try's leadership. This, despite that, starting in the 1960s, precisely because of that anxiety, Israel began to establish itself as a regional superpower.

In the early 1960s, Israel's body politic was ensnarled by a scandal after Mossad agents alleged that German scientists were helping Egypt to develop chemical and biological weapons. The German/gas association fueled a public hysteria, which did not die down even when the allegations proved to be fictitious and the head of the Mossad had to resign. Indirectly, the scandal also led to Ben-Gurion's resignation because it made it even more difficult for him to justify his policy of increased cooperation with West Germany.

Then came the "waiting period," the three weeks prior to the 1967 war during which people everywhere talked not about being invaded, but rather "exterminated," by the Arabs. Nasser was repeatedly compared to Hitler and gallows humor abounded. After the war, a young Israeli soldier was quoted in the book *The Seventh Day* saying, "People believed we would be exterminated if we lost the war. We got this idea—or inherited it—from the concentration camps. It's a concrete idea for anyone who has grown up in Israel, even if he personally didn't experience Hitler's persecution. Genocide—it's a real possibility. There are the means to do it. That's the lesson of the gas chambers."[23]

When the war finally broke out with a preemptive Israeli attack, it took the IDF only six days to defeat the combined armies of several Arab countries and to capture Egyptian, Jordanian, and Syrian territories three times the size of Israel. Years later, the magnitude of this victory led some historians to conclude that while the fear of extermination had been real, the threat had not. As put by Tom Segev, "More than any other factor, fear had prompted the war."[24] That fear, Segev and others observed, was rooted in the Holocaust.

After the war, some Israeli leaders, including bookish dove Abba Eban, began to refer to Israel's pre-1967 borders as the "Auschwitz lines." While the euphoria of the following year or two masked much of Israel's Holocaust anxiety, the 1973 war brought it back with a vengeance. In that war, in spite, or perhaps because of, its more secure borders, Israel was caught off guard and came into real danger. Among other things, this threat brought home to Israelis their complete dependency on the United States, whose political and military support proved crucial in turning the war around. As pointed out by former IDF deputy chief education officer Colonel Ehud Praver, the Yom Kippur War made Israelis feel what the Diaspora Jews they had so despised felt so many times before— isolated, abandoned, and unable to fight back on their own. Praver believes that the 1973 war decoupled in the Israeli mind the words *Holocaust* and *heroism*. Whereas prior to that war, Israelis identified with the handful of partisans who heroically resisted the Nazis, they now tasted the limit of heroism.[25] At the time, historians and media pundits labeled that war an "earthquake." From a psychological perspective, however, it was merely one more milestone in a long-term process in which Israeli overreliance on the sabra defense mechanism of heroism gave way to the more pervasive, if not always conscious, Holocaust- and other Diaspora-related anxieties.

In 1977 Israel elected the long-standing opposition-party leader, Menachem Begin, to become its first Holocaust-survivor prime minister. This was no coincidence. As demonstrated by a 1990 Ben-Gurion University study, starting in the late seventies, the Holocaust became an event common to all Israelis regardless of their origins or cultural background.[26] A similar 1992 study of Israeli identity among university students preparing to become teachers found that close to 80 percent identified with the statement "We are all Holocaust survivors."[27] Indeed, in subsequent years, Holocaust-based persecution and annihilation anxieties have become even more pervasive, easily turning out to be the most salient psychological factor influencing government policy. Begin, who publicly dramatized and exaggerated his personal survivor story, referred to the Holocaust repeatedly when discussing security and foreign affairs. In 1981 he justified the Israeli bombing of the Iraqi nuclear plant, saying, "We must protect our nation, a million and a half of whose children were murdered by the

Nazis in the gas chambers."[28] On the eve of Israel's 1982 invasion of Lebanon, he told his cabinet, "There is no way other than to fight selflessly. Believe me, the alternative is Treblinka, and we have decided that there will be no more Treblinkas."[29]

This kind of resolve—bolstered by the same basic fear—also guided the Israeli response to the first Palestinian intifada. The mass demonstrations in the Palestinian territories, even when violent, did not threaten the state of Israel. Carried out by young teens, women, and other unarmed civilians hurling stones at Israeli soldiers, the uprising could have been treated as civil disorder. Instead it was perceived as an existential threat and met with beatings and bullets.

In 1991, during the first Gulf War, when American pressure deterred Israel from responding to Saddam Hussein's missiles, and the US military was searching in western Iraqi for Scuds aimed at Israel, Israelis were left with their fear, minus their resolve. Heightened by this forced passivity, their Holocaust anxiety was in full view. Saddam was referred to as "little Hitler." The gas masks, distributed in preparation for a possible chemical attack, reverberated for everyone with an unmistakable connotation. An Israeli teenager waiting with his peers in the airport for their flight to Poland was heard joking that they didn't need to worry because when Saddam's chemical missiles hit Tel Aviv, they would be in Auschwitz. And as in the early sixties with Egypt, false reports alleged German involvement in the development of Iraqi chemical weapons. Only this time, there was no preemptive or even retaliatory action. There was only fear. For the first time in Israel's war history, thousands of Israelis left their homes and fled south, out of the missiles' range.

A version of this dynamic took hold of the Israeli mind during the second Palestinian intifada. As we shall soon discuss, the 2000–2005 uprising precipitated an assortment of anxiety-related conditions in a huge number of Israelis. But in addition, the

apparent lack of a military solution to the relentless waves of terrorist attacks tearing at the heart of the country reactivated the
same old association of fear and passivity. And worse than in the
Gulf War, this time there was no place to escape to, and for a
while, no end in sight. Under these circumstances, the widely
held feelings of helplessness turned into a national depression of
sorts, a broad sense of gloom accompanied by a vague cognition
that the "end is near." While these feelings subsided when the
intifada faded away, the subsequent Israeli drive to separate
from the Palestinians—spearheaded by the unilateral withdrawal
from Gaza and the erection of the West Bank barrier—was,
among other things, an attempt to return to the Zionist psychological defense of springing into a bold action when confronted
by an unyielding reality. It is again no accident that this drive was
led by Ariel Sharon, a classical Zionist character, who for better
and for worse made a career out of rejecting fear, passivity, and
helplessness by taking a daring, grand action, with major personal,
national, and international consequences. In this case, since a unilateral separation on terms unacceptable even to the most moderate
Palestinians was unlikely to result in progress toward peace, it
was hard to imagine that redrawn, narrower borders, marked by
a tall fence, would alter the fundamental Holocaust anxiety residing within the Israeli psyche. The subsequent wars with Gaza-based
Hamas—an organization equipped with rockets and missiles that
could reach deep into Israel and driven by an Islamist and anti-
Semitic ideology—naturally made matters worse. And it did not
help that during those years, the president of a country on the
verge of attaining nuclear weapons would repeatedly declare that
the Holocaust was a myth construed by the West to justify Zionist
colonialism, and that Israel should be wiped off the map.

As David Grossman once observed, in Europe, when people
mention the Holocaust, they talk about "what happened *then*," that
is, in the past. In Hebrew, or Yiddish, people say not *then*, but

rather, *there,* in those other places or human conditions, as if it is not quite over, at least not for the Jews.[30] Indeed, in Israel at present, as in the last two to three decades, hardly a day goes by without some mention of, or allusion to, the Holocaust in the media. When an Israeli soldier confronts a rock-throwing Palestinian teenager, in his less-than-conscious mind's eye he is confronting an all-powerful, dangerous Nazi. Likewise, when an Israeli diplomat visits Washington to discuss Israeli security concerns, consciously or unconsciously he is thinking Auschwitz. Clearly, the pendulum had swung. Very much like the author Ka-Tzetnik, Israel as a whole has undergone a therapeutic catharsis bringing the repressed horrors of yesterday to the consciousness of today. Now we know why nobody wanted to hear the stories the survivors didn't want to tell. If the Eichmann trial marked the onset of Israel's national therapy, at present the country is mired in the dangerous, seemingly interminable middle phase of treatment, struggling against a steady current of debilitating anxieties, with intermittent existential flash floodings.

Israeli psychologist Ofer Grosbard, among others, posits that to reach maturity and stability, a nation, much like an individual, must acquire the capacity to tolerate and process, without necessarily jumping into action, just such emotional turmoil.[31] Therein lies the danger for Israel and the international community. If the Israeli mind cannot contain the fear and rage that emerged from the long shadow of the Holocaust, Israeli governments may continue to find themselves pressed to act too forcefully or prematurely. This could translate into a more aggressive military course, possibly escalating all the way to a nuclear confrontation—with Iran, Pakistan, or other hostile countries that may acquire weapons of mass destruction in the future. Or, it could mean further unilateral withdrawal or otherwise unwise retreats that may well undermine Israeli security and ultimately lead to a similar escalation. A poorly calibrated combination of aggression and retreat—perhaps the most dangerous outcome—is also a likely scenario. Finally, the opposite type of danger is to be overwhelmed by emotions and failing to act when necessary. Indeed, a prolonged period of indecisiveness and paralysis seems to have settled in the land since the 2008 invasion of Gaza.

To the extent that Israeli society will someday develop the capacity to tolerate, accept, and integrate the trauma of the Holocaust—rather than continue to be subjugated by it—Israel, the Middle East, and the rest of the world will be less susceptible to these dangers. Unfortunately, this capacity is unlikely to emerge anytime soon. A major obstacle is one particular defense mechanism, mobilized by the Israeli mind to cope rather specifically with what is perhaps the most troublesome psychological legacy of the trauma—the sense of utter helplessness experienced by the victims and survivors as their lives were devoured by the powerful Nazi machine. Because it is structuralized deep within the Israeli psyche, this defense does not bode well for a speedy or smooth integration.

WHEREVER THERE IS HUMANKIND, THERE IS AUSCHWITZ

The parallel between Ka-Tzetnik's journey and the Israeli mind's comes to an abrupt end, with the analogy falling short in one critical respect. Unlike Ka-Tzetnik, by and large the Israelis have not arrived at the point of seeing themselves in Nazi uniform. Over the years, a handful of Israeli intellectuals on the fringes have raised the question, but for the vast majority of Israelis, this is a notion that should earn its holder a permanent residency in a psychiatric ward. While Israelis are relatively quick to label atrocities committed by other nations as Nazi-like, and whereas extremists on both sides of the political map within Israel occasionally slip into reciprocal labeling as *Nazis,* Israelis in general rarely apply the same labels to their own behavior. This is understandable, not only because of the subjective sufferings of the survivors in Israel's midst, but primarily because absolutely no moral, political, or reality-based equivalence exists between what the Nazis did and Israeli behavior—even at its worst. However, from a psychological, character-developmental perspective, the picture is more complex.

The preposterous, unthinkable Nazi-Israeli comparison in the eyes of practically all Israelis explains why it took almost forty years to publish in Hebrew one of the most important books about the Holocaust, Hannah Arendt's *Eichmann in Jerusalem: A Report on the Banality of Evil.*[32] Arendt's main thesis, which grew out of her coverage of the Eichmann trial for *The New Yorker,* was that Eichmann was no monster, but rather an ordinary person—a typical bureaucrat who, like countless other people, was corrupted by the Nazi regime. Arendt felt the same way about the Judenrats, the Jews who collaborated with the Gestapo in administering the ghettos and who were often cruel and sadistic toward their fellow Jews. In her view, so powerful and penetrating was the Nazi evil that even the victims were not immune. Arendt's philosophy did not divide the world into good and evil but, instead, rather pessimistically shared Ka-Tzetnik's final insight that wherever there is humankind, there is Auschwitz.

When *Eichmann in Jerusalem* was first published in 1963, it provoked an intensely emotional, almost hysterical reaction in Israel. It was received more calmly when it finally came out in Hebrew in 2000, but it still created a controversy. One of the things that riled the Israelis to their core was Arendt's contention that the Jews' best strategy to defeat Hitler's final solution would have been to do nothing. Rising up against the oppressor, she argued, could have achieved nothing and has not been attempted by other peoples in even more dire circumstances. Yet collaborating with the Nazis to save oneself also couldn't have and, in fact, didn't work. Doing nothing, however, would have increased the chaos and made the task of mass extermination more difficult. To support this argument, Arendt pointed out that had the Judenrats not helped the Nazis to assemble the Jews in the ghettos, many would have been saved.

Whatever the merits of such a strategy, the two possible paths of action, divergent as they may have been in moral terms, for the Jews in the ghettos and concentration camps—resistance or collaboration—effectively resulted or would have resulted in the same outcome for the vast majority of the victims: torture and death for self and others. Helplessness was a near-absolute reality, a rare condition for most adults even in totalitarian societies or institutions. However, this is not at all a rare circumstance for children, certainly not for abused children, so psychologists know a great deal about what humans do to cope with helplessness when an action-oriented escape is out of the question. While children and adults alike resort to a variety of defense mechanisms to deal with helplessness, one such mechanism is particularly relevant to the type of total control exercised by the Nazis over the Jews. This defense gained notoriety in the 1970s following an incident in which a group of Swedish hostages emerged from captivity only to resist the police and support their kidnappers. Dubbed the Stockholm syndrome, the technical name of this defense is *identification with the aggressor*. Rather then accept his helplessness, the victim of sustained, repeated, or severe abuse finds a way to justify or understand the thoughts, behaviors, or characteristics of the abuser and make them available for himself. He thus turns a passive experience into an active one, mastering the trauma of powerlessness by doing to others what has been done to him. In most cases this is not achieved in a single conscious decision but rather through a cumulative process of unconscious or preconscious resolutions arrived at and reinforced over a long period. Identification with the aggressor is one of the mechanisms through which physically or sexually abused children grow up to abuse their own kids.

Because identification is a universal developmental process—children as well as adults in all cultures aspire to model themselves after, internalize, and become like their more powerful authority figures—it is natural, almost automatic, for people made powerless by authority to employ some version of identification with the aggressor. Like all psychological defenses, this one, too, comes in degrees, ranging from the healthy to the pathological as defined by a particular culture. But given the nature and magnitude of the Nazi control, and the zero tolerance for helplessness of the early Israelis, identification with the aggressor was a particularly compelling and functional choice for the Israeli character. One would think that the national Holocaust-related catharsis of the last several decades, coupled with Israel's newly found power, would have expelled most residues of powerlessness and helplessness from Israeli consciousness. However, much of the catharsis has focused on the emotions of fear and rage, both of which motivate action, typically of the fight-or-flight variety, rather than reflection. Feelings of loss have also been prominent, and these are more reflective in nature and indeed closer to the experience of helplessness—no matter what, you can't bring the dead or pre-Holocaust Europe back. But the mourner still has control over his life and future. So virtually none of the feelings dredged up from the trauma of the Holocaust in the past several decades resemble the kind of helplessness experienced by the victims and survivors. Yet, precisely the reexperiencing of such helplessness could have prevented identification with the aggressor from becoming an integral part of the Israeli national character. As for Israel's newly found power, ironically though logically, this only afforded the Israeli mind the opportunity to exercise the defense, thereby reinforcing its usefulness in warding off the dreaded Jewish tradition of helplessness.

But what evidence do we have that the Israeli mind has taken on any of the mental or behavioral characteristics of the Nazi machine or ideology? While it is worth repeating that *there is absolutely no moral, geopolitical, or reality-based equivalence between what the Nazis did and Israeli behavior,* over the years a number of Israeli intellectuals, scholars, and artists have likened Israeli treatment of the Palestinians to Nazism. Unlike the purely political and sometimes anti-Semitic motivation of Arabs and Europeans who draw this analogy, the motivation of these Israelis, at least consciously, has been a deep concern for Israel. They often speak in humanistic terms but at times used psychological concepts not dissimilar to the analysis offered here. To complicate matters, on a less conscious level, these individuals might have been motivated by another type of adaptation to powerlessness, a self-destructive form of masochistic appeasement. I will discuss this further in chapter 6, "There's No Place Like Masada."

On the evening of the first day of the 1956 Sinai campaign, a group of about fifty Arab Israelis were walking back from work to their homes in the village of Kfar Kassem near Jerusalem. The men, women, and children in the group were not aware that a new military curfew had gone into effect that day. At the entrance to the village they were confronted by a border-police unit who identified them as residents of the village, lined them up, and, following an order from their superiors, shot them. Almost all were killed. A few survived by pretending to be dead. The Israeli government, we now know, tried but failed to cover up the incident.

The subsequent public debate raised the question of "following orders," with an apparent though initially only implicit allusion to Nazi Germany. When details of the incident began to emerge, several newspaper articles made the analogy explicit. But the country as a whole rejected it out of hand. Some columnists treated the incident as an understandable consequence of the political conditions on the ground. One wrote, "This is not the time for a mournful lament that the Nazi beast has wakened within us."[33] The Kfar Kassem killers eventually faced justice and were sentenced to prison terms ranging from seven to seventeen years. While the verdict contained what would later have become a hallmark legal guideline for when a military order must be defied, the government ultimately followed popular sentiment, rejecting the Nazi comparison. The families of the victims received minimal financial compensation, and the killers were pardoned and freed within three years. From that time on, light sentencing and/or pardoning of soldiers and civilians who have murdered Arabs has become the norm. To be fair, as mentioned before, relatively light sentences have also been applied in Israel to those committing violent and sexual crimes against other less than equal victims, including women and children. Perhaps the application in general of such sentencing to crimes against the more helpless members of Israeli society reflects a narcissistic lack of empathy for "the weak" being tinged by a shade of identification with the aggressor.

The 1982 Lebanon war, which many Israelis viewed as the country's first true war of choice, also aroused comparisons to Nazi behavior. Yeshayahu Leibowitz, a religiously orthodox scholar and one of Israel's most brilliant and provocative thinkers at the time, denounced the Israeli government for its "Judeo-Nazi policy" toward Lebanon. Years later, these remarks, among others, cost Leibowitz the Israel Award, the country's most prestigious state prize. He was named a winner but declined the award after a storm of public protest. After the Sabra and Shatila massacre, in which an Israeli-controlled Christian militia slaughtered hundreds of Palestinians at a Lebanese refugee camp, respected Israeli poet Dalia Rabikowitz wrote, "Back to camp, march! shouted the soldier / To the screaming women from Sabra and Shatila. / I had orders to follow."[34]

The debate over that war also produced what historian Tom Segev called one of the strangest paragraphs ever printed in the Israeli press. It came in response to an Amos Oz op-ed that challenged Prime Minister Begin's justification for the bombing of Beirut.

"Mr. Prime Minister, Hitler is already dead," wrote Oz.[35] But defending Begin's comparison of Arafat to Hitler, the editor in chief of Israel's largest daily wrote, "Arafat, were he only to gain enough power, would do to us things that even Hitler never imagined. This is not rhetoric on our part. If Hitler killed us with a certain restraint—were Arafat ever came to power, he would not merely play at such matters."[36] This line of thinking illustrates not only the psychologically obvious—that, to paraphrase British psychoanalyst D. W. Winnicott, what Israelis are so afraid of had already happened—but also the severity, harshness, and hypermasculinity inherent in the defense of identification with the aggressor. *Hitler killed us with restraint. What Hitler did to us was child's play compared to what's coming, so we'd better toughen up.* According to this analysis, toughening up requires that we view even Hitler as a softy.

In 1984, Rabbi Meir Kahane, former leader of the militant American organization Jewish Defense League, was elected to the Knesset. Referring to the "lessons of the Holocaust," Kahane's political platform called for the expulsion of Arabs from Israel and the occupied territories. Once in the Knesset, Kahane introduced legislation stripping Israeli Arabs of their political rights, separating Arab and Jewish communities, and barring sexual relations and marriages between Arabs and Jews. During the parliamentary debate, one Knesset member went over the proposed bill, comparing it item by item to the Nuremberg laws. The political establishment as a whole was shocked and sought to restrict Kahane's Knesset activities. However, the Israeli high court upheld his right to propose legislation. Eventually, the Knesset passed a law barring overtly racist candidates from running for office, and Kahane was unable to run for reelection.

Notwithstanding his ultimate failure, public-opinion surveys showed that Kahane had significant support among the less educated and the young. Indeed, as periodic terrorist attacks continued to take place through the 1980s, each was followed by throngs of Israeli youths roaming through Arab neighborhoods and shouting, "Death to the Arabs," which to the ears of at least one Knesset member and Holocaust survivor resonated with "Death to the Jews." One 1990 Ben-Gurion University study concluded that Israeli youth in the late 1980s had a much lower level of democratic consciousness than their German counterparts.[37] Eventually, this rise in "Kahanism," especially among the young, led the government to introduce in schools and the military special educational programs designed to fight racism and protect democracy. During those years several Israeli intellectuals began to attribute Israeli "aggression" to the trauma of the Holocaust. Most notably, and consistent with the hypothesis proposed in this chapter, playwright Yehoshua Sobol displayed onstage the process through which the victim had become the victimizer. His plays were met with widespread hostility and occasional violence.

The first Palestinian intifada of 1987–93, even more acutely than the war in Lebanon, brought home to Israelis the moral dilemmas involved in using force to control another nation. Though many of the demonstrators were equipped with stones and large rocks, which posed some threat to individual Israeli soldiers, on the whole this uprising pitted the powerful Israeli army against a relatively helpless Palestinian population. Persisting near daily for more than six years, this struggle set off some of the more extreme forms of identification with the aggressor among Israeli soldiers. In 1988, the IDF decided to suspend visits by soldiers to the Ghetto Fighters Museum in southern Israel. The official reason given was that guides at the museum were poorly trained, but other accounts indicated that some soldiers had planned to apply what they've learned in the museum about Nazi brutality to their dealings with Palestinian rioters. In the following year, the press reported on military units calling themselves "the Auschwitz platoons" and "the Demjanjuks," the latter, namesakes of the Ukrainian Nazi guard accused of extremely cruel and sadistic war crimes.[38] These were clearly isolated incidents. Nonetheless, they revealed something about the state of mind of the young Israeli soldiers whose job it was to subdue the Palestinian population.

Indeed, the more general, officially sanctioned application of force, which included the use of live ammunition to disperse crowds, resulted in the death of 1,124 Palestinians, including hundreds of children and teenagers. The comparison to the number of Israelis dead, 90, is part of the story. Even when the military tried to minimize Palestinian casualties, its methods betrayed a callous or cruel attitude. This was certainly the case with Defense Minister Rabin's publicly issued order to literally break the bones of demonstrators, which effectuated unsightly beatings of defenseless men, women, and children. Quite often, when Palestinians were killed from a shot to the chest or head, the IDF's official response was that the soldiers had followed the normal procedure, aiming at the rioters' legs. In recent years this type of violence has subsided, replaced perhaps by the more common, and often more legitimate, military response for Palestinian terrorist acts and other provocations. The result, however, continues to be the disproportionate killings of innocent Palestinians. In the 2014 Gaza war, for example, more than 2,100 Palestinians have been killed, most of them civilians, including about 500 children. At least 11,000 people were injured, and more than 17,000 homes were destroyed or badly damaged. Around a third of Gaza's 1.8 million residents have been displaced. Israeli fatalities consisted of 65 soldiers and 7 civilians. Israeli injuries included 450 soldiers and 80 civilians. With the exception of a few ultraliberal columnists and academics, one of whom received serious threats on his life, the Palestinian toll, reported by the Israeli media, evoked little by way of public sympathy in Israel.

In the early 2010s Kahanism seems to have returned to the fringes of the right, with retaliatory actions by the group Price Tag against Palestinian civilians, first in the West Bank, and ultimately within Israel proper. Anti-Arab hate graffiti and the torching and defacing of a mosque in Galilee smacked not merely of random rage, but of a racist ideology. In August 2012, in what was widely described as an attempted lynching, a mob of Jewish youth beat to near death a seventeen-year-old Arab boy in Jerusalem's Zion square. Reuven Rivlin, a politician from the right-wing school of Greater Israel and then speaker of Israel's Knesset, condemned the incident and labeled it a microcosm of a national problem. Rivlin also denounced fans of the popular soccer team Beitar Yerushalayim after they held up signs reading "Beitar Forever Pure" to protest the signing of two Muslim players from Chechnya. And later, he cancelled a scheduled performance at the president's official residence of a popular singer who released an overtly racist, anti-Arab song. Once again, in a tacit acknowledgment that racism is a threat to Israeli democracy, the education minister instructed all junior high and high schools in the country to dedicate a class period to a lesson on the attempted lynching episode. But this did not prevent, in the aftermath of the brutal murder of three West Bank Jewish teenagers in the summer of 2014, the revenge killing of a sixteen-year-old Arab boy and an accompanying wave of anti-Arab incidents of lesser violence. That summer there were once again crowds shouting "Death to the Arabs" as well as a large, racially tainted Facebook campaign that included pictures of soldiers posing with their weapons and calling for revenge upon the Palestinian community. During the subsequent military conflict with Hamas, more than thirty known incidents of violent attacks on Arabs and leftist activists occurred across Israel, including an attempted lynching by ten Jews of two Arab youths. Throughout that war, "Death to the Arabs" was joined by "Death to the leftists" as well as actual death threats to left-leaning public figures. And as reported on Facebook and in television interviews by, among others, an Israeli soldier serving in Gaza, those disagreeing with government policies toward the Palestinians were commonly met with "You belong in the gas chambers," and in the case of women, "Hope you get raped by an Arab or a Sudanese." In one case, right-wing extremists wearing neo-Nazi shirts popular in German and other neo-Nazi circles physically attacked a group of left-wing demonstrators in Tel Aviv. In another, the kindergarten of Jerusalem's only joint Jewish-Arab primary and high school was torched and its walls were spray-painted with the epithets "Kahane was right" and "No coexisting with cancer."

In the fall of 2014 the government banned West Bank Palestinians working inside Israel from express buses used by settlers to commute from Israel proper to the West Bank, even though the IDF opined that they paused no security risks. Minutes from the parliamentary committee that debated the issue later revealed that the settlers lobbying for the ban were concerned with such matters as overcrowding, sexual harassment of Jewish girls by Arabs (despite a paucity of actual complaints), and a lack of courtesy on the part of the Arab passengers. The settlers also complained that allowing Palestinians on these buses gave them "a win" against "the Jewish occupier." When these minutes became public, Israeli justice minister Tzipi Livni stated that, to the extent that the government decision was in response to these concerns, it was a policy of apartheid. At about the same time, in the aftermath of a terrorist attack in Jerusalem, the mayor of one major Israeli city, Ashkelon, directed a government contractor to discontinue the employment of Arab-Israeli construction workers in kindergartens. Finally, that fall Israel's agriculture minister Yair Shamir called on the government to consider policies that would reduce birth rates among Israeli Bedouins, a formerly nomadic Arab tribe with a particularly high rate of population growth residing in southern Israel. As pointed out by the *Haaretz* columnist B. Michael, under both international and Israeli law, carrying out such a policy would constitute genocide, and according to Israeli law would be punishable by death.

On a larger, legal and philosophical scale, in November 2014 the government debated a so-called Nationality Law, to be added to Israel's Basic Laws—the country's equivalent of a constitution. Proposed by members of Netanyahu's Likud party the law would subjugate Israel's democratic system to the principle of Jewish nationality. It would enable courts to rule on the basis of Israel's Jewish identity over its democratic tradition when the two values are in conflict, codifying discriminatory practices such as subsidizing Jewish housing but not Arab. It would also demote Arabic from its current status as one of Israel's two official languages. The law was condemned by Israel's attorney general and criticized by the American Jewish establishment. It played an important role in the collapse of Netanyahu's third government.

At least in terms of attitude and philosophy, if not in action, a 2012 survey suggests that systemic racism is entrenched in large segments of Israel's Jewish population. According to the study, about a third of the Jewish Israeli public supported an official and open government policy of racial discrimination toward Arab citizens. Additionally, almost 70 percent of respondents supported an apartheid state in the event that Israel annexed the West Bank.[39] In the aftermath of the 2014 Gaza war, the perception that racism, along with its political incitement, had moved into the mainstream has become so widely held that Rivlin, by that time Israel's president, or nominal head of state, announced that combating it would be his first initiative in office. This did not stop Prime Minister Netanyahu from making seemingly racist comments toward Israeli Arabs on the eve of the 2015 elections, which appeared to have contributed to his decisive reelection victory.

As in the Lebanon war, during the first intifada, a large number of Israelis expressed serious moral reservations about how the government and the military were handling the uprising. At that time the phrase *crying while shooting* came into being, ostensibly to describe the conflicted emotions of the Israeli soldiers. They were killing, it was said, but with great remorse. The political left saw this as a vindication of the personal integrity of Israel's youth, as well as an indictment of the occupation policy that placed them in this predicament. But the right viewed it as a dangerous weakness that had to be eradicated. From a psychological perspective, the phrase, like the phenomenon it captures, is a poignant rendition not only of a moral conflict but also of a deeper problem: because his present aggression rests on a historical foundation of victimization, the aggressor is unable to experience himself as such.

Years ago, at the onset of the Egyptian-Israeli peace talks, Golda Meir famously addressed Arab violence against Israel by saying, "We can forgive you for killing our sons. But we will never forgive you for making us kill yours." While this statement foreshadowed the kind of conscious moral regret later expressed by many Israeli soldiers, it also appears to be an assertion of moral superiority not inconsistent with an aggressor seeking to justify his actions. More important, however, it also represents the aggressor's underlying sense of helplessness. In 1988, Doron Rosenblum, an Israeli columnist known for his brilliantly sarcastic insights into Israeli society, suggested that perhaps it wasn't a coincidence that while Israel was violently putting down the Palestinian riots, a new Yiddish theater was about to open its doors in Israel with a production of *It's Hard to Be a Jew*. After all, wrote Rosenblum, even when we break our clubs on the heads of women, children, and the elderly, we can't help but feel sorry for ourselves. " 'Gevald,' we yell, 'it's hard to be a Jew! It's hard to beat up and shoot people and hold on to our moral integrity! Oy vey, what have they done to us that we became so cruel?' 'Help' we cry, 'we are beating up people, good Lord! We are shooting straight at their kishkes!' "[40]

Rosenblum wrote this a couple of months into the intifada. At that time, as he noted, whereas foreign television networks were showing indiscriminate beatings of hundreds of Palestinians, Israeli television only covered the Israeli side. A striking example was a high-profile interview with an Israeli soldier recounting in great detail every bruise he had suffered from Arab hands, while the loud sobbing of family and friends was heard in the background. Finally, highlighting a news report that along with the purchase of ten thousand new clubs the IDF was attaching psychologists to the units subduing the demonstrations, Rosenblum wrote: "These psychologists will offer emotional support not to the stricken but to the unhappy strikers, the poor Jewish children who are fated to beat up the Palestinians. The truth is, they really do need it, due to the schizophrenic dissonance in which they find themselves: from the outside, in the foreign television networks, it looks as though we are beating up others, but from a cognitive-emotional perspective we are actually being led, like a lamb to the slaughter house."[41]

While clearly criticizing the Israeli government from the left, Rosenblum also correctly identified the central psychological experience of the *crying while shooting* syndrome: the aggressor cannot help but perceive himself as the victim. For him, aggression is not only a war against an external enemy. It is also a battle against internal feelings of powerlessness. He is therefore unable to internalize his aggressive behavior and to form a view of himself as a powerful, "in control" individual. *What choice do we have? We are forced to do all this! We have to defend ourselves! We don't have another country!* These common Israeli refrains are not simply defensive propaganda statements, but rather an accurate reflection of often unconscious feelings of powerlessness and helplessness, which, try as it may have, the Israeli psyche has been unable to shed. That some of these statements are based on external reality does not diminish what they tell us about the insides of the Israeli mind. If anything, in the cycle of character development, external reality—sometimes the result of a self-fulfilling prophecy—tends to reinforce preexisting internal structures.

Blaming others for one's behavior is a symptom of helplessness, and blaming the very people one is victimizing is a classic form of identification with the aggressor. The aggressor holds the victim responsible for the aggressor's own bad behavior, in the same way that his own abuser had held him responsible for his, the abuser's, bad behavior. Finally, due to the defensive nature of their aggression, the thick skin developed by the Israelis to adopt the abuser's mentality forms an additional layer of insensitivity regarding the suffering they impose on others. Most Israelis have little empathy for the thousands of innocent Palestinian civilians injured and killed as "collateral damage" during the army's campaigns and operations in Gaza and the West Bank. And they have even less sympathy for the humiliation, economic hardships, and anxiety they inflict on many West Bank Palestinians through checkpoints, barriers, nighttime incursions, investigations, and arrests. Though many of these tactics target terrorists and militants, in reality they are also used to control the Palestinian population as a whole. Regardless of their intention, they are the cause of a thousand little traumas for innocent Palestinians every day. On the other hand, as noted earlier the Israelis have a rather thin skin when it comes to their own sufferings, not tolerating it without instant or excessive retaliation.

The Israeli identification with the Nazi aggressor does not only appear to be a preposterous proposition, it also feels that way. That is why underneath this defense is a deeply unconscious yet pervasive sense of guilt. Some Israelis are aware of feelings of guilt over how their communities treated the Holocaust survivors in the decade or two following the war. Some also have conscious guilt over the inaction of the Zionist leadership of the Yishuv when news of the extermination in Europe first arrived in British-controlled Palestine.[42] But farther below the surface a more profound layer of guilt can be traced back to a strange affinity of Zionism and Nazism: both viewed the Jewish Diaspora as infected, plagued, and emasculated, and both sought to eliminate it, though obviously in very different ways. Reviewing Israeli fiction films dealing with the Holocaust, Judd Ne'eman, a filmmaker and professor emeritus at

Tel Aviv University, describes scenes in which young Israelis are visually juxtaposed with Nazi youth or symbols.[43] According to Ne'eman, in the context of these movies' plots, such visuals illustrate the protagonists' conflict between identifying with the victim and identifying with the victimizer, the latter of which is reinforced by the Zionist ideal of the aggressive new Jew. Ne'eman was not the first or only one to note these aesthetics. Indeed, a disturbing imagining of the ideal sabra physique as Aryan goes all the way back to Herzl.[44,45] Even before the Holocaust this physical ideal represented a version of identifying with the aggressor, as the early Zionists sought to create a little Europe in swampy Palestine while projecting their despised inner Jew onto local Arabs, and later "Oriental" Jews, treating both groups with the same contempt the Europeans had treated them. But Ne'eman takes this analysis to another level, concluding that "Zionist Israel appears to be living in a tangled 'dead-end future,' obsessed with endless bleeding and bloodletting to expiate the six million dead for whose death it innocently and unconsciously puts the blame on itself."[46]

We will explore a related hypothesis in chapter 6, "There's No Place Like Masada," but whether or not the massive sense of guilt underlying the Israeli identification with the aggressor plays such a role in Middle East violence, there's little doubt that it, too, erodes whatever empathy Israelis may have for the Palestinians. As a soldier at the end of the 1948 war, Yoram Kaniuk was stationed at Ramle, an Arab town on the outskirts of Tel Aviv, much of whose population was expelled or escaped during the war. When his fellow soldiers did not allow a crowd of sobbing, begging, and angry Palestinians back into their city, the young sabra was overwhelmed by feelings of guilt and threw up. Two days later he witnessed a fleet of trucks unloading mobs of European survivors, who, like locusts, ran over the city and broke into the empty houses. These young Jews, wrote Kaniuk, grew up in the camps and were far stronger than the sabras. "Compared to them," he concluded, "we were two-legged jokes, full of self-importance, having won a Mickey Mouse war. For them, war was the Wehrmacht, Nazis, Gestapo, tanks, freight trains, gray barracks, and marching towards God through the crematoriums."[47] When Kaniuk challenged his fellow Jews about taking over the homes of the Arab families standing farther away behind a barbed-wire fence and longing to return, they dismissed him, saying these refugees were in good shape. *We've been living for more than ten years behind such fences,* they explained. These Jews came from another cosmology, thought Kaniuk; they are beyond morality and did not give a damn. But he noted the unconscious guilt belying their lack of empathy: "They came from the garbage can of history. They were moral because they survived, that is, they considered themselves such sinners that they could not pass judgment."[48]

Like these survivors, their Israeli heirs as victims and victimizers to a large extent still fail to see the Palestinians as whole human beings. When we victimize people, their very presence makes us feel guilty, so we'd rather not see, think about, or empathize with them. And if what we do to them makes us feel on any level that we are acting like those who victimized us, well, we'd rather live in a bubble, as if our victims are literally not in our midst or next door to us. Israelis' inability to tolerate their guilt drives away whatever capacity they would otherwise have to see those they aggress upon as wholly human. It does not help that since the collapse of the Oslo Accords, many Israelis only encounter Palestinians during their military service. In their roles of soldiers manning checkpoints or otherwise interacting with an unfriendly population, which sometimes hosts militants and terrorists, empathy can be a dangerous thing.

Having said all this, we must now consider the opposite picture, that of the empathic, sensitive corner within the Israeli mind, which, as in the case of Jews everywhere, is, too, a consequence of having been victimized. Israelis understand sufferings and do have a soft spot for those experiencing national or personal traumas. They are often among the first to send emergency and medical assistance when other countries are struck by national disasters. And many Israelis—when they allow themselves to experience guilt and to imagine what it was like for their own parents or grandparents to grow up as a powerless minority—do go out of their way to help individual Palestinians who are struggling. The connection between such acts of generosity and the Holocaust was made explicit by Prime Minister Menachem Begin back in 1977. Shortly after he took office, he granted Israeli citizenship to some sixty-six unwanted Vietnamese boat people, comparing their situation to the plight of the Jewish refugees during World War II.

So how do we reconcile this with the observation regarding Israelis' overall lack of empathy? First and foremost, the Israeli identification with the aggressor is partial and incomplete. Israel's aggressive response to the horrific terrorist attacks of the second Palestinian intifada, for example, cannot be seen as part of that syndrome. You don't have to go through the Holocaust to respond as Israel did. Under similar circumstances, most civilized nations would resort to similar measures, including targeted assassinations, unlimited detentions, territorial closure, and bombings in civilian areas. The American response to 9/11 is a case in point. When Israelis see themselves as both victim and victimizer rather than one or the other, they are able to experience fear, anger, strength, and, yes, empathy.

Second, individual Israelis are just as empathic or unempathic as people from any other culture. This book highlights the collective character shared by all Israelis, but individual psychological differences within a culture are ultimately greater than its shared psychology. The corollary of this is that what psychologically unites individuals from different cultures is greater than what divides them.

A small, but growing counternarrative with respect to the Holocaust exists within the Israeli psyche, and many of the artists and intellectuals mentioned here represent that trend. It can be witnessed nowadays nowhere more convincingly than in . . . Berlin, Germany, which boasts a large Israeli expat community. Many of the Israelis residing in Berlin are artists and intellectuals drawn by the city's international art scene, affordable living, and welfare-state system. In a recent Israeli newspaper exposé about that community, several Israeli Berliners expressed sentiments to the effect that unlike Israel, Germany has learned the right lesson from the Holocaust. One young man left Israel in 2005 because he couldn't make it financially in Tel Aviv. In Berlin, he learned German and eventually found a job as a translator. He described his acculturation as follows:

"You arrive from Israel with existential fears and a constant tension about your Jewish identity. You think you are in the center of the universe, but when you leave, you find out otherwise. It's easier for me to deal with my Jewish identity and the Holocaust here. They don't pound its remembrance into your head with a sledgehammer. You realize there was another Germany here before 1939, and the memory of the Holocaust is present on a daily basis."[49]

Another resident in the community, a thirty-five-year-old writer/actor and a former decorated IDF soldier whose great-uncle and namesake was murdered in Treblinka, moved to Berlin in 2010. He explains, "Israel has been taken over by rudeness and malice. . . . Berlin is not a utopia, but there is thoughtfulness here because of the Holocaust. . . . In Israel, on the other hand, you can see how they treat Holocaust survivors. This comparison makes me realize that the Germans won—they got what they wanted. Unlike in Israel, here, individuals, the elderly and the weak, are respected.

"You tell yourself you gave Israel thirty-five years. And you can choose to give it another thirty-five, or you say, 'I prefer not to be a victim, and if this country behaves like all others, why not live amongst a different people, one whose past might be awful, but its present is not.'"[50]

This community is hardly neutral in its relation to Germany, as no Israeli or Jew can be. But unlike most Israelis, they seem to exist both in the past and the present, both in the other planet and on earth. It is not a coincidence that through a direct encounter with the victimizer, or his culture, these Israelis are better able to come to terms with the Holocaust. One of the most poignant stories along these lines is that of Israeli documentary filmmaker Tomer Heymann. Seventy years after his maternal grandfather escaped Berlin to Palestine, Heymann returned to the city to present a movie at the Berlin International Film Festival. There he met and fell in love with Andreas Merk, a German man who eventually moved to Israel to live with Heymann in Tel Aviv. Their relationship, as well as their triangulation with the filmmaker's mother, is the subject of Heymann's most recent film, *I Shot My Love*. While the Holocaust is always in the background, the movie is clearly about the present-day relationship and how it changed the filmmaker's life.

Notwithstanding, as Heymann tells the story, on the day Andreas arrived in Israel, Heymann had a screening, so he asked a few friends to spend some time with his boyfriend, pleading with them in advance not to bring up the Holocaust. He knew it was a sensitive subject for his lover, who at age thirty was clearly not responsible for the sins of his forefathers. But as soon as Heymann left, his friends started joking about Hitler and the Holocaust, rendering Andreas pale as a ghost. So even in these circumstances, when the past is being integrated into, rather than dominating, the present, Israelis are unable to avoid the duality that has always plagued them with respect to the Holocaust—it's still an all-or-none proposition. It's either too sensitive to talk about, or, more likely, something to use and abuse with no sensitivity.

This counternarrative, while not predominant in Israel, is actually in line with the classical Zionist goal of normalization, as well as the Jewish religion's notion of redemption. As pointed out by

Don Handelman and Elihu Katz of the Hebrew University, in structuring the Israeli calendar, the Jewish state chose to bunch together, in that order, Holocaust Day, Memorial Day for the fallen Israeli soldiers, and Independence Day. This gave the calendar a narrative advancing from darkness to light, mourning to rebirth.[51] All Israelis continue to strive for this progression, even if in reality the vast majority of them are stymied by the inability to mourn. At present, and for the foreseeable future, this sequence is likely to be achieved only on the fringes that consist largely of artists and intellectuals, whose function in many societies is to highlight and foreshadow the forbidden truths of the unthought known.

During the first Palestinian intifada, when many Israeli soldiers and their families wrestled with the application of excessive force by the IDF, there appeared to be a potential sea change with respect to aggression within Israeli society. Writing in the aftermath of that intifada and the subsequent Oslo Accords, political scientist Yaron Ezrahi suggested that the IDF's decision to employ rubber bullets in response to rock-throwing Palestinians represented a turning point in Israeli attitudes. Though the rubber bullet—a steel bullet coated with rubber—proved to be lethal, and in Ezrahi's mind was a fantasy that could be neither effective nor moral, Ezrahi believed it represented a moment when a large number of Israelis began to view the Palestinians as civilians living in their midst, and as a nation with a collective voice. Ezrahi still questioned, however, whether, as a new iconic image of contemporary Israeli civilization, the rubber bullet merely inverted the classic prickly-on-the-outside-but-sweet-on-the-inside sabra mythology.[52] Or as my wife once complained to me, "I'm still waiting for the sweet part."

Unfortunately, the second Palestinian intifada was so brutal, and the Hamas rockets from Gaza so threatening, that even the rubber coating has now vanished from the Israeli character armor. Each new trauma has reactivated the previous one. With the new regional threats unleashed in the aftermath of the Arab Spring, the original Holocaust complex, including the Israeli identification with the aggressor, is not likely to recede anytime soon. With this sense of foreboding, during the first intifada—Ezrahi's optimism notwithstanding—another Israeli scholar and educator, Holocaust survivor Yehuda Elkana, wrote in *Haaretz* that the actions of Israeli soldiers in the occupied territories reminded him of his past. Arguing that the mistreatment of the Palestinians originated from a misinterpretation of the Holocaust, Elkana concluded his article with a radical recommendation: "I see no greater danger to the future of Israel than the fact that the Holocaust has been instilled methodically into the consciousness of the Israeli public, including that very large part that did not endure the Holocaust, as well as the generation of children that has been born and grown up here," he wrote. He then went on to describe the psychological impact of sending "every child in Israel to visit Yad Vashem over and over again," urging them to "Remember," which could be interpreted as a call for long-standing, blind hatred.

"Each nation, including the Germans," Elkana concluded, "will decide for itself, in the context of its own considerations, whether it wishes to remember. We, on the other hand, must forget. I do not see any more important political or educational stance for the country's leaders than to stand up for life, to give oneself over to the construction of our future—and not to deal, morning and evening, with symbols, ceremonies, and lessons of the Holocaust. The rule of historical remembrance must be uprooted from our lives."[53]

Elkana's article, titled "For Forgetting," drew furious reactions, one of which branded it "a moral, educational, and psychological atrocity."[54] From a psychological perspective, forgetting is not an option. Nor is it truly desirable. Not only is there unfinished business in proper mourning, along with positive residues of Jewish humanitarian concerns for fellow sufferers consistent with remembering, but also some good in identifying with the aggressor.

When you live in a brutal neighborhood, an extra dose of aggression is sometimes the right medicine. Nonetheless, when you consider the three-way collision among the narrative of ancient Jewish history, the story of Zionism, and the Israeli identification with the aggressor, Elkana's larger point, that the Holocaust is now the greatest danger to the state of Israel, can hardly be denied. Yet in 2014 the Israeli Ministry of Education extended mandatory Holocaust instruction into kindergarten. When challenged, the ministry responded with the rationale that it's not as if kids that age weren't already exposed to it. That year, the ministry also increased the portion of the high school curriculum devoted to the Holocaust.

FIVE

ANATOMY OF A CLICHÉ: SABRAS AT WAR

THE UNBEARABLE LIGHTNESS OF DEATH

The patient, an Israeli professional in his thirties, mentioned for the first time in his psychotherapy that when he was about twelve he had "a secret sexual relationship with another boy." Clearly struggling with feelings of shame and guilt over this relationship, he avoided my gaze. He seemed unsure, as in "Should I avoid these feelings and change the subject, or should I confront them head-on?" But then, in an apparent compromise between the two options, he looked up at me, smiled, and volunteered the following story:

"I was in seventh grade, so it must have been 1972 or early '73, a relatively quiet period with not much terrorism or anything like that going on. But one afternoon we heard in school that earlier in the day a Katyusha rocket fell somewhere in Jerusalem. Walking home from school, this boy and I—the same one I had the sexual thing with—got into an argument about the death penalty for terrorists. I was for it, he was opposed. At some point I challenged him, saying, 'How would you feel if it were your house that was hit by this Katyusha?!' Well, when I got home, I found out that it *was* his house, and that the rocket had punctured a wall in his room. My mother thoughtfully suggested that I invite him to spend the night in our house. 'There's an extra bed in your room,' she said. If she only knew . . ."

This took place in my New York City office around the time of the first Gulf War, when Saddam Hussein showered Israeli cities and suburbs with Scud missiles. While Israelis in general were panicking that these missiles could be armed with chemical warheads, Israeli psychologists were also worrying about the "transference implications" of having to interrupt a session during a Scud attack. How would the therapeutic relationship be affected by having to put on a gas mask and spend the afternoon together with the patient in a small, sealed room?

War permeates the most personal and private of realms. Like addiction, it is often a secondary process, the result of preexisting conditions of significant magnitude. But it takes over and metastasizes, obscuring the original pathology, becoming the cause of new and pervasive afflictions. In a country so small, with a society of such permeable social boundaries, as Israel, what's public often turns private and back again. Probably nothing reflects more tragically and poignantly this nexus of public and private worlds than the art and life of Israeli author David Grossman. In 2003, Grossman published a collection of articles he'd written in the preceding ten years, since the signing of the Oslo Accords. Grossman titled this volume *Death as a Way of Life*. Writing about Israeli-Palestinian relations in the preface, Grossman noted, "Sometimes, viewing the atrocities that these two peoples inflict on each other, a person loses not only his desire to live in this region, but his desire to live at all."[1] In an article he wrote after Rabin and Arafat shook hands on the White House lawn in 1993, Grossman expressed the wish that Israel would be integrated into the Middle

East. If we Israelis can live with this vision, he wrote, we would permit ourselves to believe that we have a future. "Perhaps we will be able to free ourselves from that sense of doom that lies deep down in our collective consciousness, that for us, life is only latent death."[2] Later in the decade, however, when waves of suicide bombings made it clear that peace was not on the horizon, he wrote, "We Israelis are accustomed to living in the vicinity of death. I'll never forget how a young couple once told me about their plans for the future: they'd get married and have three children. Not two, but three. So that if one dies, there will still be two left. This heartwrenching way of thinking is not foreign to me, it is the product of the unbearable lightness of death that prevails here."[3] In another piece he noted, "I may well be wrong, but I know that something in me is dying. I no longer have that spark inside that life here always ignited in me."[4] He then concluded this piece, written on the eve of the Jewish New Year: "May we wake up at last, may we stop straying through this nightmare, which is no one's dream. Shana Tova, Happy New Year."[5]

This was Grossman the columnist, the pubic commentator on Israeli life. The other public Grossman was the internationally acclaimed author, whose most famous novel, *To the End of the Land*, or in the Hebrew original, "A woman escaping an Annunciation," was published some five years after *Death as a Way of Life*. Grossman started working on that book shortly after the publication of *Death as a Way of Life*, and a few months into the writing, his son Uri, the youngest of three boys, was drafted into the IDF. As Grossman put it in an addendum to *To the End of the Land*, during the writing he had a feeling, or really a wish, that this book would protect Uri from harm. In the novel, too, the main character is trying to protect her son, who volunteered to extend his army service so that he could take part in a combat mission in the West Bank. Separated from her husband, who has taken off to South America with their older son, and terrified that her younger son, Ofer, would be harmed in action, Ora superstitiously decides that if she is not home to receive a message of loss, it would simply not occur. She thus sets off on a long hike with a former lover, Ofer's biological father, traversing the Israel Trail, which crosses north to south the entire length of the country. The book's English title alludes to the geography of the trail, but also to the possible end of a country where escape from death is not an option even temporarily.

Though this is the novel's framework, the real concerns of *To the End of the Land* are love, family, and motherhood, in other words life, not death. Nonetheless, even on the isolated hiking trail, Ora cannot fully escape. She tries to keep Ofer alive by telling his story, three-dimensionally, to the father who never met him. But she has the inevitable recollections of Ofer dressing up at age three as a cowboy, complete with guns and an ammunition belt, or his discovery of mortality, fairly typical for prekindergarten boys the world over, but a different matter for a Jerusalem family navigating exploding buses and other terrorist attacks in their neighborhood. Or she tries to keep Ofer alive by avoiding thinking about where he is at present, except that the trail inevitably crosses a memorial for a fallen soldier, or a village with people talking about "the news." In the end, we do not know if Ofer survived his mission or not. But not so with Grossman's son. On August 12, 2006, as Grossman was putting the finishing touches on his book, Uri was killed when his tank was hit by a missile in the last few hours of the second Lebanon war. In a brief postscript to the book, Grossman wrote, "After we finished sitting Shiva, I went back to the book. Most of it was already written. What changed, above all, was the echo of the reality in which the final draft was written."[6] Getting back to writing a day after the shivah, he later explained, was "a way of fighting against the gravity of grief. It was a way of choosing life. It was so good that I was in the middle of this novel, rather than any other. A different book might suddenly have seemed irrelevant to me."[7]

As a psychologist who has worked with such patients, and as a father, I know that losing a child, to paraphrase Grossman, can make you feel exiled from your own life. In Israel, Grossman's art and life tell us, all Jewish parents who send their sons to the army must navigate this potential terrain in their heart. As remarkable as David Grossman's personal tragedy is, in a small country such as Israel, it is hardly singular. In 1996, for example, one of Israel's most popular journalists, Nahum Barnea, arrived in the center of Jerusalem to cover a suicide bombing for his newspaper only to discover that his son was one of the dead—which did not stop him from continuing to work on the story. Perhaps the most famous case in the blurring of the lines between the private and the public in this domain, and in the role of personal mourning in the country's overall trajectory, is that of Prime Minister Benjamin Netanyahu. The loss of his brother during the Entebbe operation launched his career as a commentator on terrorism, a diplomat, and eventually the nation's leader.

Psychologically speaking, however, Grossman's writings take us to a much deeper place. Whether, to borrow Picasso's famous dictum, *To the End of the Land* is the lie that tells us the truth about life, or whether the author's loss of his son is a case of life imitating art imitating life, it is hard to digest this tale without losing one's sense of reality. This is precisely what Grossman tackled head-on in his next novel, *Falling out of Time*. Evidently wrestling with his loss, in *Falling out of Time* Grossman tells the story of a group of parents who had lost their children and are embarking on a desperate journey to reunite with their dead. The novel takes place in an unspecified European town, where the Duke, the Town Chronicler, and a number of other stick-figure characters encircle and re-encircle the town and descend underground, all in an interminable search for their loved ones. Unlike in *To the End of the Land*, the book has no real plot or flesh-and-blood protagonists for the reader to identify with. Rather, employing both prose and poetry, the characters echo each other's grief and engage in a cerebral quest to understand death. As suggested by Israeli literary scholar Avraham Balaban, the location, the mythological allusions, and the fantastical nature of the novel, among other things, construct a remarkably constrained, even distant, study in bereavement.[8] It was as if to write about his loss, Grossman had to divorce it from reality, most particularly the Israeli reality. Through this dissociated framework Grossman makes the most penetrating observations about the experience of loss, presumably his own, but certainly that which permeates the wounded Israeli psyche.

"All that's present / from now on / will only echo / Absence," says the Duke.

At another point, the entire group cries out to their lost loved ones:

"And how is it that you are / Dead, and we / Managed / to stay alive? / Did you ever think / What this means? / Perhaps it's not a coincidence that / You are there / and we are here? / Perhaps you did something / to make this-s-s happen?—/ You know what? / We don't want to bother / with these thoughts / We don't want to think about you! / We thought about you enough. . . . So take, take your pack / of bones—and get out / Get out of our lives! / Do you get it? / You / You there / Die already!"

The void, the rage, and the implied survivor's guilt are all there. But the suffering also turns existential. Addressing his dead son, the leader of the march, the Walking Man, says, "And forgive the stupid, pointless / Question I must ask / Because for five years already / it's been eating at my soul / Like a disease: / What is death, son?" Not surprisingly, their walk toward death is reminiscent of the death marches of the Holocaust. The Town Chronicler's description of the procession evokes the death march depicted by Elie Wiesel in his classic, autobiographical book *Night*: "They walk the hills . . . moaning and falling, rising, hanging on to each other, carrying the sleeping, themselves falling asleep, nights, days, again and again . . ."

Speaking of his dead son, the Centaur, a writer of sorts—perhaps representing the author—decrees to the Town Chronicler, "Please note in large, giant letters: I must create him anew in the form of a story! Got it? Yes, him, and that horrible thing that happened to my son and me, yes, I must weave it into the story. With imaginative tales! And fantasies, freedom and dreams! Fire! A boiling caudron!" In other words, the dead must be kept alive, but in Technicolor fantasy, because delving into the loss in a real way is emotionally unbearable. Nonetheless, and just in case the reader doubts that this book is very much about the Israeli reality, Grossman chooses to enlighten him in the title. Without mentioning it, but clearly alluding to the Hebrew language, the Walking Man relates to his dead child a story he was once told "by a man of a distant land / in whose language the war dead / are said to have 'fallen' / and you too fell / Out of time, out of my time."[9]

Time as we know it stops for the dead, but it does, too, for those in perpetual, unresolved mourning. Because of their inability to mourn the loss of the homeland, the pre-Zionist, Diaspora Jews were trapped in the past. The devastation of the Holocaust made a full mourning even less possible, and Israel's history of war and terrorism have piled on another layer of unresolved grief. To appreciate the centrality of time in Grossman's book, and in the Israeli psyche, consider the ubiquity of war-related post-traumatic stress disorder in Israeli society. Reuven Gal, former chief psychologist of the Israeli Defense Forces, and later deputy national security adviser in Ariel Sharon's government, told me that in his estimation, hundreds of thousands of Israeli men suffer from nightmares, intrusive thoughts, emotional numbness, anxiety, and depression, all post-traumatic stress reactions precipitated by combat-related military service. These numbers, which equate to dozens of millions in America, do not even include the civilians exposed to the 1991 Iraqi missile attacks, the 2000–2005 suicide bombings of the second intifada, the 2006 Lebanon war and other campaigns in the West Bank and Gaza, and the 2014 summer of Hamas rockets and terror tunnels. In a tragic return to 1948, some of these wars have extended the battlefield back into the country's population centers. Thus, in recent years, the Israel Ministry of Education has published a growing number of books and manuals intended to help parents, educators, and mental-health professionals to cope with conditions of sustained trauma, stress, and emergency in the school system.

In their most benign manifestations, psychological symptoms related to past combat can enter the most casual of dinner conversations anywhere in Israel. In a recent family get-together, when someone mentioned the first Lebanon war, a relative in her early thirties volunteered that after he came back from Lebanon, her husband suffered several months from violent nightmares reliving his war experience. On the more debilitating end of the spectrum, where symptoms are more likely to be kept under wraps, a retired Israeli brigadier general who fought in the 1967 and 1973 wars tells the following story about his son's military service in the West Bank during the first Palestinian intifada. The son, nineteen years old at the time, would come home once a month for a weekend pass, but would say absolutely nothing about his missions. At night, however, the family would hear him crying or screaming in his sleep. He had put them on strict instructions never to wake him up abruptly, but once, when his little sister did, he jumped out of bed violently and almost strangled her. This state of affairs continued until he finished his service a couple of years later, refusing all the while to talk about it, even when probed. Then, a few months after he completed his service and left home, the parents received a call from his roommate, asking them to come quick. They arrived to find their son lying on the floor in the corner of his room, hitting his head against the wall and crying, "I can't take it anymore." Consenting at last to get help, he told his parents what had triggered his breakdown. A couple of days earlier he had been interviewed for a documentary film about the intifada. He was asked by a psychologist to describe what he did during his service. Watching the movie, you see this young man in close-up, speaking haltingly, as tears keep rolling down his cheeks. "When my children will ask me what I did in the army, I'm going to have to tell them that I beat women and children."

Post-traumatic stress symptoms are a psychological time machine. They are an ill-fated attempt to recapture past experience in order to overcome it, via flashbacks, dreams, the startle response, or depressive preoccupations; or, they are an equally ill-fated attempt to escape the past—through emotional numbness—which results in a dissociated approach to the present. But if living in a different time zone is one outcome of war trauma, another is to act in some extreme manner, ranging from the heroic through the aggressive to the dangerous. In his memoir, Amos Oz sweetly describes how at age eight, during the last year of the British Mandate, he and two friends built a rocket in his backyard, aiming it toward London's Buckingham Palace. Using his father's typewriter, they drafted a letter with an ultimatum demanding that His Majesty King George VI withdraw his military from Palestine. Failure to do so within six months, they warned, would turn Yom Kippur into a day of judgment for Great Britain itself. While they were developing the necessary missile-guide and fuel technology, Oz reports, the British came to their senses and left the country. Such a letter was not an unusual make-believe play for an Israeli child; sometimes, such fantasies travel into the future, materializing, so to speak, as heroic actions in adulthood.

As a teenager, Moshe Amirav, later an adviser to Prime Minister Ehud Barak during the Camp David negotiations, was caught up in a dream about liberating the Old City of Jerusalem. On Yom

Kippur of 1961, without telling their parents, he and a fellow youth movement member traveled from their homes in central Israel to Jerusalem, planning to sneak across the border deep into East Jerusalem and blow the shofar by the Western Wall. They reasoned that even if they were caught, and all the more so if they were killed, their pilgrimage would stir the people to rise up and free Jerusalem from the Jordanian occupier. On the way, they sought the blessings of one of their heroes, the nationalist poet Uri Zvi Greenberg, who every Yom Kippur prayed on Mount Zion from a location overlooking the border and the Old City. Greenberg, who apparently understood the difference between fantasy and reality, angrily sent the two teens back home, but not before promising that not too far in the future Israeli soldiers would enter and liberate the occupied city. Six years later, on June 5, 1967, Amirav arrived in West Jerusalem as a young soldier in the paratroop brigade heading toward the Old City and the Western Wall. During fierce combat with Jordanian legionnaires just outside the old Ottoman walls and a stones's throw away from the Western Wall, Amirav was hit in the face by shrapnel. To his great chagrin he was evacuated to Hadassah Hospital just outside West Jerusalem, where he was told that a piece of shrapnel was lodged in his head and would have to be taken out surgically in a couple of days, once his condition stabilized. The following day, when he heard on the radio that his fellow soldiers had just reached the Western Wall, he got out of bed and decided to head to the Old City. With one eye shut, a painful, swollen face, and a bandage around his head, he jumped out one of the hospital's ground-floor windows. Joined by another wounded soldier, he somehow commandeered a military jeep, in which they also found a pair of helmets and submachine guns, and drove to East Jerusalem. Limping, running, and with Amirav barely seeing, they finally made their way, amid shootings and explosions, to the Western Wall. After the war, Amirav received the paratroop brigade medal awarded to the soldiers who liberated Jerusalem.[10]

From that same paratroop brigade that fought so brilliantly emerged another famous, or to the vast majority of Israelis, infamous, figure, Udi Adiv. Born to a founding family from a venerable kibbutz, Adiv was disillusioned by the socialist party his kibbutz was associated with and in the aftermath of the 1967 war joined a fringe communist movement. He later traveled clandestinely to Damascus to meet with members of the PLO, then an anti-Zionist terrorist organization, and in 1973 was convicted in an Israeli court of spying for Syria. Adiv acknowledged it was wrong of him to travel to Syria, but he insisted that his intentions were merely to form relations with Palestinian representatives, and that he never gave the Syrian authorities any information. Nonetheless, he was also convicted by the Israeli media and public and spent seventeen years in jail.

The Adiv affair came as a huge shock to Israelis, as the idea that one of them would spy for an Arab country could hardly be contemplated, and it was a trauma for the Adiv family. Their kibbutz was also home to Uri Ilan, an Adiv family friend with the opposite type of legacy preceding Udi Adiv. Ilan was captured by the Syrian army along with four other soldiers when his unit conducted a covert operation in the Golan Heights in 1954. After brutal interrogations and torture, Ilan hanged himself in his prison cell, using a rope made from his mattress cover. When his body was returned to Israel several years later, a few notes were found hidden in his clothing, the most famous of which read, "I did not betray my country, I killed myself." When Ilan's fate was disclosed to the public, the national grief was overwhelming. But his suicide has also become a cause for pride, an inspirational symbol of heroism for a generation of Israeli youth. Setting aside the value of such self-sacrifice for a society, from a psychological perspective it is reasonable to view this soldier's tragic choice—to kill himself rather than betray his country—as an extreme response to the trauma inflicted on him by his captors. It is also possible to interpret Udi Adiv's version of extraordinary action as a reaction to trauma. This is what Adiv's sister, now a psychoanalyst in New York City, believes. In the battle for Jerusalem, she told me, her brother lost several of his buddies, and shortly after the war, he was ordered to shoot at Palestinian civilians endeavoring to return to their homes. She believes he failed to process these events emotionally and therefore took extreme and, in his own words, "stupid" action in an attempt to undo the trauma.

These two opposite if rare responses to trauma are two sides of the same coin, representing something of the proclivity for grand action residing within every Israeli. One course of action is in total loyalty to the national status quo, the other a total rejection of it. A more ordinary version of this can be seen in Grossman's *To the End of the Land,* where two of Ora's three sons express opposite last wishes in case they are killed during their military service. One requests that his parents place a bench in his name outside the Jerusalem nightclub he had performed in; the other, that the family leave Israel.

This action-oriented coping style is also a subset of a larger mental structure, namely the hypermasculine disposition of the Israeli national character. From the start, the Zionist enterprise depended on the willingness to become a soldier and fight for the national home, for at its base was the idea that the Jews had no other place but Palestine. As noted by American-born Israeli writer Haim Watzman, the early sabra culture—the cornerstone of Israeli identity—was based on masculine ideals. The myths of the farmer, military commander, adventurer, and even poet and writer were explicitly male.[11] Since then, the continuing state of war has resulted in an oversize military establishment whose culture exercised a penetrating, all-pervading influence on Israeli society. This is evident everywhere in Israel, and in everything, from the lyrics of popular music, where a girl might be "conquered" with the assistance of an artillery battalion, to paramilitary training in youth movements, to roadside monuments. One such monument just outside Jerusalem consists of about 150 tanks, inviting children of all ages to climb on and be photographed with them. A fourteen-year-old Israeli boy told me that during one calendar year in middle school, he was exposed to six visits from representatives of military intelligence units. Explaining what they do, he reported, these soldiers would reassure the kids "not to worry if intelligence does not sound like combat service—there's one super combat unit within the intelligence community." Bullying in Israeli schools is often about perceived weaknesses associated explicitly with the avoidance of war-related play. Kids advocating for peace or human rights for Arabs are also likely to be bullied.

Directly or indirectly, this hypermasculinity is also prevalent in modern Hebrew literature as well as in Israeli movies—from those depicting the human and cultural dimensions of the military experience, such as Shimon Dotan's 1982 *Repeat Dive,* to those of more mixed genres, such as Eytan Fox's 2004 *Walk on Water.* In the popular television drama series *BeTipul,* or *In Treatment,* which premiered in 2005 and revolved around the professional and personal life of a psychologist played by Assi Dayan, son of famed Israeli general Moshe Dayan, one of the most poignant characters is an air force pilot struggling with unconscious guilt over the bombing of a school in Gaza, as well as with his masculine identity. This patient's bravado, his haughtiness, and his underlying vulnerability are quintessentially Israeli. By comparison, in the American adaptation of the show, the patient, a fighter pilot who was involved in a similar action in Iraq, is not prototypically American, just a man caught up in the trauma of war. The IDF and its wars, unsurprisingly, have also been a regular fixture in Israel's highly sophisticated fine-arts scene. One of the most striking pieces hanging in the permanent collection of modern Israeli art in the Israel Museum in Jerusalem is a large Adi Nes photograph in which Israeli soldiers are staged as replacements for the characters in Leonardo da Vinci's *Last Supper.*

Israelis are famously direct, if not combative, in their communications. When my daughter was eight, one of her Israeli cousins, who had just completed his military service as a noncommissioned officer, pulled her aside at a family event to give her life advice. "Always be direct!" he instructed. This greatly impressed my daughter because, as she put it when she grew old enough to understand what he meant, "in America, when people give you advice, it's often something like 'Always be yourself,' which is completely useless because who else can you be?" Israeli sociologist Oz Almog suggests that Israeli *dugri,* which means "straight" in Arabic and refers to this direct speaking style, is speech under fire, originating from or mimicking the language of army radio communications.[12] I see this in my Israeli patients all the time. Their resistance to treatment, for instance—a universal feature shared by all psychotherapy patients—is typically more overt than that of their American or European counterparts. On the flip side, my Israeli patients are also much quicker to open up and expose their inner world. One such patient made himself quite vulnerable in the initial consultation. But predictably, as the session came to a close and I was pleased to be able to make what I considered a pretty good observation about a pattern in his relationships, he shot back, "Well, it doesn't take a psychologist to see that."

New York Times columnist David Brooks put it this way: "Israel is a country held together by argument. Public culture is one long cacophony of criticism. The politicians go at each other with a fury we can't even fathom in the U.S. At news conferences, Israeli journalists ridicule and abuse their national leaders. Subordinates in companies feel free to correct their superiors. People who move here from Britain or the States talk about going through a period of adjustment as they learn to toughen up and talk back."[13]

Israeli psychologist Avner Falk views it less kindly, suggesting Israelis often leave their homes feeling like soldiers going into battle.[14] Like many others, he describes daily life in Israel as full of friction, tension, and pressure, with verbal discord and shouting matches punctuating the continuous noise of radios and televisions blasting loud music and terse news bulletins. All this directness and blare does have an aggressive edge. As suggested by David Grossman, starting perhaps in the nineties, visitors who have returned to Israel after a long absence have been struck by, along with the huge buildup and infrastructure development, the brutality, vulgarity, and insensitivity of the culture.[15] Israeli commentators on the left have attributed much of this daily aggression to the socialization of young Israeli soldiers and reservists while on tours of duty in the occupied territories. Enforcing roadblocks, searching houses, bulldozing homes, uprooting vineyards and olive groves, conducting large-scale arrests and deportations, confiscating land, and supporting law-breaking, sometimes violent Jewish settlers, not to mention the killing of civilians, all require the suppression of loving, sensitive emotions and the hardening of one's outer shell with angry disregard for others. Social modeling alone—the human tendency to copy and generalize—can explain how such practices are imported back into Israel proper to reinforce the hypermasculine disposition and influence interpersonal transactions.

But another, deeper dynamic is at play here. Israeli psychologists, including Falk, Shalit, and Grosbard, have noted that the everyday belligerence in Israeli society is rooted in unconscious anxiety.[16,17,18] Ever fearful of suicide bombings, rockets, bad news from the front lines, and even car accidents—driving on Israeli highways can be unsettling—Israelis live in a hypervigilant state of mind, often exercising a first-strike option in anticipation of an attack. Collectively, they can't quite believe that the miracle of the Jewish state will endure. Indeed, a tiny country surrounded by hundreds of millions of Muslims, many of whom reject its very existence, and one threatened from within by a growing Arab minority and an intra-Jewish secular-religious struggle, can never feel safe. Throw in the specter of a nuclear Iran and bioterrorism, not to mention the multiple historical layers of existential anxiety discussed earlier, and it's easy to see why such fears are difficult to contain. So like the psychotherapy patient who can't tolerate his or her anxiety and "acts out" in aggression toward other people, or the parent who angrily—but out of fear—yells at a young child who is about to hurt himself, Israelis deny or repress their anxiety and take it out on others in anger.

Many Israeli children have a clear developmental trajectory along this hypermasculine dimension. Describing his own development as a boy, political scientist Yaron Ezrahi recalls how at age twelve he realized what it meant to be an Israeli. Sensing that his mother's primary concern was for his safety, he realized that her worldview was consistent with the traditional Jewish idea of surviving by walking away from trouble or literally leaving for a safe haven elsewhere. His father, on the other hand, viewed Palestine, and later Israel, as the home in which the family would live or die, but would certainly not abandon. He thus sided with his father. "As the voice of private family values, my mother stood for all the things Zionism derided and our schoolteachers taught us to reject," he writes.[19] Whereas in most Western countries in the transition from adolescence to adulthood one leaves home for higher education or a civilian job, in Israel, in this transition most youngsters, certainly boys, join the military, where the collective experience focuses on getting armed and becoming a warrior. As pointed out by Ezrahi, the word for firearms and the vernacular for the male organ have a strong linguistic affinity in Hebrew. This illuminates the connection between carrying a gun and being a potent male.

On the battlefield, Ezrahi notes, soldiers who are afraid to fight are mocked or criticized for acting like women. There is nothing particularly Israeli about this military machismo, but unlike in other Western countries, it ends up shaping both the individual and the social values of the society at large, outside the confines of the army.

As in all cases of hypermasculine identification, an underlying, unconscious desire exists for the disavowed mother and what she represents, i.e., comfort, safety, acceptance, softness, and femininity. But such desires threaten to undermine the boy's sense of evolving masculinity and must therefore be squashed. The typical boy in this kind of environment therefore doubles down on his efforts to preserve his psychological maleness, and hence the hypermasculine outcome. In Israel, this means an unconscious wish to return to the passive, dependent, bookish, and traditionally feminine ways of the Diaspora, desires that are so antithetical to the heart of the national enterprise, they must be crushed. In the ever-changing Israeli society, however, these desires are much less forbidden than they used to be. The reduced stigma associated with leaving Israel, the growing number of yeshiva boys who do not serve in the military, and even the pleasure-oriented, gay-friendly, easygoing, and intellectually bent elements of the Tel Aviv lifestyle are all testaments to this trend. Still, the predominant Israeli narrative is aggressive masculinity, and even these rising counternarratives pursue their agendas rather assertively. Finally, as individuals, try as they may, members of all these groups or with these lifestyles often fail to shake off the aggressive predisposition embedded in their culture.

The dynamics of this hypermasculinity are exquisitely packed into one symbolic moment in David Grossman's *To the End of the Land*. When Ora would greet her son, Ofer, on weekend leaves from the military with an embrace, "her fingers would recoil from the metal of the gun slung over his back and search for a demilitarized space on that back, a place that did not belong to the army, a place for her hand."[20]

As Grossman puts it elsewhere, the experience of loss is intimately associated with femininity. In *Falling out of Time*, the Walking Man likens the loss of his son to giving birth and concludes, "Thus, with a lucent chisel, his death engraves upon me anew: the bereaved will always a woman be."[21] Here we see in rough schema the feminine versus masculine reaction to trauma. The former survives it by mourning, the latter, by belligerence. To the extent that Israeli society is more masculine as a whole, the burden of trauma has no doubt exacerbated its aggressive proclivities. As suggested by psychologist and trauma expert Yuval Neriah, the move to the right by the Israeli public in the aftermath of the second Palestinian intifada is a natural political response to trauma. It is an explicitly more muscular approach to coping with fear and anger.[22]

As an individual, each Israeli woman follows her own developmental path. But as noted by Watzman, early sabra folklore viewed women less as individuals than as part of the collective, which was dominated by men.[23] Historically, many young women also separated from their families through military service. For the most part, however, regardless of their skills or intelligence, the military assigned them to secretarial or otherwise supportive positions, subjugating them to the male military hierarchy. They, along with women who did not serve, were toughened up by the hypermasculine culture and often ended up identifying with its values and behaviors. Indeed, when Israeli women stand out in a crowd, they often appear to be extremely assertive. Golda Meir, Israel's most accomplished female political leader, was thus famously described by Ben-Gurion as the only man in his cabinet. This type of what would traditionally be considered masculine identification is common among female leaders in many societies, but in Israel, many women are just as aggressive as men.

Against this general backdrop, the recent emergence of the female leader Daphni Leef, a twenty-five-year-old video editor, is remarkable. Leef, who in the summer of 2011 led the biggest social-justice movement in Israeli history, did not serve in the IDF for medical reasons. As a youth of premilitary age, however, she joined dozens of other youngsters in signing a public letter of refusal to serve in the "occupation army." When she gained fame as a leader of the movement, she openly discussed her struggles with love, overeating, the death of a friend by suicide, self-esteem, support groups, and having been raped at fourteen. And she did not hesitate to shed tears publically. She appeared to be a totally different type of leader: vulnerable, open, soft, and authentically uninterested in masculine concerns. Yet, her boldness is distinctly Israeli. The first time she spoke in public was in front of hundreds of thousands of people, the equivalent of tens of millions in the United States. As she later noted, she was so anxious that she couldn't read the prepared text. Instead, she improvised. Leef seems vulnerable, but she is nothing if not assertive and courageous. Perhaps a similar paradox lies in the combative, in-your-face, public attitudes proudly displayed by the Israeli LGBT community in Tel Aviv, and even in Jerusalem. In other words, even those Israelis not associated with traditional definitions of masculinity are hypermasculine in their own way. As demonstrated by Yaron Peleg, a Hebrew literature and film scholar, notwithstanding the weakening of Zionism as the central organizing ideology of Israeli society, the masculine model of the early Zionists endures even within the counterculture. Peleg's analysis reveals that contemporary gay literature and film in Israel have adopted that very model by using the military, soldiers, and the combat experience as the means and the context within which to normalize gays.[24]

This dynamic was underscored by one of the most touching and symbolic moments in Israel's social-justice movement and Daphni Leef's rise to prominence. At the close of one of the largest demonstrations, after Leef spoke, a thirty-nine-year-old, unemployed software programmer approached her and her parents. Telling her he did not appreciate that she had been criticized for not serving in the army, he handed over to her the war citation he was awarded in the second Lebanon war. It was a difficult decision, he explained, as this citation was something you'd want to show your grandchildren. But, he added, the war at home was more important than the war away.

Like drugs, alcohol, or other forms of acting out, the aggressive, hypermasculine response to trauma creates a secondary trauma, not only for the target of the aggressive behavior, but also for the aggressor himself. In his memoir of the 1948 war Yoram Kaniuk poignantly captures the silence, guilt, and shame suffered by the aggressor. It took Kaniuk fifty-nine years to tell the story that was at the heart of his war experience. He was seventeen and a half when his ragtag platoon won a bloody battle over a hilltop village outside Jerusalem. When the fog of war lifted, they came upon one of their buddies hanging from a tree, his body cut up and tied with ropes, and his penis sticking from his mouth. Horrified and enraged, a close mutual friend of Kaniuk's and of the dead soldier's started taking revenge on the few remaining Arabs around them. When his friend put a knife to the throat of an eight-year-old boy and threatened to slaughter him, Kaniuk pointed his submachine gun at his friend and ordered him to let the boy go. When challenged to shoot the boy or watch him slit his throat, Kaniuk aimed the gun even more carefully at his friend. Then Kaniuk heard a shot. But though he was standing merely six or seven feet away, when the puff of smoke cleared, the boy, not the friend, was dead. The bullet was meant for his friend, and he was certain he aimed well, Kaniuk writes, but somehow he had murdered the child. The next day, Kaniuk reported the incident and brought charges against his friend, but this appeared to have led to nothing other than everyone's telling him to forgive and forget. But Kaniuk couldn't.

He shaved his head with an old razor blade, cutting ugly lines into his scalp. Everyone noticed but not a word was said.

After the war, that same friend tried to help Kaniuk rationalize what had happened. We founded a state in blood, he said. We were dead ourselves, like holes in Swiss cheese. You took in some bullets yourself, you suffered enough, enjoy that you are alive. He quoted one of Kaniuk's favorite poets: *Don't say: My essence is from dust / It's from the life that died in your stead.*[25] But for Kaniuk, the boy became, as he put it, an icon, a memory of shame, carried in silence for nearly sixty years. We now know that this is but one among countless Israeli war stories, each containing a range of extremely intense experiences, emotions, and scars. These traumas have undoubtedly rubbed off on those Israelis who did not experience them directly, through personal interactions, the educational system, and the country's overwhelming collective culture of loss, mourning, and memorialization. During recent wars, front-page photos and bios of every fallen soldier, as well as television and print interviews with families or friends just hearing or processing the awful news, have permeated daily life, overwhelming many readers and viewers. While this culture is undoubtedly authentic, it has also been criticized as over-the-top. Describing it as political indoctrination, an Israeli American businessman I know labeled its institutional component "the bereavement-heroism industrial complex." Call it propaganda or call it an effective national narrative of the kind engaged in by all societies, the normative rituals it generates can sometimes add another layer of trauma to the already traumatized individual. Yuval Neriah, Israeli clinical psychologist, author, and expert on PTSD, noted a phenomenon along these lines, which he called *mosad ha-iturim,* or roughly, "the institution of war decorations." Neriah, who was injured during the 1973 war and received the highest medal of honor awarded by the IDF for acts of bravery in combat, struggled himself with depression in the aftermath of the war. In his mind, medals and decorations are an artificial construct that prevent the recipients from gaining insight into the behavior and circumstances for which they were labeled heroes. The celebration of heroism and the public exposure that goes with it, Neriah argues, impose a superficial, John Wayne–like theory of motivation on a person who internally struggles with a totally different reality, most specifically, profound feelings of loss, whether it's a loss of limbs, best friends, or the capacity to appreciate the small joys of everyday life outside the war zone. The circumstances of the heroic act may also generate in the hero feelings of self-doubt, survivor's guilt, and anxiety. In the face of the John Wayne–like public recognition and community admiration, such raw emotions must often be suppressed, and at a great psychic cost.

After 9/11, Neriah accepted a prestigious academic position in New York. Notwithstanding the magnitude of his personal sacrifice for his country and his training and expertise as a psychologist, several years later he acknowledged in a newspaper interview that he couldn't enjoy the success and personal peace that this extended sabbatical had brought to his family without a heavy sense of guilt—and an ongoing dialogue with that emotion—over taking a break from life in Israel.[26]

MICHELANGELO, LEONARDO DA VINCI, AND THE RENAISSANCE

In the classic 1949 film *The Third Man,* Harry Lime, the Orson Welles character, famously rationalizes his criminal behavior in postwar Berlin as follows: "In Italy, for thirty years under the Borgias they had warfare, terror, murder, and bloodshed, but they produced Michelangelo, Leonardo da Vinci, and the Renaissance. In Switzerland, they had brotherly love, they had five hundred years of democracy and peace, and what did that produce? The cuckoo clock."

Much of what Israel has produced and accomplished in its short history should unquestionably be attributed to its existential struggle. With death never too far from consciousness, Israelis choose life every day and live it as intensely as possible. The air in Israel is filled not only with strife and tension, but also with excitement and vitality. In Jerusalem, the passions are often religious, nationalistic, and historical; in Tel Aviv, secular, business-bound, and hedonistic. Other places are hybrids, but all share an intensity of experience and a compulsive engagement in, or escape from, meaning-making. Thus, while spending time with Israelis is not particularly relaxing—unless they are engaged in some form of extreme relaxation—it is often stimulating. The Israeli existential drive, the need to live life to its fullest because the reality of death and loss cannot be denied, is another reason Israel has produced a culture of high achievement in the arts, business, high tech, literature, music, the sciences, and of course the military. As a direct result of its ongoing experience with the reality of war, the Israeli character is vibrant, creative, intellectual, and enterprising. The positive corollary of hypermasculinity or aggressiveness is assertiveness. This dimension of the oedipal rebellion of the Zionists has benefited not only the Israeli, but also the American and other Diaspora-based, Jews. Inspired, in part, by Israel's assertiveness in the second half of the twentieth century, these Jews, too, have rejected their history of passivity and submission and are now acting on the world stage with greater public confidence than ever before.

Sometimes, the experience of loss is directly inspiring, not only in producing a life-affirming counterreaction, but also in demanding creative expression as a way of coping with intolerable psychic pain. An American couple I know comes to mind. After losing their twenty-two-year-old son to cancer, the wife, previously a commercial illustrator, immersed herself in painting, generating a series of dark portraits of loss and mourning, while the husband, a businessman, bought and developed a couple of brownstone communities for creative youth, to commemorate or keep the artistic legacy of his son alive. Though without such a personal tragedy in their own lives, it is perhaps no coincidence that the designers of both the new One World Trade Center, or Freedom Tower, and the National September 11 Memorial at the World Trade Center complex in Manhattan are Israeli (as well as American) citizens. The designer of the tower, Daniel Libeskind, is a celebrated Polish-born Jewish architect who spent three of his formative years in Israel. The designer of the memorial, Michael Arad, is the son of an Israeli diplomat. He grew up in several countries and served in the Israeli military. In both cases, it seems, a creative character imbued with the sensibilities of, and sensitivities to, loss may have played a role in their selection for these historical projects. The case of Michael Arad is of particular interest, as this thirty-four-year-old, previously unknown architect bested fifty-two hundred competitors from sixty-three countries in an anonymous contest, the largest design competition in history. Like David Grossman's *Falling out of Time*, the name of Arad's design, *Reflecting Absence*, and the concept it represents capture the universal paradox of loss, but can at the same time be said to specifically illuminate and project the Israeli mind.

War-related Israeli creativity is not limited to the artistic articulation of trauma, nor to the well-established proclivity of the Israeli art-scene elite to critique Israeli society's embrace of war as a way of life. In *Start-Up Nation*, another book title aptly representative of the Israeli psyche, Dan Senor and Saul Singer attribute much of Israel's extraordinary success in the start-up world to the experiences and training acquired by young Israelis in their military service. Such concepts as experimentation, innovation, initiative, and interdependency—all dictated by the need to adapt to the constant but ever-changing landscape of the military threats faced by the IDF—are inculcated deep into the minds of the young recruits.[27] The IDF, in a way the most direct social expression of Israel's existential geopolitical condition, has contributed other positive elements to the Israeli character. An equalizer of all socio-economic classes, and a true melting pot, it propagates a set of communal responsibilities. It instills a lasting sense of belonging. The social bonds it fosters are based on and tested by shared experiences of challenge, threat, and danger. Even now, notwithstanding the ascent of American-style individualism, and Middle Eastern–style, sectarian strife, the attachment to a group emotionally and as a value remains a distinctive and lovable Israeli trait.

As discussed by sociologist Oz Almog, the Israeli culture of the circle, with the hora and *kumzits* (campfire) as its most well-known, nostalgic, and historical examples, goes back to the days of the pioneers and the prestate military platoons of the Palmach. Almog holds the hora, a new pioneer dance, which imitated the old Hasidic one, as a symbol of that feeling of togetherness, where the circular dance "symbolizes the centripetal attraction of the individual into the communal circle."[28] For the Palmach fighters, the circular campfire with its public singing, the telling of jokes, and the all-important Turkish coffeemaking ritual, formed or represented a sense of home and family in the wilderness. Critically, Almog also traces this early, intense wish for belonging to the pioneers having left their families in Europe and needing to create new, familylike bonds with fellow pioneers. This wish, reinforced by the need to depend on the collective for survival and support, trickled down to subsequent generations. Deep in their hearts Israelis are still refugees, immigrants, and pioneers searching for a home. The growing orthodox communities in Israel have a greater continuity with the Diaspora culture in the type of the communal bonds practiced, less so with those of the IDF and its precursors.

But when you put the secular and the religious social bonds together—which, one way or another, history actually did—you get the kind of observation offered by economist and psychoanalyst Bruno Boccara. Working with a group of Israelis in a group-relations conference, Boccara noticed that unlike other conference participants, who viewed their breakout work group as a perverse organization that was antithetical to individual freedom and innovation, the Israelis felt protected by, and protective of, their group. Alluding to the small Jewish town of Central and Eastern Europe that prior to the Holocaust provided for a traditional, close-knit, safe-home environment, they characterized their group as a start-up operating in a shtetl. Consistent with Senor and Singer's analysis of Israel's high-tech economy, Boccara suggested that in their minds, the Israelis were experiencing their innovating yet safe work group as though it were the IDF, the ultimate Israeli social organization, which tackles its central mission—survival—through a strategy of adaptation and innovation.[29]

SIX

THERE'S NO PLACE LIKE MASADA

A FOUR-STATE SOLUTION

"His one eye glimmered with an enormous lust for life, his other eye was extinguished beneath the black patch, dead. At times he seemed to symbolize Israel itself, in which life and death are close partners, and which draws its courage from its very willingness to die in order to live."[1] Thus wrote biographer Shabtai Teveth about Moshe Dayan, one of Israel's most iconic historical figures. Moshe Dayan himself said once, "Death in war is not the end of warfare, but its pinnacle, and since war is part of life, and sometimes its entirety, death too, when it is the pinnacle of war, is not the cessation of life, but its ultimate expression."[2]

At the height of the second Palestinian intifada, when suicide bombers ripped into buses and restaurants almost daily, depression and despair settled in the minds of many Israelis, numbing the rapid cycling of panic and relief experienced with each new bombing. During that period in a phone conversation from Jerusalem, my mother lamented, "*Mayle* [Hebrew indicating acceptance with resignation], so we won't have a country, but what about our music?" Israelis are deeply identified with their popular Hebrew music. The Israeli experience, be it war, immigration, or settling the land, often intrudes on even the most intimate of love songs. An instructive if random example is popular singer Rami Kleinstein's brooding "Nothing But You." Proposing to cope with loss and depression by means of lovemaking, it cries, "And my cock is expanding like our country when I embrace you." In addition, many popular Israeli songs are devoted explicitly and self-consciously to the Israeli experience. But of the fleeting array of musical associations that crossed my mind when my mother spoke of "the end," two Hebrew songs, connected with my own, perhaps more sober, assessment of "the end," stood out.

First came the 1969 "Song for Peace." Written by one of Israel's earliest pacifist songwriters and performed by the military pop group Nachal, the song's soulful, defiant melody and antiwar lyrics broke with the well-established tradition of the upbeat, sweet, pro-military, or triumphant Hebrew song. When released, many Israelis considered it sacrilegious or treasonous. One of Israel's top generals, who would many years later become the first Israeli cabinet minister to be assassinated by a Palestinian terrorist, banned the Nachal group from singing for his troops altogether. This prompted a parliamentary debate, which called more attention to the song and helped turn it into a huge hit, and with time a rallying song for the Israeli peace movement. Twenty-six years later, when hundreds of thousands of demonstrators came out to support Prime Minister Yitzhak Rabin's peace policy, Rabin and his supporters sang "Song for Peace." After Rabin was shot in the back at the end of that rally, a folded sheet of paper with the song's lyrics was found in the inner pocket of his jacket. It was stained with his blood.

Whereas the writer of "Song for Peace" developed his antiwar vision after losing a leg in combat, the writer/performer of the second song that came to my mind, Aviv Gefen, never served in the army. He avoided the draft by threatening suicide. From the start, Gefen was an antimilitary, antimachismo, and antiestablishment performer. Androgynous, wearing makeup, sometimes even dresses and pink hair, Gefen's career took off at age twenty with the album *We Are a Fucked Generation*. While way out of the mainstream and outright offensive to most middle-aged adults at the time, within a couple of years Gefen became a rock star, selling hundreds of thousands of albums and receiving every conceivable music award. He was twenty-three when he found himself face-to-face with Prime Minister Rabin minutes before the commencement of the fateful peace rally in Tel Aviv. Learning that Aviv Gefen was in attendance, Rabin personally approached him and asked if he would sing for the demonstrators. Gefen consented. "I have no idea why I chose to sing 'Crying for You,'" he later had to explain to the media, because the song—written to mourn the death of a friend in a car accident—seemed to have foreshadowed the assassination, which took place only minutes after it was performed. Later, thousands of mourners joined Aviv Gefen for an unbearably sad tribute to Rabin, singing and recording "Crying for You." The song thus became a permanent musical memorial for all that was lost as a consequence of the Rabin assassination.

Rabin was neither a charismatic leader nor a lovable character, yet his loss has become an intensely intimate experience for many Israelis. I personally never liked him, and at the time of the assassination I was thousands of miles away, physically as well as mentally. Notwithstanding, the assassination took center stage in my life. It even became a diagnostic tool in my work with my American patients. A seemingly disturbed artist who expressed his condolences and brought me a copy of an Israeli newspaper with news of the assassination as a banner headline suddenly appeared capable of human connection; but a smooth and successful Jewish executive with business dealings in Israel who didn't even mention the assassination revealed his lack of empathy and his narcissistic character. Even now, when I listen to Gefen's song, I am moved to tears, and likewise when I unexpectedly find myself thinking about the assassination. Without question, for most Israelis, Rabin's assassination was a singular emotional event, fraught with historical implications and symbolic meanings. But what was the central meaning of this event in the Israeli mind? Did it, like the Kennedy assassination, signify a loss of innocence and optimism—in the Israeli context, the loss of hope for peace? Or was it about the loss of the person, the leader, the father figure? Surely, it was the latter for most people and the former for many, especially those in the peace camp. But for practically all Israelis the assassination evoked an even graver, more troubling sort of anguish. Moments after the murder, one of Rabin's closest aides put it this way on television: "They killed our country." This was also the first thing my father—who opposed Rabin's peace initiative—said to me when I reached him on the phone that night.

When Yigal Amir pulled the trigger, he killed not only Rabin, the Oslo peace process, and the peace camp, but also himself and all those who opposed Oslo. More than anything else, the assassination of Rabin highlighted the self-destructive potential lurking at the base of the Israeli national character. While the murder shocked the entire country, it shouldn't have been a surprise. Not only had there been an unprecedented amount of public incitement against the person of Rabin and a sharp increase in the number of threats on his life in the preceding year, but just a few months before the assassination, one of Israel's top former intelligence and security officials, General Yehoshafat Harkabi, submitted a manuscript for a book in which he predicted the assassination. But Harkabi's editors felt that the prediction was too far-fetched and edited it out of the published book. Theirs, as well as most Israelis' denial, in this case consisted not only in declining to comprehend a scary possibility, but also, and perhaps primarily, in refusing to face their own potential self-destructiveness.

Whereas the Zionist revolution succeeded in creating a new Jewish melting pot, it failed to resolve at least two major historical rifts, which have undone the Jews in the past and are once again threatening their national sovereignty. The destruction of the First Temple (and to a lesser extent the Second) was a consequence of an internal political division in which might was the enemy of right. The polarization between the "realists," i.e., the kings who advocated increased power and sovereignty for Judea, and the "moralists," the prophets who sought accommodation and compromise, led to the de facto acceptance of the realists' agenda, which provoked the Babylonian empire to destroy the Jewish kingdom.

In the case of the Second Temple, religious sectarianism and extreme political infighting created a power vacuum, which the Romans filled by appointing Herod, an authoritarian and brutal governor, who decimated the entire Jewish elite. After Herod's death, the power vacuum and the renewed internal strife gave birth to the anti-Roman revolts, which ultimately led to the extermination and exile of the Judean Jews. In modern Israel, the "realists" appear to be winning the argument both in terms of refusing to succumb to international pressure and in the use of power rather than accommodation in relation to the Palestinians. But the threat they pose to the traditionally unifying state institutions, and the bitterness they generate on the other side of the political divide, cannot be understated. In recent years, right-wing settlers and their supporters have extended their traditional campaign of intimidation and low-level violence against West Bank Palestinians to Israeli Arabs, Israeli Jews on the left, and finally the IDF. In 2010, the increase in death threats toward, and the actual harassment, of left-leaning public figures led Israel's internal security minister, Yitzhak Aharonovich, to warn the Knesset of the risk of a political assassination. For the first time, Jewish resistance to the IDF, which is in charge of security in West Bank areas affecting the settlements, has morphed from passive or sometimes aggressive civil disobedience to proactive, physical confrontations. Most brazenly, in December 2011 dozens of settlers took part in an organized raid on an army base, blocking its entrance, vandalizing military vehicles, and injuring a deputy brigade commander. While such attacks have been denounced by the settlers' establishment, the ideology on which these fringes act is shared by this establishment. Furthermore, these fringes represent an authentic, historical voice within the Zionist vision, taken to an extreme. The more moderate Zionist and post-Zionist Israelis disagree with the application of the Zionist project to the West Bank. They condemn the settlers' methods and resent the allocation of vast state funds to the settlements. They are also frightened and angry about the increased number of right-wing settlers within the army-officer ranks, which in their minds raises the possibility that the IDF will be unable to enforce the dismantling of settlements if a peace accord is ever achieved.

While the left arguably protests and provokes as much as the right, by its very nature it is less likely to rely on force to advance its goals—after all, its agenda is peace through reconciliation, not force. But if the right overreaches in hubris to deny the reality of the Palestinian and Muslim ascent, and to further isolate Israel from the world, the left has its own hubris. This is where Israeli narcissism meets its masochism, resulting in another potential form of self-destructiveness. The left, if it ever takes the reins of power again, is perfectly capable of trading everything, including Israel's basic security interests, for what would ultimately turn out to be a piece of paper. It would do so out of desperation, or in a grandiose and heroic gesture to give peace a chance and the Palestinians what they deserve. And it could well end up being a grand and foolish appeasement of historic proportions.

While it is not impossible to imagine an ultimate peace accord with the Palestinians and a subsequent easing of the external threat, the second, internal conflict unresolved by the Zionist movement, the secular-religious divide, offers no such pathway in the foreseeable future. While the overlap of the right wing with the religious, and of the left wing with the secular, is growing, the secular-religious divide goes to the core of Israeli identity and to the struggle over the basic character of the Jewish state. As noted by the Israeli as well as the international press, the demographic explosion and growing political power of the ultraorthodox communities in Israel are challenging the country's liberal-democratic foundation. A 2012 *New York Times* article, for instance, described how Israeli women are now sometimes barred from being onstage during state ceremonies and have to resist being segregated from men while using public transportation in certain neighborhoods. In a particularly controversial case, a pediatrics professor was to accept a Health Ministry prize for her work on hereditary diseases common to Jews. Knowing that the acting health minister was ultraorthodox, the professor dressed modestly, but to her surprise she was not allowed to sit with her husband and was instructed that a male colleague would have to accept the award for her, because women were not permitted onstage.[3] Such cases, and that the Haredim—as the ultraorthodox are known ("those who tremble before God," in Hebrew)—live on state subsidies and are exempt from military service and value religious studies over employment; as well as the lack of separation between church and state, mandating secular Israelis to submit to halachic law on personal matters such as marriage, divorce, and burial—all generate profound resentment among secular Israelis. Adding insult to injury, over the years ultraorthodox public officials, recently even a government minister, have publicly suggested that Israel had suffered military setbacks because soldiers had failed to pray, or that a devastating terrorist attack was a divine retribution for violating the Shabbat.

Critically, the liberal, secular identity of many Israelis is just as fundamental to their sense of self and way of life as the religious one is to the Haredim's. The longer such secular Israelis feel that their civil liberties are trampled upon and eroded by the Haredim, and the greater the cumulative erosion, the greater the likelihood that one day they will take up arms for their cause. This is the conflict in which the secular, peacenik community is most likely to manifest the Israeli aggression, the worrier mentality that they share with their fellow Israelis on the right. I sometimes joke that the ultimate path to peace in the region is a four-state solution, a secular Israel in the greater Tel Aviv area, a religious Judea in the Jerusalem area, a secular Palestine in the West Bank, and a religious Hamastan in Gaza. But jokes aside, a self-destructive civil war of sorts between the religious and the secular in Israel cannot be ruled out. As we have seen, the Israeli national character is ensnared by a dialectical relationship with its religious origins, so the psychological, inner world equivalence of such a war is already familiar to every Israeli.

Literary scholar Yael Feldman notes that in biblical narrative, certainly in Genesis, the family model of expressed aggression is not necessarily based on aggressive masculinity and the associated father-son oedipal competition.[4] This surprising absence of binary gender roles, Feldman speculates, correlates with the Diaspora tradition (or stereotype) of the assertive Jewish mother and the conflict-avoidant father who submits to the only true paternal authority, God. This submission, according to Feldman, blocks "vertical" aggression in the family and redistributes it "horizontally," at least in biblical stories, between siblings. Indeed, taken at face value, there are no biblical stories of patricide or filicide, yet fratricide occurs in the story of Cain and Abel, the first and only instance in the Bible in which family aggression is acted on. As discussed before, the Zionist revolution was in a sense an oedipal, Freudian rebellion against the passive Jewish father. Now, however, we are witnessing the fraternal conflicts of the father revisiting the son. In his book *Fratricide in the Holy Land,* psychologist Avner Falk extends this concept to an in-depth analysis of the self-defeating nature of the Israeli-Palestinian conflict. Psychologically, he explains, these two are brothers, believing in fact that they are the descendants of Abraham's sons, Isaac and Ishmael, fighting with each other over the motherland.[5] Along with colleagues Ilan Kutz and Sue Kutz, he evokes one of Spanish painter Francisco Goya's most famous paintings to convey the fraternal aspect of the Israeli-Palestinian conflict.[6] In this dark classic, two men are furiously swinging their clubs at each other while sinking, knee-deep, in a quicksand or mud. This conflict both aggravates and is aggravated by the other fraternal conflict, the one within the Jewish Israeli community. A relatively benign example: in January of 2012 the ethics committee of Israel's parliament suspended a lawmaker for dumping water on a colleague during a heated debate over whether an Arab Israeli school had the right to take its students to a human rights march in Tel Aviv.

THE ETERNAL DNA HELIX OF THE AQEDAH

As a nation born in reaction to nineteenth- and twentieth-century European anti-Semitism, the survival of the Jews, perhaps of the fittest among them, has been Israel's raison d'être from the beginning. Officially and otherwise, the Zionists defined Jewish self-destructiveness rather narrowly, as the passivity and learned helplessness of the European Diaspora. In 1903, Hebrew poet Hayim Nahman Bialik, later Israel's most prominent national poet, was sent by the Jewish Historical Commission in Odessa to Russian-controlled Bessarabia to investigate the Kishinev pogrom against the Jews. At the conclusion of his investigation, rather than writing a report, Bialik penned a disturbing epic poem, "The City of Slaughter," in which he used the language of Jewish martyrdom (*kiddush hashem*) to condemn the victims for their passive submission to the local mob and the authorities.

In the face of this perceived Diaspora helplessness—magnified exponentially by the Holocaust—the early Israelis looked elsewhere in Jewish history to be inspired. What they found was that against a near-constant backdrop of cautious or passive leadership, small, underground, or paramilitary groups have always advocated resistance and rebellion against all odds. Many of these movements failed, and their members often paid the ultimate price, but that was an essential feature of their appeal. Indeed, from the beginning Zionism has consciously incorporated into its nation-building strategy the belief that individual self-sacrifice can advance the interests of the collective. The concept of self-sacrifice has not only historical but also religious roots in Judaism. In the biblical tale of the Aqedah, the binding of Isaac, Abraham was willing to follow God's inexplicable order to sacrifice his only son, Isaac. Throughout Jewish history, this theme repeated itself in the practice of *kiddush hashem*—the sanctification of the name of God—whereby individuals and communities chose to die rather than denounce or abandon their faith. The early Zionists adopted this tradition with one important modification—instead of being ready to die for religion, they were now ready to die for the homeland. Israeli commemorative literature, as well as Hebrew poetry and prose in general, have made frequent use of the Binding of Isaac as a metaphor for the willingness of the new sabra to die in battle. Joseph Trumpeldor, the one-armed Jewish hero from Tel-Chai, who died fighting throngs of Arab attackers in 1920, exemplified this spirit. "It is good to die for our country," he is said to have uttered while dying. To this day Trumpeldor remains one of Israel's most mythical figures, and the site of the Tel-Chai battle is a major draw for Israeli youth. And of course there is the story of Masada, the mountaintop fortress overlooking the Dead Sea in the Judean desert, where, in the first century, a group of Jewish rebels put themselves and their families to the sword rather than face imprisonment and slavery by the Roman army. While the historical accuracy of this event has been questioned, decades of archaeological digs, state and military ceremonies, and ritual youth hikes have fixed the symbol of Masada deep in the consciousness of all Israelis. Embracing this history, Israeli society has incorporated the Masada martyrs and similar heroes into its cultural hall of fame. Naming sports teams, youth movements, businesses, and city streets after them, it has ensconced their legacies in all facets of Israeli reality.

The affirmative, survival value of the Zionist reinvention of Jewish self-sacrifice cannot be underestimated, especially as it relates to the formation of group morale and individual motivation during the early years of the state and at times of war. It has manifested, for instance, in the legendary leadership of young army officers who would, during ground or trench combat, cry out, "After me!" and charge ahead of their platoons to near-certain death. Much of the Israeli success story in reversing the misery of the Diaspora can be attributed to this ethos. However, in their search for historical evidence of Jewish power, the Israelis have blinded themselves to the fact that these heroic rebellions led to the same self-destructive outcomes brought about by the timid helplessness of the Diaspora. With this history in mind, Shabtai Shavit, former head of Israel's Foreign Intelligence Service, the Mossad, warned in a 2014 *Haaretz* op-ed that Israel is marching blindly down a time tunnel back to the Bar Kokhba's confrontation with the Roman Empire. That confrontation, he wrote, ceded one hundred years of national sovereignty to two thousand years of exile. Speaking in a Peace Now demonstration at about the same time, Carmi Gillon, former head of Israel's Internal Security Service, the Shin Bet, echoed that concern in even stronger words.

As noted by A. B. Yehoshua, one of Israel's most celebrated authors and essayists, the Jewish people's distinctive linkage between religion and nationality began on Mount Moriah, the site of the Aqedah, where Abraham waved his knife over his son's head. According to rabbinical tradition, this was where God gathered the dust to create the first man, Adam, and where the two Jewish temples were later built. Identified now as the large plateau above the Western Wall in Jerusalem's contested Old City and considered the holiest place in Judaism, the area is known to Israelis as the Temple Mount. Referring to the connection between religion and nationality first established in that site, Yehoshua writes, "This special connection is recreated anew by a forced repetition of the Akedah ritual. Abraham's descendants bring themselves to situations of conflict with their surroundings, in which they are threatened with extermination and destruction, with a knife waving overhead."[7] Perhaps both symbolically and historically it is no coincidence that the second Palestinian intifada—the overwhelming, murderous violence that more than anything else foreshadowed the emerging capability of the Palestinians to bring an end to the Zionist enterprise—started at the Temple Mount. Though clearly not the underlying cause, what triggered the violence was a visit by then opposition leader Ariel Sharon to the Temple Mount. As Islam's third-holiest site, hosting the Dome of the Rock and the al-Aqsa Mosque, the Temple Mount has been managed by the Jerusalem Islamic Waqf authority without interruption since 1187. Secured by over one thousand police officers, Sharon entered the Temple Mount and declared that the site, occupied by Israel in 1967, would remain part of Israel forever. On a smaller scale, subsequent such visits by Israeli politicians also precipitated Palestinian violence, including at least one terrorist attack with an overtly religious tone. In 2014 these visits also added fuel to the Islamist flames raging in the broader Middle East. To use Yehoshua's concept, Sharon figuratively, if not literally, forced the Israelis to return to the birthplace of Jewish nationality and its central metaphor, the Aqedah. Why and how such a "forced repetition" occurs, and to what extent it is truly self-inflicted rather than the result of external circum-stances, is a central, indeed critical, psychological question about the Israeli national character.

Historically, the Binding of Isaac has been viewed as an impor-tant philosophical marker in the moral development of the early Israelites. Since God commanded Abraham to stop the sacrifice and save Isaac, the story was interpreted to signify the differentia-tion of the Israelites from the surrounding peoples, who, in fact, continued the barbaric practice as part of their religions. Unlike the Jews, none of these ancient people survived, and perhaps this is no accident, the work of their own self-destructiveness. In the Diaspora the Jews have interpreted the tale as a theological dia-logue between the people and their God about self-sacrifice. In the Zionist version, the dialogue is between people, specifically fathers and sons, and it's about the line between altruistic self-sacrifice, murder, and suicide. The early Zionists, who were raised on the annual retelling of the Aqedah story in synagogue every Rosh Hashanah, adapted its message of self-sacrifice to the birthing of the new nation and the conquering of the land. A good exam-ple was the popular 1942 play *Ha'adama Hazot,* or, *This Earth,* which tells the story of a tiny 1890s settlement and its struggle with deadly malaria. As discussed by Yael Feldman, the play "affirms the priority of land over the sanctity of life."[8] While this is a case where the degree of self-sacrifice and the extent of the reward do in fact mark the line between self-sacrifice and self-destructiveness, conceptually a straight line runs between that ideology, which was mainstream at the time, and the self-confessed position of the extremists among today's West Bank settlers. Once again we see the meeting place between narcissism and masochism: this land replaces God as the one and only because it is special and indivis-ible even if in reality no God has ever promised it to his people and others have equal claims to it by virtue of their own histori-cal residence.

But having used self-sacrifice to win the war against the land, the Zionists then needed to employ the same ideology to win the war against those other inhabitants of the land, the Arabs. Interpreting the Aqedah as an act of free choice rather than of submission to a God, they argued there was inherent happiness in self-sacrifice. As highlighted by Feldman, when the War of Independence was coming to its glorious end in 1949, the concept of *osher aqeda,* "the bliss of binding"—which was coined decades earlier by a Labor Party leader to celebrate and secularize the joy of altruism—popped up in the Passover Haggadah of the celebrated kibbutz of Na'an.[9] That this kibbutz had served as the IDF's headquarters for the operation to free Jerusalem and that this concept reemerged at that particular moment in Israeli history demonstrate yet again how much the Aqedah retained its supremacy as the eternal DNA helix of the Jewish nation and the Israeli mind.[10]

In a comprehensive and complex volume titled *Glory and Agony: Isaac's Sacrifice and National Narrative,* Yael Feldman delves into Hebrew literature, art, philosophy, psychology, and politics to trace the development of Israeli attitudes toward what she calls the trope of the Aqedah. Among other things, she analyzes the biblical story of Jephthah's daughter, suggesting that the concept of sacrifice applies to women as well. One of the main narratives Feldman explores involves the shift, for many Israelis, in the interpretation of the Binding of Isaac from a symbol of the willingness to sacrifice one's self to that of the willingness to sacrifice one's son. Indeed, beginning in the 1960s and early 1970s, Israeli authors and artists— mostly lone voices on the margins—began to use this foundational myth to critique the trajectory of the Zionist project at the time. Playwright Hanoch Levin, author A. B. Yehoshua, and painters Menashe Kadishman and Uri Lifshitz, among others, confronted the political leadership and Israeli society at large regarding their eagerness to sacrifice, not themselves but their sons, by sending them to die at war. In Levin's satirical play *The Queen of the Bath-*

tub, which the government banned shortly after its opening in 1970, Isaac mocks his father, Abraham, for "his"—the father's—presumed sacrifice. He admonishes the father to seek forgiveness from *him,* the dead son.

To understand how this dynamic works in today's Israel, consider Jeffrey Goldberg's 2004 *New Yorker* report from the West Bank, titled "Among the Settlers: Will They Destroy Israel?" Goldberg interviewed a Hebron settler, a mother of ten who was allowing one of her children to play outside amid soldiers, barbed wire, and Palestinian snipers. "Hebron is ours," she told Goldberg, "why shouldn't he play?" "At least his death here would sanctify God's name. . . . You don't live just to keep living. That's not the point of life."[11] In a different conversation, she also expressed admiration for Abraham and recounted the legend of Hanna and her sons as the rationale for her own, present-day choices.

The story of Hanna, the pious mother of seven sons and partisan of the Jewish revolt against the Greeks some twenty-seven hundred years ago, is known to nearly every Israeli child. Brought before the Greek king Antiochus, Hanna's sons were ordered to eat pork as a test of loyalty to the crown. When they refused, their tongues were ripped out and they were boiled alive. Just before the seventh boy was thus martyred, Hanna gave him a message to deliver in heaven: "Go and say to your father Abraham, 'Thou didst bind one son to the altar, but I have bound seven altars.'" After her last son was killed, Hanna threw herself off the roof, at which point, according to the Talmud, a voice came from heaven, singing, "A happy mother of children."

Contemplating this, Goldberg speculates that the settler he interviewed suffers from the "Moriah complex," the desire to match Abraham's devotion to God in binding Isaac at Mount Moriah. Now as in the case of young Moslem suicide bombers—and no equivalency, moral or otherwise, is implied—it is misguided to assume that a mother who approves of her son's martyrdom does not love him. Rather, as illustrated by the story of Hanna, she sees her children as an extension of herself and is therefore primarily self-sacrificing. Indeed, from a national-character perspective, the distinction between the Aqedah as a potential suicide and a potential murder is insignificant, because if progeny is sacrificed so is the future of the self. This, along with the pain of loss associated with the reality of war in Israel, was beautifully rendered in a popular 1997 song recorded by then groundbreaking young musician Evyatar Banai. Called "Fathers and Sons," the lyrics capture this intergenerational tragedy with a refrain expressed by a soldier dying at war, "a father crying over a son crying over a father."[12]

But if this is right, and Abraham's descendants, as A. B. Yehoshua put it, have returned to the site of the Aqedah only to repeat the ancient trauma in an endless loop, what is the psychological process and the reasons underlying this repetition? How and why we cling to past threats, losses, and masochistic behavioral patterns is a much-discussed topic in psychoanalytic theory. One school of thought is that when such early experiences are at the core of our attachment to others, we return to them later because they are better than nothing. More than anything else, we humans need a connection, and if all we have known is a relation of abuse, then that's how we connect to others. This makes sense in the context of individual development, but less so, in the lives of nations. Nonetheless, there is perhaps a kind of nostalgia in the Jewish and Israeli attachment to a wrathful God or other, larger-than-life projects demanding self-sacrifice. Or maybe the nostalgia is for a special sadomasochistic attachment to the persecutory gentiles, somewhat like the free slave's attachment to his master, which is hard to let go of. Another theory, however, originating in Freud's concept of the *repetition compulsion*, is more applicable in the case of nations. This theory holds that the victim unconsciously attempts to reexperience the trauma in order to master it, in Robert Stoller's words, by "turning trauma into triumph."[13,14] To overcome the trauma, the victim goes about finding someone to whom he can do what has been done to him. But while now he acts as the victimizer, if he is to master the original trauma, his choice of object or circumstances at present must resemble his own past victimizer or situation. This, by definition, guarantees his own, repeated traumatization. Israeli psychologist Avner Falk lays out a powerful argument as to how this plays out in the Israeli-Palestinian conflict. In trying to master their respective historical traumas, he writes, the Israeli Jews and the Palestinian Arabs unconsciously continue to inflict upon each other, and therefore themselves, the very horror they have consciously sought to avoid. In his analysis Falk quotes from the classic W. H. Auden poem, "September 1, 1939"—the date associated with the beginning of World War II—which notes that everyone, even schoolchildren, know that "Those to whom evil is done/Do evil in return."[15]

Add to this concept the logic of A. B. Yehoshua and the predictable vicious cycle of war's attack and retaliation, and you can see how the Jewish state ends up doing evil—upon itself as much as others. Consistent with the psychology of the repetition compulsion, the Jews have settled in the center of a hostile sea of gentiles—Arabs in this case—and engaged in a war that in the long run they cannot really win. It is just a matter of time before the Palestinians have a majority in the Holy Land and Iran or another such state has nuclear weapons capable of reaching the Jewish minority there. This is why in early 2014, as John Kerry was making a last-ditch effort to push his peace initiative, Thomas Friedman wrote in *The New York Times*, "So that's where we are: Israelis and Palestinians need to understand that Kerry's mission is the last train to a negotiated two-state solution. The next train is the one coming at them."[16]

But the odds were against the Zionists from the beginning, and chances are good that the Israelis have been unable to learn from their Jewish past precisely because they unconsciously need to repeat it. The more they have tried to escape the weakness of the Diaspora by amassing power, the more vulnerable they have become. Or as David Grossman put it, "As in an old science fiction story, an entire nation has been caught in a time warp, where it spins round and round, doomed to relive all the worst evils of its tragic history. Maybe, for that reason, when Israel is at the height of its military power, Israelis themselves lose their ability to act. They become nonpersons, victims in fact; only, this time, they are their own victims."[17]

A few months after the 1967 war Moshe Dayan took a few hours off and went to an archaeological dig outside Tel Aviv. Looking (illegally) for antiquities at the site, he climbed up a mound of sand, which collapsed and buried him alive. He later recalled that before he was rescued, he thought it was the end. He ended up in a hospital with serious injuries and stayed for three weeks. Observing that Dayan's sister had killed herself about four months earlier, psychologist Falk, who wrote a psychoanalytic biography of Dayan, concluded that this was an unconscious suicide attempt.[18] Be that as it may, this story has a poignant, even tragic symbolism, emblematic of the Israeli national character. Undermined by the nostalgic archaeologist within, the heroic, new Jew is trapped in the past, in a near-death experience of his own making. As pointed out by Yael Feldman, it is no coincidence that historically the Hebrew word *qorban* meant both "victim" and "sacrifice." This semantic overlap is another representation, perhaps an oversimplified one, of Feldman's overall thesis, that the "glory and agony [of the Aqedah] are forever bound together."[19]

A SECOND GENERATION OF . . . SOMETHING

Some years ago, while terminating my personal psychoanalysis, I was reading Amos Oz's memoir, *A Tale of Love and Darkness*.

Already then I considered it one of the finest literary portraits of the Israeli mind, and I told my analyst that once it came out in English, I would send her a copy. "There is a part of me, the Israeli part," I told my American analyst, who was Jewish but philosophically closer to Buddhism than to the Jewish religion, "that I'm not sure you ever really understood. This book might do the trick." So, a couple of years after our last session, I sent her a copy of the book in English. I also gave copies of the book to several close friends, all American Jews. Interestingly, most of my friends were unable to get past the first fifty pages—too dense, too intellectual, too slow, they said. My analyst, however, went on a long vacation to Antarctica, and I suppose there was not much to do there. She wrote me in a long note, *The book did remind me of our work together. I felt that like you, the author spent a lot of time and energy hiding from me in his sophisticated intellectualizations, though he eventually did reveal some of his true self.* Remaining true to her own analytic self, she had a point, I thought, both about Oz and me. But I felt that she still didn't get the Israeli part of me. I also wondered, was it merely a coincidence that when Oz "reveals himself," especially toward the end of the book, it is the suicide of his mother that unfolds? It is absurd to think that Israelis, as individuals, are more self-destructive than people of other nationalities. Israel, in fact, has a lower suicide rate than the United States and most European countries. The same goes for alcohol-related, and to a lesser extent drug-related, death rates. But the knife of self-sacrifice does seem to have settled in the deep recess of the Israeli mind. Yet if Israelis are no more self-destructive as individuals than other people, how meaningful is this trait of the Israeli national character? The same question can be posed about many of the other Israeli traits discussed in this book, which once again brings into doubt the utility, if not the validity, of the very concept of the Israeli mind. While as a psychologist I believe that people are ultimately more alike than different, this book focuses on cross-national differences, not similarities. From a practical standpoint it is reasonable to assume that both similarities and differences across the national divides, as well as individual differences within a national character, can explain potential behavior. Scientifically, we could probably even devise a way to measure the relative validity of all three factors in predicting actual behavior. But philosophically, the answer to the question lies in a paradox. Yes, culture or national character is destiny, and, yes, individual psychology is destiny, and if you take each concept to its logical conclusion, they become mutually exclusive. Yet both are true. This paradox was beautifully captured by a dialogue in Etgar Keret's and Shira Geffen's movie, *Jellyfish*. The film takes place mostly in Tel Aviv, but there is virtually nothing Israeli about its poetic, mystical themes, with the possible exception of one quick dialogue toward the end of the movie. Lying in bed next to each other, one of the two female protagonists tells the other that her parents were Holocaust survivors. "Are you a second generation?" asks the friend. "We are all a second generation," comes the answer, "of something."[20]

The extent to which the self-destructive tendencies that occupy the Israeli mind impact on individual Israelis is an open question. It is not hard to argue that the narcissistic, internally conflicted, self-hating, and acrimonious individual Israeli engages in self-defeating behavior. It is more difficult to pinpoint an individual narrative of either positive or negative self-sacrifice unless we conclude that simply by committing to stay in Israel, Israelis—at least those who can afford to leave—are in fact sacrificing themselves. This is a debatable proposition, yet as the years go by, developments in the Middle East seem to add, not detract, credibility to such a notion. In 2011 Israeli video artist Tom Pnini built and filmed a huge, fire-spewing volcano on top of an apartment building in central Tel Aviv. Ultimately an illusion, the movie is a compelling, indeed haunting, reminder of the reality of life in Israel.

In 2012, a fiercely Zionist, right-of-center Jewish American friend, whose teenage son was spending a high school semester in Israel, called me with some alarm. She wanted to discuss news reports regarding the approaching conflict with Iran that spring.

"I don't believe it's imminent," I dared to predict. "My family in Israel is not concerned, and the Israelis are not as panicked as the media would have you think."

"They are in denial," she retorted. "I'm bringing my son home in March. Would you let *your* daughter go now?"

"Yes." I did not hesitate.

But objectively speaking, perhaps she is right. Perhaps they are in denial, putting themselves and their families at great risk for a noble idea and a questionable future. A similar dialogue was initiated at about the same time in an Israeli newspaper book review. Based on an in-depth analysis of both external, geopolitical, and internal Israeli circumstances, the book in question, *Does Israel Have a Future?* by Belgian scholars Richard Laub and Olivier Boruchowitch, concluded that, absent a radical change of course by the state, Israel's existence as a national, Zionist entity would be in serious jeopardy sooner rather than later—within a decade or two. In a less academic but equally as instructive response to a sympathetic review of the book by Israeli sociologist Joseph Hodara, an online reader commented, "The authors are saying nothing new, but they have neglected the main parameter. 'In every generation they rise to destroy us but Hashem rescues us.' Logically, we have no chance. But throughout all of history, the people of Israel have proven to be above the laws of nature."[21]

CONCLUSION

SAYING NO, GETTING TO YES

S
o, to oversimplify the already simplistic portrait of the Israeli mind offered in these pages: Emerging from the depth of Jewish history and the drama of the Zionist project's counterhistory, Israelis are still struggling to forge an identity. Like a perpetual adolescent, they are at once passionate, rigid, adaptable, and unstable. They are grand and grandiose, visionary and delusional, self-centered and generous. Appearing self-confident in the extreme, they actually suffer from low self-esteem. They are condescending and disdainful, thinking they are the best of the Chosen People, yet they are often self-hating. Extremely generous out of their desire to please others, and often deeply caring because of the history of Jewish victimization, they also exhibit a lack of empathy, a shocking indifference to the sufferings and perspectives of others. Conflicted, divided, and self-doubting on the inside, they are action-oriented, assertive, and combative on the outside. They admit no self-doubt and think they are always right, only to argue the opposite if you agree with them. Saying no is their first, second, and third line of defense, even as they are totally capable of

complete and sudden capitulation. Enterprising, vibrant, and self-reliant, they are also frightened and mistrustful. Cunning, conniving, and aggressive, they project these impulses onto others and then feel persecuted or taken for a ride—the latter being one of the worse things short of tragedy that can happen to an Israeli. They perceive themselves as both victims and (benign) victimizers. They have little respect for rules and authority and live life to the fullest. They are vulnerable, traumatized, and compartmentalized survivors as well as hypermasculine warriors and harsh oppressors. From the Holocaust—the formative and omnipresent building block of the Israeli psyche—they have internalized the categorical imperative that it's better to be aggressive than helpless, even at the risk of harming the innocent, the ally, or themselves. This tendency amplifies the Zionists' wholesale rejection of the passivity and timidity of the old Diaspora Jew. Finally, Israelis are willing to sacrifice themselves for the collective, but also to sacrifice that very collective—for a higher and likely unattainable ideal.

Given the disproportional, though hardly inexplicable, centrality of their tiny country in world affairs, this interwoven cluster of personal traits has profound implications not only for the future of Israel, but also for that of the Middle East and the world at large. To be clear, some psychological variables other than national character, not to mention economic, political, and military factors, may be more determinative in these regards than the Israeli national character. But the latter can interact with or even mobilize such factors in a decisive manner. Finally, this personality portrait can be potentially useful for anyone involved with Israel as a country, or with Israelis as individuals and a group—from diplomats, to businessmen, professionals, and academicians, whether they are foreign or themselves Israeli. (Anyone who read Raphael Patai's *The Arab Mind* in the aftermath of 9/11 would have concluded that had it been studied at the Pentagon before the US military went into Iraq, we would quite possibly be living in a different world now.)[1]

Additionally, several psychologists, including Falk, Grosbard, and Sucharov, have already studied in some depth how various elements of the Israeli psychology, some overlapping with the concept of national character, impact the Middle East conflict. They have outlined the kind of psychological changes Israeli society would have to make to embrace reconciliation with its enemies.[2,3,4]

Therefore, in closing, I will limit the discussion here to only two case histories, and a single, more narrow question that has received less attention than others: How can Israel's allies, primarily the United States and the American Jewish community, and its adversaries, primarily the Palestinians, use this psychoanalytic understanding of the Israeli mind to encourage more cooperative and peaceful policies on the part of Israel? Much of what I will propose with respect to the United States, it should be noted, also applies to the European Union. While on the surface, Israelis pay far more attention to what comes out of Washington than Europe, they can never divorce themselves from their sensitivity to and admiration for European culture, which gives Europe an opportunity to play a constructive role—on its own or with the United States. However, Europe's history of anti-Semitism, as well as the various forms in which it has resurfaced in recent years, make any such role more complicated. But exploring Europe's role meaningfully is outside the scope of this book.

Finally, before proceeding, two notes of caution, taken from the clinical practice of psychology, are in order. First, as the old joke goes, it only takes one psychologist to change a lightbulb, but the lightbulb has to want to change. Or as I sometimes tell couples in marital therapy, you cannot will love, but you can create the conditions that may facilitate it. In other words, understanding Israel and acting on such insight may facilitate a change, perhaps even a dramatic change, but the pursuit of peace must be internally motivated. And second, it takes only one party to start a war, but two to make peace.

THE IRANIAN CONUNDRUM

Starting in the early 1990s, Israel began to warn the world that Iran would soon reach a point of no return in its reported efforts to develop nuclear weapons technology. In the winter of 2012, the Israelis raised the stakes with more explicit pronouncements that by June of that year, Iran would enter a "zone of immunity," at which point its nuclear materials would be stored underground and be immune to Israeli air strikes. Israel and the international media, as well as the US government, began to suggest that the Jewish state was contemplating a series of massive air strikes on Iranian nuclear targets by the spring. Iran, which appeared to have already retaliated for the assassination of several of its nuclear scientists with attempts on the lives of Israeli diplomats in Asia, threatened preemptive and retaliatory strikes against Israel and the West. The risk of attacking Iran for Israel would have involved, most significantly, being hit by thousands of missiles from Iran and its proxies on Israel's borders, particularly Hezbollah, from Lebanon. The risk for the West would have been a spike in terrorism and oil prices, which would jeopardize the slow economic recovery in America and the struggling European economies. The United States, whose stated policy is that Iran will not be allowed to develop nuclear weapons, and that "all options are on the table," has military capability that significantly extends the "zone of immunity," as delineated by Israel. It has thus counseled patience. But the Israelis balked. Even though Israel acknowledged that air strikes would only set back the clock by a couple of years at best, the Israeli leadership—enjoying strong general support from the public, if not backed specifically by a majority preference for an imminent attack—threatened to take action before summer.

This type of situation raises the question of whether the United States was and now is capable of stopping Israel from acting on its threats. Recent history tells us that America got Israel to do what it wanted in one of two ways. During the first Gulf War, Israel uncharacteristically agreed to refrain from springing to its own defense because the US Air Force was actually acting on its behalf, searching for and destroying Iraqi missiles aimed at Israel. In this case guaranteeing—in action, not merely in words—Israel's security did the trick. In 1992, when Secretary of State James Baker threatened to withhold loan guarantees unless Israel agreed to halt settlement expansion, Israel's right-wing government lost the election and the new Labor government announced a settlement freeze. In that case, a specific and credible threat of economic sanctions worked, even if less directly. In more recent years, for both ideological and political reasons, American pressure on Israel has been limited to the realm of verbal diplomacy and therefore had little or no effect.

But Iran is a different matter. Whereas Israel, the United States, and the Europeans agree that Iran should not be allowed to go nuclear, at least in the short term their interests diverge. Even in the long term there may not be a complete convergence of interests as the West might be more likely than Israel to resign itself to a nuclear Iran. For one thing, the Israelis are generally more aggressively against nuclear proliferation in the Middle East—Israel had struck both Iraq and Syria when they made advances in the nuclear arena. But for the Jewish state, Iran is one of a kind. When an adversary headed for many years by a Holocaust denier who has stated that Israel is a cancer that must be wiped off the map, and whose Supreme Leader continues to cast doubt as to the historical existence of the Holocaust, calls on Twitter for Israel to be annihilated, and appears to be developing nuclear capabilities and/or weapons, is there any doubt that Israel would attack? And given Israel's abandonment anxiety—*the whole world is against us and the world is silent*—is there any doubt that absent an ironclad guarantee it would act preemptively before its window of opportunity, as it alone perceives it, closes?

Generally speaking, an aggressor might keep his aggression in check if the risk to himself is greater than the benefit. The Israelis logically believe that a nuclear Iran would represent a greater risk than whatever retaliation they would have to endure for attacking it preemptively. So they are willing to sacrifice hundreds or even thousands of civilians at present for the survival of the collective in the future. Yet, other factors, i.e., that they can only delay, not prevent, a nuclear Iran, and that attacking Iran would only inten- sify the vicious cycle of violence in the region and would expand the ring of their already intractable conflicts with their Muslim neighbors, suggest that such self-sacrifice might well border on the self-destructive. That, however, would not stop them, for it is better to die with the Philistines than wait to be killed or even merely depend on others for rescue.

Noting the public objection on the part of the United States to an Israeli strike, Israeli author and columnist Sefi Rachlevsky wrote early in 2012, "When Netanyahu binds Tel Aviv on the altar by demolishing the strategic alliance with the United States, perhaps he sees the sunken Irgun ship *Altalena* there rather than his son. But no divine hand will descend to prevent this madness, the way an angel prevented Abraham from sacrificing Isaac. An Israeli hand must therefore be the one to refuse the order and stop the madness."[5] In a subsequent article, Rachlevsky speculated that in planning to strike Iran, the Israeli leadership actually hoped that an Iranian retaliation against American interests would force the United States into a war that would finish off the Iranian nuclear threat once and for all. If this seems like a far-fetched scenario, manufactured by an overly imaginative Israeli mind, it's because it is—but perhaps not only by Rachlevsky's mind. After all, as noted by Rachlevsky, this scenario is mild compared to what Israel actu- ally did, say, in 1954 when it dispatched secret agents disguised as Egyptian nationalists, Islamists, or communists to bomb American and British targets in Egypt to influence American policy toward

Israel's then biggest Muslim threat and to induce the British government to keep control of the Suez Canal. Known in Israel for many years as *the unfortunate business*—a revealing misnomer in Hebrew, implying it was only a problem because it was exposed and failed—this affair was certainly not the only, though perhaps the most blatant, case of Israeli violation of the self-protective rule of not biting the hand that's feeding you.

Politically speaking, even as the Israeli public was divided on the idea of striking Iran unilaterally, at least back in the long winter days of 2012, no Israeli hand appeared to have been capable of, or willing, to stop the self-sacrificial drums of war. Israel might have been bluffing, at least about the timing of the attack, to pressure the West to increase the economic pressure on Iran. Bluffing or not, this seemed to have worked as the Americans and Europeans for the first time put in place serious financial and oil-related sanctions on the Iranian regime. By the summer of 2013 it appeared that these sanctions, which caused significant damage to the Iranian economy, played a role in the election of a somewhat more moderate successor to Ahmadinejad. While as a candidate, the new president vowed to continue Iran's nuclear buildup, both before and after the election he adopted a more conciliatory tone toward the West. By the spring of 2014 an interim agreement with the West had been reached and a long-term deal appeared to be more feasible.

As reported by *The New York Times* in January 2012, Israeli officials have concluded that the Iranian threat of retaliation was itself largely a bluff.[6] Given the Israeli proclivity for narcissistic projection, this would lend some support to the hypothesis that Israel itself was bluffing—in a grand, sophisticated, and bold manner, also entirely consistent with the audacity, chutzpah, and brilliance of Israel's narcissistic streak. My thought process here sheds light on the limitation of the psychoanalytic approach in predicting human behavior. While the hypotheses generated by the discipline often ring true and may help guide our decision making, even in retrospective analysis the predicted behavioral outcome does not prove the hypothesis, as it could have been the result of equally compelling yet competing explanatory hypotheses, not to mention nonpsychological variables.

But concluding at the time that the most relevant psychological principle within the Israeli mind was the trauma of the Holocaust, what could the West have done to stop Israel in its tracks? Here's how, with the Israeli national character in mind, a White House policy memo, or more likely oral briefing, could have been drafted in preparation for what was then deemed a critical meeting between President Obama and Prime Minister Netanyahu in Washington on March 5, 2012:

> The first thing President Obama needs to know is that, facing an adversary who denies the Holocaust, calls for wiping Israel off the map, and is developing weapons-grade nuclear capabilities, the question is not whether but rather when Israel will strike. Assuming that the West's strategic interest is in fact at stake and that the United States will not allow Iran to go nuclear, the president should offer Netanyahu a deal aiming at the soft underbelly of the Israeli bravado.
>
> First, though, the president will have to find a way to reassure Israel's real as well as paranoid anxieties. An informal understanding, a promise, or the usual public statement reiterating America's "unshakable commitment" to Israel's security won't be sufficient. Israeli leaders don't always keep their own words and therefore do not trust others'. So the president would have to find a way to commit in a formal letter or equivalent, possibly through a

bipartisan mechanism, that the United States would itself resort to military force if Iran in fact immunes itself to an Israeli strike in the coming months. That would be difficult but not impossible. The only time we were able to stop Israel from taking military action in recent history was when we did the job *for* them, in western Iraq during the Gulf War.

But along with such a guarantee, the president should take advantage of the great paradox underlying the ideal of the new Jew. Try as they may have, or precisely because they have tried too hard, the Israelis have not been able to escape the Jewish affliction of vulnerability and dependency. Underneath their tough, combative exterior, the Israelis know that in the long term, they cannot survive in their neighborhood without the support of the United States and NATO. A surgical, strategic pressure, such as the one delivered by Secretary James Baker to the intransigent Shamir government in the aftermath of the first Gulf War, would play on this psychology without triggering in Prime Minister Netanyahu the default oppositional defense of the Israeli national character.

Making clear that striking Iran now would seriously jeopardize the flailing economic recovery in the United States and the fragile economy of Europe, all during a contested election year in America, would send a strong and clear message. A likely reelected Obama, hint, hint, and a sinking European economy would exact a heavy toll from Israel for such a poorly timed attack. Furthermore, potentially forcing the American president into yet a third, unpredictable war in the Middle East—a likely outcome if Iran retaliates against American interests—would divide the American people. At the very least, it would raise a serious question over the value of Israel's friendship if it cannot even be persuaded to delay military action for a few months. On this point the president should be quite explicit, as Israelis do not comprehend subtle communication cues. To sweeten the deal, the president should tell the prime minister that we would try to find a way to help Israel push back Iran's "zone of immunity" beyond this fall's elections.

Laying out these consequences in detail for the prime minister would engage the Israeli mind's fear of abandonment and would outweigh what remains of its current annihilation anxiety vis-à-vis Iran. That the concession demanded is relatively minor would allow the Israeli leadership to save face and alleviate this anxiety by saying yes, rather than resorting to its oppositional self and choosing to self-sacrifice and/or self-destruct. Of course, if our policy—along with those of our European allies—was such that we were strategically willing to contain a nuclear Iran, we would have to say so to Israel in concert, letting the Israelis know they are on their own. That would trigger a nuclear clash within the Israeli psyche between the new and the old Jew, the outcome of which would dramatically weaken Israel, whether it goes it alone or blinks.

In reality, a few days before his meeting with Netanyahu, President Obama struck a similar note in a well-placed interview, stating that the United States would use military force if necessary to stop Iran from possessing nuclear weapons. He also said that as the president of the United States he doesn't bluff. This was meant to send a strong message to both Iran and Israel, presumably with a deliberate choice of words, taking into account both parties' penchant for reciprocal bluffing. In the same interview he warned Israel about the consequences of a strike at this time, saying, among other things, that he didn't know how the American public would react. On that basis, I believed at the time that notwithstanding its highly focused campaign of warnings and threats, Israel would indeed not strike Iran before the American presidential elections of 2012. But then again, as we have just said, Israel is fully capable of biting the hand that's feeding it, rationality notwithstanding.

Finally, from an American perspective—and if you are Obama, certainly after his reelection—it wouldn't have been the worst outcome if Israel had struck Iran on its own, as it would have allowed the United States to distance itself from such an attack and reduced the risk to America. An even better outcome, based on the assumption that Israel would take action even without American agreement, would have been for both governments to privately coordinate a good-cop/bad-cop strategy, with the United States and its partners entering into negotiations with Iran, backed by an independent and credible threat from Israel. Indeed, in the aftermath of the Obama-Netanyahu meeting, a scenario of this type appeared to have been put in motion, as the European Union announced that the United States, along with the five permanent members of the Security Council and Germany, would reenter into a new round of negotiations with Iran. At the same time, the United States publically increased its security cooperation with Israel to unprecedented levels. This combination seemed to have done the trick. Netanyahu extended his ultimatum to Iran and the international community by a full year, and following the Iranian elections later that year, another round of negotiations was undertaken. While Netanyahu's hand was somewhat weakened in his 2013 reelection, the Israeli threat remained credible, if more elastic, time-wise. At the time of this writing, the United States and Iran have reached a six-month interim agreement, publically decried by the Israeli prime minister as a "historic mistake." With progress cited in the negotiations, this agreement was later extended by another four months with a possible path for a long-term outcome preventing Iran from developing nuclear weapons without sufficient warning time for the West. As Thomas Friedman summed it up in *The New York Times*, "Had Bibi not been Bibi, we never would have gotten Iran to the negotiating table, but without Barack being Barack, we'll never get a deal."[7]

As reported by Jeffrey Goldberg of *The Atlantic*, toward the end of 2014, the Obama administration concluded that Netanyahu was too much of a coward to pull the trigger on Iran. This conclusion, a senior administration official told Goldberg, was consistent with Bibi's reluctance to do something dramatic on the peace front with the Palestinians.[8] There is some truth to these observations, as Bibi appeared to be determined to do little more than what was absolutely necessary to survive in office. Having said that, like any Israeli, when faced with the trifecta of Holocaust denial, a call for Israel's destruction, and a nuclear development program, Bibi was fully capable of springing into radical action. Indeed, as the negotiations were about to conclude, he did not shy away from a serious public confrontation with the Obama administration about the issue. Perhaps more important, as Leo Tolstoy argued in *War and Peace,* national leaders, even more so than the seemingly powerless masses they lead, are themselves prisoners of large historical processes whose causes we as humans can never fully comprehend. One of these forces, I submit—and Tolstoy would have probably agreed— is national character, or the sum of the individual psyches forming the collective wills of all the national groups cooperating or colliding to move history forward. All this is to say that unless Iran goes through a revolutionary change, the question of whether Bibi is a coward or a man of courage is ultimately immaterial. Sooner or later he will strike, or else be replaced by someone else who would.

THE ISRAELI-PALESTINIAN QUAGMIRE

If the Iranian conundrum is about preventing or delaying war, the Israeli-Palestinian conflict is about attaining peace. In this area the question is not only how to say no to Israel more effectively, as for example, no more settlements, but also how to get Israel to say yes—to a contiguous, viable Palestinian state with a capital in East Jerusalem and to a moral acceptance of Israel's historical role in the creation of the Palestinian refugee problem. In other words, yes to the only real peace option with the Palestinians, endangered a species as it is becoming with every passing year.

If you believe that the continuing settlement expansion is rapidly closing the window on a two-state solution—a point first made more than two decades ago in a study by former Jerusalem deputy mayor Meron Benvenisti—and that, as noted by, among others, Israeli columnist Shmuel Rosner, a one-state solution is a nonstarter for virtually all Israeli Jews, the first question is how to influence Israel to finally put the brakes on the settlements.[9,10] Here, both history and psychology agree. The international community, including the United States, has objected to and condemned the Israeli settlement project from the start, yet has been unable to stop it. The only exception was when James Baker put some bite behind the bark. More recently, President Obama, relying on mere persuasion, got Netanyahu to agree to a partial and time-limited freeze in 2009. On a tactical level, Baker was more successful because Israelis understand action better than words. Also, unlike Obama's, his approach did not allow the Israeli mind to outfox him with various Talmudic arguments and Machiavellian evasions. Strategically, both failed equally, because contrary to the conventional diplomatic wisdom about international conflict, the objective of that freeze—to bring both sides to the negotiation table to "keep the dialogue going"—was never going to work. The Palestinians had their own reasons, psychological and otherwise, to sabotage the talks, but for the Israelis, the deepest reason was self-sabotage. Israel's Abba Eban famously said, "The Palestinians never miss an opportunity to miss an opportunity," but whereas, historically speaking, this may have been true for a time, it is perhaps another example of a narcissistic projection on the part of Israel. In previously saying no to peace, the Palestinians may have been playing the long game, inflicting suffering on themselves while waiting for the demographic destiny to unfold. In this sense, it is the Israelis who have missed opportunities, certainly those that arose after they gained leverage in 1967 and once the Palestinians became more accommodating starting in the late 1980s. Israeli self-sabotage is thus one of the reasons the list of failed Middle East peace initiatives is so long and varied, inhabiting people, places, and plans such as Rogers, Jarring, Geneva, the 1979 Palestinian Autonomy section of the Israel-Egypt peace treaty, the Shultz initiative, Madrid, Oslo, the 1993 Washington Peace Conference, the Wye Plantation, Camp David, Taba, Sharm el-Sheikh, Amman, Mitchell, Tenet, Zinni, the 2002 Saudi Peace Plan, the Quartet, the Road Map, and the Kerry Initiative, to name just a few. These third-party interventions have ignored the inherent, basic logic of self-destructiveness: to the extent Israel is bent on self-destruction, its leadership must, by definition, reject the helping hand.

Here, too, James Baker, the Texan with the tough-love approach, understood something about Israeli psychology. In seeking to break down Israel's long-standing refusal to negotiate with the PLO, Baker approached Israel's oppositional behavior head-on. Instead of proposing yet one more plan, he asked the Israelis to come up with their own proposal, giving them the "opportunity" to initiate rather than respond. That way, they couldn't quite respond with a no. He subsequently put forward a negotiation plan only in response to, and as an elaboration of, Prime Minister Shamir's own initiative. At a later stage, Shamir regained his footing and found a new way of saying no, at which point—after consulting with journalist Thomas Friedman, who knew a good deal about Israeli psychology—Baker made his famous "Call us, we won't call you" comment to Congress. In so doing, he once again put the ball in the Israeli court, which meant that Israel had nothing to oppose and no help to reject. Most important, it now had to face the consequences of its self-sabotage. Baker's tactical diplomacy led to the 1991 Madrid Peace Conference, which, arguably, laid the groundwork for Israel's de facto and later de jure recognition of the PLO, and the 1993 Oslo Accords.

Yet Baker's efforts ultimately failed, yielding little in Madrid, and ultimately even more bloodshed in the chimera of the Oslo Accords, because he didn't take his approach to its logical conclusion. As in most third-party interventions, he focused on the tactical and incremental, rather than the strategic and differential. It is hard to find success stories in the Arab-Israeli conflict, but if there are any, they lie in the 1979 Egypt-Israel Peace Treaty, and in the initial dynamics of the 1993 Israeli-Palestinian Oslo Accords, both of which were initiated by the players themselves, not third parties. Having said that, in both cases external changes in geopolitical conditions created a facilitating environment. In the latter case, it is reasonable to assume that Baker's final "Call us, we won't call you" contributed to the inception of the secret and endogenous Israeli-Palestinian negotiations that led to the Oslo Declaration of Principles. Indeed, as Thomas Friedman observed, the United States was only able to advance peace in the region when it was invited by the parties themselves. The flip side of this was the Camp David Summit of 2000, which brought the Oslo Accords to a violent end because President Clinton apparently wanted a peace treaty more than the Israelis and the Palestinians wanted it themselves.

From a strategic standpoint, therefore, the best third-party intervention is no intervention at all: leave the Israelis alone and let them deal with the consequences of their own behavior. To the extent that an Israeli-Palestinian peace is the top priority for the American government, reducing or eliminating its military and financial support to Israel would be part of such a strategy—assuming that American politics would ever allow such a move. The logic here is clear. If Israel cannot rely on America to guarantee its security, it would ultimately recognize that it could not survive in the neighborhood without peace. As with any self-destructive behavior, the risk of such an approach, however, is grave, as Israel may not "hit bottom" but rather continue to deny reality all the way to its ultimate defeat. Nonetheless, the other side of the self-destructiveness/self-sacrifice Israeli paradox is survival. So given an undeniable threat, the life force that drove the early Zionists to leave Europe and give birth to a new nation-state is also likely to reemerge. In reality, none of this appears to be in the cards, at least as long as America is even partly dependent on Middle East oil and the American body politic remains receptive to the influence of the powerful, right-of-center Jewish lobby. In any case, America and the West do not need to go to such lengths. They can continue to guarantee Israel's security but walk away from the "peace process," by now little more than a dangerous delusion enabling Israeli denial. This would have a significant impact, reducing Israeli opposition to peace and placing its existential anxiety in a more contemplative frame of mind. In short, if Israel is a perpetual adolescent, it's time for the parents to let go. The only element missing from such a strategy is a sense of drama, a bold action of sufficient magnitude to shake the rigid but unstable grid of Israeli identity, to confront its grandiose character and to break through its narcissistic denial. As a left-leaning Israeli businessman once asked me, how do you help someone see that they are out of touch with reality when they think that *you* are?

One idea debated in the Obama administration and supported by many Israelis on the left was for America to put forward its own final peace proposal and use it to put pressure, or perhaps even impose it, on the parties. In practical terms, primarily because of American politics, any such move would ultimately be reduced to the art of persuasion, not real pressure, and certainly not an imposed settlement. It would therefore easily be defeated by Israeli gamesmanship and resistance. It would also bounce right off the hard core of the Israeli conviction—illusional as it may be—that Israel must always be the master of its own destiny. So unless America is willing to back up such a proposal with a credible threat of immediate and serious consequences, it shouldn't bother. It is also better if the drama required to challenge Israeli psychology comes from reality itself—the reality on the ground in Israel-Palestine, that is—rather than from external powers whose shifting policies could provide a good target for an Israeli public relations or political offensive. In other words, the answer must come from the Palestinians.

So if America and the West should basically leave it alone, what should the Palestinians do to get Israel to a yes? First, as we have seen, Israel's tough rhetoric notwithstanding, the only times the Palestinians or Arabs in general wrested concessions from the Israelis were when they used force to inflict pain. The near defeat in the 1973 war incentivized Israel to enter negotiations with Egypt prior to Sadat's visit; the first intifada brought Israel to the Oslo Accords; and the second intifada prompted Israel to withdraw from Gaza. There is a critical difference, however, between the first and second intifadas, both in their psychological and political impacts. The first intifada consisted largely of aggressive demonstrations and civil disobedience, driving home the demographic reality of occupation while at the same time awakening the old Jew within, the one not able or wishing to conceive of himself as a victimizer. As demonstrated by political scientist Mira Sucharov, seeing themselves—through the mirror of the media and the international community—in the new reality created by the Palestinians, the Israelis suffered from a severe cognitive dissonance. They suddenly experienced a painful gap between their perception of themselves as victims or defensive warriors and the reality of having been turned into forceful occupiers battling unarmed Palestinians, many of them children. To realign this dissonance, Israel had to take radical action with respect to the most obvious cause of the new reality, the Palestinians. This translated into opening negotiations with, and formally recognizing, the hitherto despised and hated enemy, the PLO.[11]

By contrast, the horrific violence of the second intifada only reinforced the symbiotic relationship between the old and the new Jew. If the former was struck with fear, anxiety, and despair, the latter sprang into action. The result was the ill-conceived hybrid of retreating from Gaza and thereby rewarding the violence, but doing it unilaterally and thus quarantining the poorest and most desperate of the Palestinians in a chaotic and devastated strip of land with an economy and borders harshly controlled by Israel. This combination further radicalized the Palestinians, resulting in the Hamas takeover of Gaza and the subsequent, repeated confrontations between Hamas and Israel, which only further devastated the Palestinians and pushed Israel to the right. From an Israeli perspective, the smart thing to do would have been to negotiate this withdrawal with the PLO leadership, giving them a political win so as to demonstrate to their constituents the value of negotiating with Israel. Instead, the most violent and hateful element within the Palestinian national movement won the day, and the cycle of mutually assured traumatization received another shot in the arm, a lose-lose proposition for both Palestinians and Israelis. The separation barrier in the West Bank, while generally less cruel than the eventual blockade of Gaza, was also a classic Zionist solution. Both offered a great tactical answer, bringing terrorism to a halt, but were also employed to deny the tragic strategic challenge rooted in the Jewish return to Zion. The fences around Gaza and the West Bank serve as one more psychological defense against the reality that the Jews have returned to a land already occupied by another people. They similarly represent a defense against the reality that the Israelis are, and will always be, a tiny island in a vast sea of anticolonialist and potentially anti-Western Arabs and Muslims. And a defense against the reality that these neighbors are heavily invested, psychologically and otherwise, in the Palestinian cause.

So what should the third Palestinian intifada look like? As proposed by Thomas Friedman in a *New York Times* op-ed, assuming that the Palestinians are still interested in a two-state solution, it should take a page from Tahrir Sqaure.[12] Every Friday, thousands and thousands of Palestinians should march peacefully from the West Bank, through the checkpoints, and into Jewish Jerusalem, demanding their sovereign rights alongside a Jewish state based on the 1967 borders and mutually agreed-upon land swaps. A relentless and a relentlessly nonviolent movement of this kind would once again penetrate the Israeli defenses. It would alert the Israeli mind to take notice of what goes on just a few miles down the road that no fence can diminish. If Israeli security forces respond with force, the Palestinians must be willing to self-sacrifice and not escalate. Their only strength in such a case would lie in their weakness. Indeed, if they are able to maintain a nonviolent posture—no rocks, no knives, no charging at police—in the face of a violent crackdown, the cognitive dissonance they would provoke within the Israeli mind would result in a splitting headache for the Israelis. This would ultimately put into motion a more powerful reconciliation process than the one precipitated by the first intifada, when no such zero tolerance for violence was observed.

Whether the Palestinians are sufficiently motivated by misery, national dignity, politics, or psychology to actually do this appears to be questionable. The conduct of Hamas during its 2014 confrontation with Israel renders this proposition positively utopic. However, if and when the Palestinians, especially those in the West

Bank, are ready for such action, they should do it with a genuine peaceful intent. They should demonstrate this intent with emotion. Here the second ingredient required for shifting the ground upon which the Israelis walk comes into the picture. If during such an intifada or in its aftermath, a Palestinian leader emerged who would offer the Israeli public the same acceptance, validation, and love showered on them by Anwar Sadat, the Palestinians would realize their national aspirations soon thereafter. The Israelis want nothing more than real acceptance and legitimization, though an extra dose of admiration wouldn't hurt. Once they receive these emotional gifts of empathy, they would respond with sincere empathy of their own. They would reciprocate and validate the Palestinians not only as a nation, but also as the collateral historical victims of Zionism. This type of love can hardly be expected from occupied or traumatized people, on either side, which is why it could only come from the leadership, and only after a perceived win for their constituents, as was the case for Egypt after the 1973 war. Anwar Sadat believed that much of the Arab-Israeli conflict was psychological, and while his assassination at the hands of Islamist fanatics after he made peace with Israel underscored the limits of this belief, his success in negotiating with Israel—to this day unmatched by anyone else—did demonstrate its validity. Sadat was hardly perfect, as he failed to sell true reconciliation to his people—not that Israel did anything to help, or at least to avoid undermining him. Indeed, the Palestinian leadership would have to do better, as unlikely at it sounds, and one particular way they could do it would be to meaningfully embrace the Jewish sufferings in the Holocaust and the singularity of that genocide and its ideology among all others. Equally as important would be an unequivocal recognition of the Jewish historical link to the land of Israel. All these would have to be rooted in an intellectual and historical foundation but delivered with affect and drama if they are to connect with the Israeli mind.

The third Palestinian intifada, then, must combine the strength of demographics and the weakness of a peaceful submission. This is not simply a version of the stick and the carrot principle. It is rather a psychologically integrated presentation of the Palestinian reality, which would challenge the Israeli mind to rebalance its own divided self. It would be good not only for the Palestinians, but also for the Israelis.

In conclusion, it would appear that it is up to the Palestinians to save Israel from itself. If they won't rise to the occasion, or if they frankly give up on a two-state solution and simply mark time until Israel-Palestine becomes an apartheid entity, then the future is darker than the darkest days of the past for both them and the Israelis. In the long haul, Israelis, along with their chief supporter, the American Jewish community, would not tolerate running and advocating for such an entity, and one way or another, it would ultimately follow the path of South Africa. In our context this would mean the end of the Zionist project and the eventual implosion of the Israeli mind explored in this book.

LAST BUT NOT LEAST: THE AMERICAN JEWISH COMMUNITY

If America is politically unable to help Israel face reality, or worse, if, as it approaches energy independence and Middle East fatigue, it loses interest in resolving the Israel-Palestinian conflict; and if the Palestinians are too divided, hateful, or violent to do what they should, one other powerful group can make a difference. In what would be the ultimate irony and a slap in the face to the ideal of Zionism, it might be up to the Jews who did not follow the Zionist path to save Israel from itself. The American Jewish community, like other Jewish communities around the world, is not simply a friend of Israel like the United States. Obviously, it is also not an adversary like the Palestinians. If anything, it's more like a sibling, representing an alternative and successful path that is at once admired, envied, and despised by Israelis. Sharing deep if ambivalent bonds of love with Israel, American Jews therefore have the access of an insider. For that reason their influence need not be strategic and differential. Instead, it can be tactical and incremental. Another added advantage is that any constructive criticism they level at the Israeli government cannot be seriously construed by the latter as anti-Semitism.

However, to exercise its influence, the American Jewish community must practice what it preaches, that is, psychologically if not politically, to own its dual identity, to claim Israel as its second home. This means, first and foremost, getting involved and being willing to critique Israel when necessary. If Israel is a safe home for all the Jews in the world, as both Israeli and Diaspora Jews agree, then in the spirit of "I can say anything about my mother but you can't," American Jews should treat Israel, not only America, as their homeland. More than thirty years ago, when my wife and I first visited Israel together, one of my closest Israeli friends asked her, whom he had just met for the first time, what she as an American Jew thought about "the situation." "The situation" back then was totally different and yet exactly the same, depending on one's historical perspective and consistent with the paradoxical environment that gave birth to the Israeli national character. My wife declined to take a position, and in typical Israeli fashion my friend criticized her for her reluctance. At the time, I understood and supported her, but in retrospect, my friend was ahead of his time.

Notwithstanding the strength and pride that the American Jewish community drew from Israel's post-1967 power, Israeli Jews are ultimately more dependent on their American siblings than the other way around. This is not only because of the latter's financial and moral commitment to Israel, but perhaps primarily due to their political and socioeconomic status in America. Given their electoral clout in a couple of crucial swing states, their deep pockets, and their powerful lobby, should they choose to do so, American Jews could change the course of American policy toward Israel. Over the past three to four decades, in a shift from its historical focus on liberal, domestic causes, the American Jewish community—or more accurately, the major organizations that claim to represent it—has redirected its attention toward more exclusively Jewish causes. Along with this transition, these organizations, embodied perhaps by the powerful lobbying group American Israel Public Affairs Committee, or AIPAC, have by and large reoriented themselves to provide uncritical support to the emerging Israeli right. Whereas in the 1960s and early 1970s mainstream Jewish leaders such as then president of the World Jewish Congress, Nahum Goldmann, sometimes criticized the Israeli government for its policies toward the Arabs, at present such criticism among similar figures is practically nonexistent. In current psychological parlance, this support, with its public, moral, financial, and political dimensions, both enables and disables the Israeli national character.

Now notwithstanding the recent emergence of J Street and other progressive Jewish groups that advocate—for the sake of both Israelis and Palestinians—ending the occupation of the West Bank and applying democratic principles in Israel to Jews and Arabs alike, American Jewish politics continue to be dominated by an establishment that equates support for Israel with support for the policies of the Israeli government. Indeed, as recently as 2014, the Conference of Presidents of Major American Jewish Organizations rejected J Street's application for membership. J Street, it should be noted, is not a radical, fringe organization. It is a small, but growing, explicitly pro-Israel and pro-peace advocacy and lobbying group. From a psychological perspective, the current Jewish establishment in America is identified with the Israeli maxim that the whole world is against us and the world is silent.

In part, this is because some of its leaders are children of Holocaust survivors and in part because they are of a generation that grew up in an era tolerant of, if not suffused with, anti-Semitic sensibilities. Not unlike the Israelis, these American Jews have been unable to internalize Israel's and their own newly, or not so newly, found power. Many of them still cling to the ideology of affliction, that ancient Jewish identity construed from the narrative of victimhood. They look for (and sometimes find) the anti-Semites hiding behind every door but ignore the incredible success, integration, and power enjoyed by Jews in America. While they are aware of it and might even brag about it in private, they are emotionally unable to own that their fellow American Jews are overrepresented on the Supreme Court, within the most senior staff of the White House, in the president's cabinet, in the presidencies and faculties of Ivy League universities and elite colleges, in the entertainment industry, on Wall Street, in real estate, medicine, law, and the other professions. Projecting their internal insecurities onto Israel, they reinforce the paranoid element within the Israeli mind. Rather than experiencing Israel as the regional nuclear power it is, they continue to see it as the powerless victim it was, and they were, decades ago.

All this is to say that for the Jewish establishment to press Israel to become more accommodating toward the Palestinians, it will first have to see that Jews in America and in Israel have become quite powerful, and that in spite of their historical narrative, they, too, like anyone else, can abuse the power they possess. In symbolic terms, Malcolm Hoenlein, one of the top officials of the Conference of Presidents of Major American Jewish Organizations, would have to replace the photo of an Israeli air force jet flying over Auschwitz that he reportedly has in his office with one of that jet flying over the extremely impoverished slums of Gaza.

If and when the American Jewish establishment lets go of the ideology of affliction, or at least recalibrates it in a manner proportional to the reality of Jews in America today, it could then reinforce other, more positive elements within the Israeli psyche. It could remind Israel that its military and economic successes make it no longer necessary to model the new Jew after historical instances like Masada, where heroic self-sacrifice ultimately led to the same self-destructive outcome brought about by the timidity of the Diaspora Jews. It could mirror, admire, and support Israeli foresight, audacity, and self-confidence. It could celebrate Israel's strength and press it to adjust its self-perception so as to rid the Israelis of their "crying while shooting" complex. It could then encourage Israel to trust its strength and to take risks in the pursuit of peace. But along with advocating for even stronger US-Israeli security ties, it would have to confront Israel's residual denial of the demographic clock. It would have to impress upon the Israeli leadership that given their own deeply held democratic values and their successful integration into all aspects of life in the United States, American Jews can never support the de facto apartheid state that is emerging in Israel and the West Bank. Reaching back into its own historical role in the civil rights movement, the Jewish establishment could also lend Israel an extra dose of empathy for both Israeli Arabs and West Bank Palestinians. The latter group is struggling under Israeli occupation with no civil and political rights to speak of.

As opined by Peter Beinart in *The Crisis of Zionism,* American Jews suffer from a sense of guilt in relation to their Israeli counterparts. Quoting Abraham Foxman, the national director of the Anti-Defamation League, that since he is not a citizen of Israel he does not bear the consequences of his opinions, Beinart argues that American Zionists feel guilty for never having emigrated to the Jewish state in large numbers. Furthermore, they feel pampered by their lives in America and vaguely effeminate in comparison with the more masculine Israeli Jews who plow through the hardships of war and send their children off to fight in the army. To ward off these feelings of guilt, Beinart suggests, Jewish leaders line themselves up behind Israeli policies and avoid criticizing Israel no matter what. To the extent that this is the case, the Jewish establishment needs to rid itself of such binary notions as historical right and wrong, strength and weakness, masculinity and femininity. American Jews would do well to note that while it has served Israel well at war, Israeli hypermasculinity is not an ideal to strive for but rather a necessary evil that must be curtailed away from the battlefield. This would help them celebrate their own, more integrated form of social aggression and get over their guilt.

The bad news is that the chances of such a transformation occurring at the upper echelons of the mainstream Jewish organizations anytime soon are rather small. For one thing, as the saying goes, it's hard to teach an old dog new tricks. Additionally, as discussed by Beinart, the old Jewish narrative of victimhood, applied to Iran, Hamas, and the danger of rising anti-Semitism around the world, is what gets elderly Jewish donors, the ones currently sustaining these organizations, going and giving. The good news is that when it comes to Israel, this Jewish leadership and their major donors do not actually represent the views of American Jews, most of whom support halting settlements and applying pressure on both Israel and the Palestinians to settle their conflict. Indeed, a large majority of Jews voted to reelect President Obama even after his confrontations and poor personal relationship with Prime Minister Netanyahu burst onto the airwaves. This gap between American Jews and their leadership is particularly large in the case of younger American Jews. It is, in my view, one of the reasons that the *Atlantic*'s Jeffrey Goldberg was correct in observing, "Those Israelis, and those American Jews, who believe that J Street, and the spirit it represents, are fleeting phenomena have absolutely no idea what is happening in the Jewish world."[13]

Furthermore, many of the leaders of the Jewish establishment are approaching their golden years, and many of their big Palm

Beach and New York donors are literally dying. The stage is thus set for a new generation of leaders to emerge. This transition, and whoever ends up heading these organizations in the next few years, will determine what influence the American Jewish community will have over American and Israeli policies toward Palestinians and the Muslim world at large. As they approach this transition, American Jews can be divided into several, though not all-inclusive or mutually exclusive, groups. The largest of the groups consists of Jews who appear to have little attachment to Israel and little interest in Zionism. Many in this group also care little about Judaism. They tend to be secular, are comfortable marrying non-Jews, and do not necessarily bring up their children Jewish. The current intermarriage rate among non-Orthodox Jews is 50 percent, and it's considerably greater among the children of such marriages, the majority of whom do not raise their own children as Jews. Unless a significant number of these Jews somehow return to their roots at an older age, as a minority of researchers in the field propose will occur, it is unlikely that they will play an active role in the leadership of the Jewish community in America. They are thus unlikely to engage with American and Israeli policy makers one way or another.

Representing the polar opposite, and rapidly growing in numbers and influence, is the second group, Orthodox Jews, a large majority of whom these days are Modern Orthodox families who seek to integrate strict religious observance with active participation in the non-Jewish community. Jews in this group are strongly attached to Israel. They visit, spend time in, and study in Israel. While they currently represent only about 10 percent of American Jews, they constitute about 21 percent of all families affiliated with a synagogue. And the children of such families constitute no less than 40 percent of all synagogue-affiliated children in America.[14] Barring a dramatic and unexpected change in the near future, this demographic trend, which as we have seen parallels a similar trend within Israel, will catapult this group to populate and assume leadership of the American Jewish establishment.

As a whole, the Modern Orthodox movement offers an authentic, morally conscious, and viable path for American Jewry. When it comes to Israel, the movement also has a historical tradition of political moderation, certainly in its pre-1967 Israeli wing. It is therefore theoretically possible that many in this group will someday reembrace the gentle, accommodating strain of Judaism described by Israeli philosopher Hugo Bergman. Should this happen, the leaders of the Modern Orthodox movement would do well to engage Israel in the manner discussed above with respect to the current Jewish establishment. An added benefit to such a turn would be that the deep connections of this group to the religious communities in Israel would have a moderating influence on the hard-core religious right there. Yet in this group, too, such a shift is unlikely in the foreseeable future. Since the 1970s, Modern Orthodoxy has trended quite heavily to the right. This evolution has a logical and a religiously legitimate aspect, namely that the West Bank, with such places as Hebron, Bethlehem, and Beit El, is just as important from a religious-historical perspective to the Jews as Jerusalem. If accommodating to the Palestinians means abandoning the homeland so deeply embedded in biblical narrative, how can a practicing Orthodox Jew advocate for it? Additionally, whereas the separation of church and state in the United States, created precisely to provide freedom and autonomy to religious groups, enables the Modern Orthodox community to practice its religion without being encumbered by or encumbering the rights of others, the absence of such separation in Israel makes it more complicated. When having to choose between the demands of democracy and those of religious obligation—with the latter potentially precluding not only political rights for West Bank Palestinians but also certain civil rights for Arabs and secular Israelis within Israel proper—Modern Orthodox Jews are more likely to choose religion. In their mind, this choice may not be as difficult as it appears because from an Orthodox religious perspective, divine guidance or intervention may settle such issues as God sees fit. In short, for Modern Orthodox Jews, a sovereign Jewish state in the biblical Holy Land gets prioritized over a fully democratic Israel. In reality, therefore, it is hard to see how the movement's religious edicts would allow it to advocate for any sort of practicable reconciliation with the Palestinians.

A third group of American Jews is also Zionist and cares a great deal about Israel. It, too, is authentic, morally conscious, and viable. However, it is secular and left leaning. This group is exemplified by organizations such as J Street and the liberal, college-campus movement. Its main challenge is that most of its potential supporters reside in the large number of assimilated or secular Jews who have little interest in Judaism, Israel, and Zionism. These potential supporters tend to agree with J Street's political agenda regarding a two-state solution, settlements, and the like, but for them Israel is just one among many progressive causes they care about, including universal health care, women's right to choose, gay rights, or income inequality. They are unlikely to join J Street or similar organizations anytime soon. Thus, at the moment, due to its small size and lack of funding, the group of Zionist, secular, left-leaning American Jews is easily squashed by the Israeli oppositional character. Dismissed by Bibi Netanyahu and his right-of-center coalition partners as outside the mainstream, anti-Israeli, or self-hating Jews, they have been denied access to most Israeli decision makers.

Finally, a small but growing group of young American Jews, identified by Peter Beinart, may in fact ascend to positions of leadership in the future, though not through the existing organizations. These are unassimilated Jews who care deeply about Jewish life. They either belong to independent temples combining religious rigor with intellectual openness and equal participation for women and members of the LGBT community, or to Jewish organizations combining Jewish education with social-justice action around the world. In either case, whether due to a lack of proper Jewish education in childhood or to the liberal values they cherish, they are increasingly alienated from Zionism and Israel. Based on recent research, some experts in the field, for example sociologist Theodore Sasson, believe that overall attachment to Israel has seen no decline but rather a change from a centralized, organizationally affiliated focus to a personal and, in fact, more meaningful engagement. Even so, Sasson concedes, since American Jews no longer speak with a unified voice, their ability to influence policy will diminish.[15]

Given the coming generational shift within the Jewish establishment, these last two groups—the secular, progressive Zionists and the non-Orthodox but religious or otherwise meaningfully Jewish individuals who are distant from Israel—represent the best chance for American Jewry to once again exercise a moderating influence on Israeli society and leadership. If enough American Jews within these groups find their way back to mainstream, organized Zionism; if enough ultimately feel shamed by the behavior of a Jewish state occupying another nation on the land sanctified by their shared scripture and prayers; and if they can then join forces with the tiny, potentially progressive wing of the Modern Orthodox movement, then more could be done to prod the Israeli mind to that end. First, American Jews could counter the negative aspect of Israeli narcissism by pressing Israel to embrace the traditional Jewish commitment to universal, humanistic values. This applies specifically, though not exclusively, to the memory of the Holocaust. A striking, if perhaps radical, example of the underlying principle was provided in 1993 by Rabbi Arnold Wolf, a disciple of renowned Jewish theologian and civil rights movement activist Rabbi Abraham Joshua Heschel. Objecting to the building of a Holocaust museum on the Washington National Mall, Wolf explained that because it was Native Americans who had endured genocide in America, a Native American museum would better represent the true lessons of the Holocaust.

As Leo Tolstoy, one of the greatest nonprofessional psychologists to have ever lived, observed in *War and Peace,* to be inspired a crowd needs to have a tangible object of love and a tangible object of hate. Currently, American Jews are inspired by their leadership to support Israel more out of hate—for Hamas, Iran, ISIS, and various anti-Semites—than by love for Israel. This is evident in the not atypical response of many Jews when someone criticizes Israel. If, for example, you support Israeli military actions against Hamas's cross-border tunnels but criticize Israel for a disproportional use of air power resulting in more than a thousand civilian deaths, the answer is often "What about *them*? What about what *they* do?"—followed by the mention of suicide bombings, rockets, executions, beheadings, and the hateful ideology of Hamas and other Islamist organizations or cultures. The problem with inspiring or motivating by hate is that it perpetuates the narrative of victimhood and weakness, which as we have seen is now threatening to overtake the original psychological mission of the Zionist movement and the Jewish state. What I am prescribing, therefore, is more inspiration by love of Israel than by hatred of its enemies. But to inspire more by love, one must first focus on the object of love, not the comparison to the object of hate. "Why care about *them*?"—the response to "What about *them*?"—should be "They are weak and cowardly, we are strong and brave."

Then, by organizing cultural exchange programs, trips, internships, and summer camps that expose American youth to specific aspects of modern, liberal Tel Aviv with its thriving intellectual, artistic, culinary, and business life on the one hand, and to Israeli organizations devoted to human rights and reconciliation with Palestinians on the other, a new American Jewish leadership would be able to recalibrate the balance between love and hate, with more emphasis on the former. Such a loving embrace of progressive, pluralistic Israel would go a long way to deepen the bonds between American Jews and Israel, and thereby further alleviate Israeli abandonment and annihilation anxieties. Additionally, the people-to-people aspect of this strategy would counter the Israeli and Jewish history of "vertical" alliance with ultimately unreliable, centralized powers, replacing, or at least enhancing, it with the "horizontal" alliance that is so lacking in Israel's current relationship with other nations. Needless to say, such a loving embrace would work both ways, potentially increasing the involvement of alienated American Jews with Israel and Zionism. Such a program should also seek to identify meaningful symbols that would augment Masada, Tel-Chai, and the Temple Mount as the primary icons of the Zionist revival. Perhaps something from the city of Haifa, the seat of Israel's MIT, the Technion, and maybe the best current example of Jews and Arabs sharing a place in peaceful coexistence, or as ridiculous as it may sound, the Tel Aviv boardwalk or its thriving LGBT community. Finally, this agenda should also expose American Jews to Israeli Arabs and West Bank Palestinians, to put a human face on "them," who are basically more like Americans and Israelis than the jihadists we view on CNN. In a way, J Street U, the college-campus arm of J Street, and organizations such as Seeds for Peace, have struggled to implement baby steps of this entire strategy. But underfunded, turned down as a sponsor for the establishment's Birthright trips to Israel, and seeking to broadcast a more explicitly political story line, J Street's efforts do not currently scale. They do not approach anything resembling the depth and breadth of the Israel-oriented programs offered by the mainstream Jewish organizations or the Orthodox community. Birthright, the Jewish establishment's massive heritage program, for example, offers all Jewish young adults in the world a free, ten-day trip to Israel, with a current annual participation of close to forty thousand.

Now as we have seen, Israelis' want for love runs deeper than that of most, connecting with an intense need for validation. This need is particularly strong in relation to American Jews, for they represent a successful, alternative path to Zionism. When upward of thirty thousand Israelis showed up to the funeral of the young American Jew who made aliyah and was killed in IDF action during the 2014 Gaza war, they did so not only to show support for and mourn a soldier without a family in Israel, but also because they were deeply touched and felt validated by a young American Jew making the ultimate sacrifice for what they feel is their profoundly moral and superior, yet often delegitimized, enterprise. So perhaps the most important thing a new generation of American Jewish leaders could do to nudge Israel to be more accommodating is to validate and legitimize in every possible way democratic Israel, that is, the Jewish state within the pre-1967 borders, and also to invalidate and delegitimize with equal force Israel's non-democratic occupation and settlement of the West Bank. As pointed out by Beinart, supporters of the BDS (Boycott, Divestment and Sanctions) movement, certainly those who would apply it to Israel as a whole, have colluded with Israeli policy makers and settlers to erase the 1967 borders, thereby placing Israel's existence as a Jewish and a democratic state at risk. Whether this collusion has been brought about unwittingly or is the result of political calculation and/or what I have attributed on the Israeli side to unconscious self-sabotage is open to debate. But regardless, American Jews should reject both the BDS movement and the Israeli settlement policy. Instead, they should press for even more engagement with Israel proper while supporting selective BDS measures applied solely to the West Bank. This could mean increasing financial contributions and investments in Israeli cultural institutions, medical technology, and start-ups on the one hand, while advocating for policies such as labeling products made on West Bank settlements, or lobbying the IRS to end tax-deductible gifts to charities that fund settlements. Fighting the BDS movement that wishes to delegitimize and dismantle the Jewish state as a whole by comparing it to South Africa must be part of the strategy, again drawing a sharp distinction precisely on the dimensions of legitimacy and validity between Israel proper and its control of the West Bank.

In terms of Iran, at least based on the stated policy of the American government, America and Israel are on the same page in their strategic goal of preventing Iran from becoming a nuclear power. Perhaps not surprisingly, surveys show that American Jews support an Israeli strike against Iran in much greater proportions than they support Israel's policies in the West Bank or toward the Palestinian Authority. However, to the extent that differences between American and Israeli policy on Iran emerge—such as the ones I explored earlier with respect to the timing of a military strike or the terms of a potential agreement between the West and Iran—American Jews should own the other part of their dual identity, the American one. Assuming they would ultimately line themselves up with the American, not Israeli, policy of avoiding war with Iran unless it is absolutely necessary—as defined by the American rather than the Israeli security establishment—they should clearly state so to their Israeli counterparts. Given the paranoid streak within the Israeli mind, American Jews must convey honestly and straightforwardly that when the chips are down, they are Americans first, Zionists second. This is critical not only with respect to Iran but in general, as Israelis need to internalize this reality in order to understand that they cannot alienate their closest, if not strongest, source of international support, the American Jewish community. This point must be made unapologetically and unequivocally because, as John Kerry found out in 2014, when it comes to effective communication with Israelis, subtlety and ambiguity are not an option.

If, as some experts propose, American Jews are indeed distancing themselves from Judaism and Israel never to return, or even if

they are merely transitioning from the model of organizational af-
filiation to a more personal engagement with Israel, their direct
impact on American policies toward Israel will ultimately de-
crease. Should this, in the long term, coincide with an American
disengagement from the Middle East, Israel would be left to fend
for itself. As frightening as this sounds for those of us who love
Israel, if it forces the Jewish state to return to the original Zionist psychology of a visionary, yet pragmatic and interdependent,
self-reliance, then Zionism itself may well end up being what
saves, protects, and presses on with the amazing experiment that
Israel has always managed to be.

EPILOGUE

DINNER IN JERUSALEM

On one of my visits to Israel while working on this book, friends in Jerusalem hosted a dinner party to discuss ideas about the Israeli national character. I knew their neighborhood well, from my youth, but as I navigated the narrow streets leading to their home, I noticed, as if for the first time, that virtually all the streets of my childhood were named after biblical figures, Hebrew conquerors, prestate defense forces, or Zionist men of letters. The hosts, a mixed American-Israeli couple, were a foreign correspondent and clinical psychologist, and the guests included authors, journalists, university professors, a lawyer, and a former member of the Knesset. I knew one of these people as the brother of a childhood friend, but when everyone was introduced, it emerged that another was a colleague of a friend I had eaten lunch with that very day, and that each was writing a book, separately, about the same Israeli author; yet another guest was a former colleague of my sister-in-law's, at whose house I had dined the previous evening; a married couple were neighbors of one of my brothers; and another guest was divorced from someone I had previously interviewed for the book. All these connections reminded me how in an earlier visit I had met with a Hebrew University professor and a couple of days later was introduced at a barbecue to a renowned Israeli historian who was her father. None of this was surprising, but it belied a point made rather emphatically later in the evening by one of the guests, i.e., that a country is not a family.

As we sat down to eat, the host suggested we apply a one-conversation rule to the evening. I chimed in, recommending an American-style conversation, quoting an Israeli sociologist who observed that an American conversation is like classical music, where instruments take their turns responding to each other, while an Israeli conversation is more like jazz, where players interrupt each other and improvise as they go along. This drew an objection from one guest, who knowingly asserted that jazz players are well aware of their fellow players' lines. I agreed that the sociologist's analogy was overly kind to the way Israelis converse. Since some of the guests were American expats, the conversation ended up being a mixed concert.

While my intention was to listen to the others' thoughts and experiences, one of the guests insisted that I present my ideas first. Unable to resist talking, I went ahead, but was interrupted within seconds by that very guest, who, in the eloquent manner befitting the university professor that he was, disputed the notion of a national character and obliterated my entire thesis. He was not a psychologist, but that did not stop him from offering, "I assume that as a clinical psychologist you are well versed with the many ways in which personality makeup cuts across national boundaries." Another participant, also an extremely articulate and knowledgeable academician, provided insights consistent with my ideas, but spoke contemptuously about the danger of "reductionist psychological concepts," i.e., my project. Applying reverse psychology, but also because I found some of their critique intellectually valid, I agreed with their observations. I pointed out that while I believe that people are fundamentally more alike than different, this does not mean we cannot talk about differences. This applied as much to national character, I explained, as to gender. In a more academic version of this book, I should add now, these issues would have been discussed in great depth. I also said, somewhat defensively, that I hoped in my writing I could be more subtle and less simplistic than in our brief encounter. As in the Israeli mind's "old baby" dynamic the substance of their critique, I believe, balances on an irreconcilable paradox: people across national boundaries are truly different; people across national boundaries are truly alike.

I expected my oppositional dinner guests to counter with one of the most ingenious Israeli inventions, the *haphuch al haphuch,* or "opposite of the opposite" debate tactic, and disagree with my agreement to force me to disagree so that they could decimate me. Miraculously, that did not happen. Yet, predictably enough, as I continued to present my outline, every few minutes the conversation turned political. It was still pretty well orchestrated, if for no other reason than with the exception of one couple, almost everyone was solidly on the left end of the political map. But also not surprisingly, this did not preclude political disagreements. One of the authors in the room repeatedly clashed with the former member of the Knesset, who more than once had to remind her that she was preaching to the converted.

Despite these digressions, the one-conversation rule had held up pretty well. But then someone told a story about a boy and a dog. Walking her small schnoodle in her trendy, secular Jerusalem neighborhood earlier that Saturday afternoon, she wandered into a bordering religious area, where she came upon a group of young, orthodox boys playing in the street. The kids approached the dog, but evinced, as she put it, an approach-avoidance conflict. "Come pat the dog," she encouraged them.

"Are you Jewish?" one of the boys asked.

"What's the difference?" she responded. "You can pat the dog."

"No," the six-year-old-or-so boy retorted, "my dad says it's *muk-tzeh.*"

A Hebrew word for "separated" or "set aside," *muktzeh* generally refers, at least in rabbinical terms, to objects one may not touch or move on Shabbat. With this on the table, the conversation erupted into a multitude of Talmudic arguments about the meaning of the word, its theoretical applicability to a dog, Arabs, and/or Shabbat. Interestingly, the two religious people in the room, a yarmulke-wearing journalist and his converted American wife, who were probably in the best position to interpret the story, remained silent. Everyone else was an expert. We eventually reestablished the one-conversation rule, but I couldn't help but wonder why a group of fiercely secularist Israelis were so emotionally engaged in such a debate. Was it simply their liberal outrage and despair at the young boy's feelings about Arabs? Their less conscious dialectic struggle with their own religious origins? Or their even deeper desire to do what the boy wouldn't, that is, defy the boundaries and break the rules, in this trivial case the one-conversation rule?

The second major interruption occurred when the host received an urgent call from his foreign-desk editor, requesting an article on the breaking news regarding the acknowledgment by the South African jurist Richard Goldstone that his famously controversial report would have been different if he had known then what he knew now. The Goldstone report, commissioned by the UN Human Rights Council to investigate Israel's incursion into Gaza in December 2008, found that Israel had engaged in a "deliberately disproportionate attack designed to punish, humiliate and terrorize a civilian population."[1] Goldstone's correction, as our host wrote that evening, fell like a bomb in Israel because his original report has been viewed there as providing spurious justification to anti-

Israeli accusations designed to delegitimize the state. As the host retired to his study to spend the rest of the evening working on the story, the rest of us discussed Goldstone and its impact on Israel. In no time this produced a consensus on Israel's singularity, which was seen not so much in the country's perennial state of war, but rather in the existential threat to its survival.

Here I posed a question as to the psychological effect of this unique threat on the Israeli psyche. To this, the religious man's spouse, a converted, formerly Christian woman from a particularly picturesque corner of Connecticut, responded, "In truth, we are all under existential threat. Not just here in Israel, but everywhere. It is part of the human condition, yet in many places people have the illusion of safety. Think about the earthquake and tsunami that hit Japan, it can happen anywhere. I grew up in a beautiful, peaceful suburb not too far from where you live now, and ultimately I couldn't stand the manicured superficiality of it all. The reason I fell in love with Israel and stayed here for thirty years is that in this place there are no illusions. It's all real, and that's why life here is so vital, so full of passion." That struck a chord with me, and I later mentioned it to my distinctly secular brother.

"Was she religious?" He barely disguised his contempt. "That's the kind of thing that religious people say."

"I think so," I said, amazed by both the perspicacity and harshness of his observation. I suppose the American in me was able to listen to the existential wisdom of her words irrespective of her faith. It actually helped me set aside any stereotypes I might have had about religious Israelis, as this couple were among the most insightful and temperamentally moderate members of our dinner group. The Israeli in my brother, on the other hand, saw it in a different light, one, he would contend—in an ironic agreement with the religious lady—that is far more real.

Though obvious in retrospect, perhaps the most remarkable moment in the evening occurred when I raised the issue of the

Holocaust. A psychologist of a grimly disenfranchised Yemenite descent said that during childhood the Holocaust for her was a screen behind which she had to hide her own sufferings. Though personally not sharing the European narrative with the Israeli elite of the 1950s and '60s, she recalled having nightmares about the Holocaust, designed, so to speak, to split off her more personal and shameful traumas as a child. The other participants said virtually nothing. One spoke derisively about the various psychological constructs that could be deployed to explain current Israeli behavior in light of the past, and the conversation moved on. When I inquired as to the reason for this group process, the message was clear: they were sick and tired of hearing, thinking, or talking about the Holocaust. It was old news, boring, a pack of psychological clichés, or, worse, a historical catastrophe turned into a government propaganda tool. Having grown up in Israel in the aftermath of the Eichmann trial, and having recently visited on Holocaust and Heroism Memorial Day, I was not unsympathetic to their apathy. But no psychologist worth his dime would take this at face value.

Just a week earlier I had been sitting in my New York office, listening to a new patient whose avoidance of the Holocaust, at least according to his wife, had nearly ruined his marriage. A prominent lawyer, the patient was the son of two Holocaust survivors, each with a harrowing story. Raised atheist and barely Jewish, the patient never discussed this history with his wife and children, who now seemed to have developed their own interest in, and anxiety about, the subject. As he told me in rather factual terms what he knew of his father's experience in Buchenwald, he suddenly and jarringly broke down in tears, sobbing uncontrollably like a young child. He hadn't talked about this in twenty years, his wife explained, and his teenage children were afraid to ask him about it, even as they were studying the Holocaust in Hebrew school. As noted in these pages, this is what Israel was like with regard to the

Holocaust before the Eichmann trial opened the floodgates. So, back to our dinner, I was now asking myself whether, at least for this group of Israelis, we have come full circle. Are Israelis so consumed by the revived memoires of this national trauma, so exhausted by it all, that they are ready to retreat into the comfort of silence and denial? I did not share this observation with the group, in part, I suspect, because I was mentally preparing for my return to America. I have little doubt that had I stayed in Israel for just a few more days, the Israeli within would have been awakened with a combative interpretation of this group dynamic.

At the end of the evening, as we said our good-byes, the articulate professor who had critiqued my notion that the Jews and Israel have had a unique psychological narrative, added insult to injury. "I think you will change course on this project as you get further along," he advised. But on his way out, as if to moderate his criticism, he related a farewell anecdote: "The other day I was stuck in a huge traffic jam, and I counted about sixty cars that circled back illegally to an adjacent highway only to cut back in somewhere down the road. When I lowered my window and reprimanded one of these drivers, a young guy, he got really upset. Now, if you can explain why *he* was upset, then you might have a book here."

Well, I think was I able to explain that, and perhaps a bit more.

The next day I was in the aisle seat on an El Al flight back to New York. I chatted briefly with the two young men who were seated to my left. One was an ultraorthodox yeshiva boy with long, twirled sidelocks, a black hat, and tzitzit. He was reading a religious Hebrew text whose title translates into "Stories from our father's house." The other was a clean-shaven, yarmulke-wearing premed college student from Ohio. A newly practicing Modern Orthodox, he was planning to move to Israel after medical school. He was reading Eli Wiesel's book *Night,* the horrific tale of the Wiesel family's experience in the concentration camps, the central story line of which tells of Wiesel's close relationship with his father and how Eli survived his death. And I, a secular Jew who grew up in Israel, but left for America, and had just concluded a three-day visit to Israel, was reading an academic book titled *Glory and Agony: Isaac's Sacrifice and National Narrative*. Simplified, this book's central hypothesis explores the historical shift in the Zionist narrative's interpretation of the Binding of Isaac from one of heroic self-sacrifice by the son to murder by the father. Coincidentally, but also as a sample of a demographic trend within the Israeli population, the three of us thus symbolized—in our relation to Israel and religion—the current reincarnation of the Zionist Israeli story. One never questioned his loyalty to his father, one contemplated leaving his father behind to return to their ancient homeland, and one had left his father at the heart of that homeland, Jerusalem, to pursue a life in the Diaspora. It is by no means a coincidence that in the previous year my sixteen-year-old daughter had, no thanks to any conscious encouragement from me, decided to spend half of her sophomore high school year in Israel. And so it goes.

In a more profound and complex chronicle, the books we three travelers were reading told the same story. And in a testament to the combined power of the unconscious mind and pure chance, their Jewish, father-son theme resonated with the main purpose of my brief sojourn to Israel this time: to visit my ninety-three-year-old father, who was undergoing treatment for advanced melanoma. I saw my father one more time shortly before he died in a hospice atop Mount Scopus, overlooking the Old City of Jerusalem to the west, and the West Bank of the Jordan River to the east. After I said good-bye for the last time, my family and I left him for the night with a sweet male nurse, who introduced himself to us with a Hebrew name. But my brother overheard that he was actually an Arab and insisted on confronting and respecting him for who he really was, not a fake Jew. Even in his weakened state, my father heard all this and scolded my brother for not minding his own business and bringing politics into everything. Defending my brother for his humanity, but also agreeing that he'd acted a tad intrusively, was the last conversation I had with my father. My father had little use or patience for psychology, but inseparably from the deep family bond we had, we also shared the profound imprint of our native landscape. When I first embarked upon *The Israeli Mind* project, it didn't occur to me that he might not live long enough to read it; after all, he had previously survived a massive heart attack and another type of metastasized cancer. But he didn't survive this one, and I now dedicate this book to him.

ACKNOWLEDGMENTS

I t would be impossible to thank all the people who contributed to my thinking about the subject matter of this book. Friends, family members, and colleagues have been particularly generous with their time and ideas. Among my friends, colleagues, and family, some of whom have significant expertise in such areas as Israeli history, culture, politics, and psychology, I am particularly indebted to Ilana Pardes, Itamar Lurie, Joe Berger, Brenda Berger, Naomi Kehati, Ethan Bronner, Ivan Bresgi, Adam Price, Beth Dorogusker, and Peter Coleman. Family members who helped me formulate my thoughts about the Israeli national character include my wife, Michele Sacks, a psychologist and a keen observer of the Israeli mind in action, and my brothers, Eli Gadot and Ariel Gratch, who regularly contributed their considerable insights and knowledge. My parents, Haya and Avraham Gratch, have been my prime motivators in life, and my own children, Jordan, who shares my joy of politics and culture, and Ilana, who shares my passion for psychology and writing, have been great supporters of my writing from a young age. The interest and encouragement from

251

my nephews and nieces, Nir Gadot, Roni Gadot, and Oren Gadot, along with Mika Gratch, Jonathan Gratch, and Daniel Gratch, are also greatly appreciated. Last but not least, I thank my wife's parents, Evelyn and the late Arthur Sacks, for their support and loving kindness.

Among the many scholars, experts, and ordinary people I have interviewed, I am particularly grateful to Tom Segev, Yaron Ezrahi, Oz Almog, Michal Ginach, Reuven Gal, Imanuel Berman, Amia Lieblich, Doron Resenblum, and Yaniv Heled. My research assistants, Eyal Pardes-Lurie, Michal Pitowsky, and Christopher Ceccolini, have provided me with much needed data as well as inspiration. My agent, James Levine, has guided me with both editorial and strategic wisdom, not to mention grace, and the team at St. Martin's Press, including George Witte, Joe Rinaldi, Steve Boldt, and Sara Thwaite have been extremely helpful and a delight to work with. The same is true for Sarah Rippins, Tirza Eisenberg, and Ziv Lewis of my Israeli publisher, Zmora Bitan. Finally, my Israeli patients in New York have trusted me with their innermost feelings and thoughts, and I have used some of our work together and material from their sessions when relevant. All patients mentioned in this book are composite cases. They have been mixed and altered, and their identities and experiences have been modified, all to protect their confidentiality and privacy. Any resemblance to actual persons, living or dead, or to actual events in these cases is purely coincidental.

NOTES

Introduction: Rabbi, I Object

1. Tom Segev, personal communication, August 2005.

2. Emanuel Berman, personal communication, 2005.

3. Martin Fletcher, *Walking Israel: A Personal Search for the Soul of a Nation* (New York: St. Martin's Press, 2010).

4. Ethan Bronner, "An Israeli Novelist Writes of Pain, Private and Public," *New York Times,* November 16, 2010.

1. Who Is an Israeli?

1. R. Cramer, *How Israel Lost: The Four Questions* (New York: Simon & Schuster, 2004).

2. David Biale, *Power and Powerlessness in Jewish History* (New York: Schocken Books, 1986), 39.

3. C. Kluckhohn and H. A. Murray, *Personality in Nature, Society and Culture* (New York: Alfred Knopf, 1948).

4. Raphael Patai, *The Arab Mind* (Long Island City, N.Y.: Hatherleigh Press, 2002).

5. Yaron Ezrahi, personal communication, August 12, 2005.

6. http://www.jewpi.com/poll-80-of-israeli-jews-believe-in-god-1327653273/.

2. It's Easier to Change a Song Than a City

1. David Biale, *Power and Powerlessness in Jewish History* (New York: Schocken Books, 1986), 28.

2. M. Botticini and Z. Eckstein, *The Chosen Few: How Education Shaped Jewish History, 70–1492* (Princeton, N.J.: Princeton University, 2012).

3. B. Beit-Hallahmi, *Original Sins: Reflections on the History of Zionism and Israel* (Northampton, Mass.: Interlink Publishing Group, 1998).

4. Ibid., 45.

5. Tom Segev, *One Palestine, Complete: Jews and Arabs Under the British Mandate* (New York: Picador, 2001), 2.

6. Beit-Hallahmi, *Original Sins,* 77.

7. Ibid.

8. http://www.jerusalemofgold.co.il/translations.html.

9. Moshe Amirav, *Jerusalem Syndrome: The Palestinian-Israeli Battle for the Holy City* (Eastbourne: Sussex Academic Press, 2009).

10. Sergio DellaPergola, "Sergio DellaPergola vs. the Authors of 'Voodoo Demographics,'" *Azure Online* 27 (Winter 2007).

11. Martin Fletcher, *Walking Israel: A Personal Search for the Soul of a Nation* (New York: St. Martin's Press, 2010), 753.

12. Nurit Gertz, *Captive of a Dream: National Myth in Israeli Culture* (Tel Aviv: Am Oved Publishers Ltd., 1995). In Hebrew.

13. Fletcher, *Walking Israel*, 753.

14. Segev, *One Palestine, Complete*.

15. Avner Falk, *Fratricide in the Holy Land: A Psychoanalytic View of the Arab-Israeli Conflict* (Madison WI: University of Wisconsin Press, 2004).

16. Fletcher, *Walking Israel*, 635.

17. Yael S. Feldman, *Glory and Agony: Isaac's Sacrifice and National Narrative* (Stanford, Calif.: Stanford University Press, 2010).

18. E. Ben-Ari and Y. Bilu, eds., *Grasping Land: Space and Place in Contemporary Israeli Discourse and Experience* (Albany, N.Y.: State University of New York Press, 1997).

19. Sidra DeKoven Ezrahi, "'To What Shall I Compare You?': Jerusalem as Ground Zero of the Hebrew Imagination," *PLMA* 122, no. 1 (January 2007).

20. Falk, *Fratricide in the Holy Land*.

21. H. Kohut, *The Analysis of the Self* (New York: International Universities Press, 1971).

22. Ezrahi, "'To What Shall I Compare You?'"

23. Gershon Rivlin, ed., *The Temple Mount Is in Our Hand: Report from General Motta Gur* (Tel Aviv: Maarachot, 1973), 317. In Hebrew.

24. Y. Ezrahi, *Rubber Bullets: Power and Conscience in Modern Israel* (Berkeley: University of California Press, 1998).

25. L. Eisenberg, ed., *Traditions and Transitions in Israel Studies.* (Albany: State University of New York Press, 2003).

26. http://www.jewpi.com/poll-80-of-israeli-jews-believe-in-god-1327653273/.

27. Tom Segev, *The Seventh Million: The Israelis and the Holocaust* (New York: Picador, 2000).

3. The Whole World Is Against Us and the World Is Silent

1. B. Susser and C. Liebman, *Choosing Survival: Strategies for a Jewish Future* (Oxford: Oxford University Press, 1997).

2. David Grossman, *To the End of the Land* (New York: Knopf, 2010), 376.

3. T. Friedman, *From Beirut to Jerusalem* (New York: Anchor Books, 1990), 126.

4. Tom Segev, *One Palestine, Complete: Jews and Arabs Under the British Mandate* (New York: Picador, 2001).

5. Ibid., 292.

6. Ibid., 291.

7. N. Gertz, *Myth in Israel: Captive of a Dream* (Portland, Ore.: Vallentine Mitchell, 2000).

8. Segev, *One Palestine, Complete*, 325.

9. Oz Almog, *The Sabra: The Creation of the New Jew* (Berkeley: University of California Press, 2000).

10. O. Grosbard, *Israel on the Couch: The Psychology of the Peace Process* (New York: State University of New York Press. 2000).

11. Y. Ezrahi, *Rubber Bullets: Power and Conscience in Modern Israel* (Berkeley: University of California Press, 1998).

12. B. Beit-Hallahmi, *Original Sins: Reflections on the History of Zionism and Israel* (Northampton, Mass.: Interlink Publishing Group, 1998).

13. *Jerusalem Post* article, May 31, 2010.

14. Yael Shilo, personal communication.

15. Amos Oz, *A Tale of Love and Darkness* (New York: Harcourt, 2003), 14.

16. Ibid., 217.

17. Ibid.

18. Ibid., 217–18.

19. Almog, *The Sabra*, 36.

20. Oz, *A Tale of Love and Darkness*, 485.

21. A. Falk, *Fratricide in the Holy Land: A Psychoanalytic View of the Arab-Israeli Conflict* (Madison WI: University of Wisconsin Press, 2004), 247.

22. Ibid.

23. Ibid., 176.

24. Gideon Levy, "A (Second) Passport for Every Worker," *Haaretz*, June 2, 2011. In Hebrew.

25. Y. Kaniuk, *Adam Ben Kelev* (Tel Aviv: Sifriat Poalim, 1969). In Hebrew.

4. Crying While Shooting

1. T. Segev, *The Seventh Million: The Israelis and the Holocaust* (New York: Picador, 2000), 4.

2. Ibid., 7.

3. Ka-Tzetnik, *Tzofan-Edma* (Bnei Brak, Israel: Hakibbutz Hameuchad, 1987), 25–26. In Hebrew.

4. Segev, *Seventh Million,* 196.

5. Ibid., 10.

6. Ibid., 196.

7. Ibid.

8. H. Yablonka, *The State of Israel vs. Adolf Eichmann* (Tel Aviv: Yediot Ahronot, 2001), 49–59. In Hebrew.

9. Segev, *Seventh Million,* 117.

10. Ibid., 106.

11. Ibid., 97–98.

12. Ibid., 168.

13. G. Hausner, *The Jerusalem Trial* (Tel Aviv: Beit Lohamei Hagetaot and Hakibbutz Hameuchad, 1980), 245, 327.

14. H. Guri, *Facing the Glass Booth: The Jerusalem Trial* (Tel Aviv: Hakibbutz Hameuchad, 1962), 73.

15. H. Yablonka and O. Cummings, *Survivors of the Holocaust: Israel After the War* (New York: New York University Press, 1999).

16. D. Grossman, "The Carrier Pigeon of the Holocaust," in *Death as a Way of Life* (Tel Aviv: Hakibbutz Hameuchad, 2003), 23. In Hebrew.

17. Steven Erlanger, "New Museum, Putting a Human Face on the Holocaust, Opens in Israel," *New York Times,* March 16, 2005, A1.

18. Yaron London, personal communication, 2014.

19. Yoram Kaniuk, *1948* (Tel Aviv: Miskal—Yedioth Ahronoth Books and Chemed Books, 2010), 25. In Hebrew.

20. Hannah Arendt, *Eichmann in Jerusalem* (New York: Penguin Books, 1994), 118.

21. Segev, *Seventh Million,* 370.

22. D. Ben-Gurion, *The Renewed State of Israel* (Tel Aviv: Am Oved, 1969), 546.

23. Avraham Shapira, ed., *The Seventh Day* (London: Andre Deutsch, 1970), 160.

24. Segev, *Seventh Million,* 392.

25. Ibid., 394.

26. D. Bar-On and O. Selah, "The Vicious Circle Between Relating to Reality and Relating to the Holocaust Among Young Israelis," research report (Beer Sheva, Israel: Ben-Gurion University, Department of Behavioral Sciences, 1990), 39.

27. Y. Oron, *Jewish-Israeli Identity* (Tel Aviv: Kibbutz College School of Education, 1992), 58.

28. Gideon Alon, "Begin: If Iraq Tries Again to Build a Nuclear Reactor, We Will Act Against It," *Haaretz,* June 10, 1981, 1.

29. Quoted in Segev, *Seventh Million,* 399.

30. Grossman, "Carrier Pigeon of the Holocaust," 22.

31. O. Grosbard, *Israel on the Couch: The Psychology of the Peace Process* (New York: State University of New York Press, 2000), 35.

32. Arendt, *Eichmann in Jerusalem.*

33. Bar-Yosef Yehoshua, "On the Kfar Kassem Incident," *Davar,* December 18, 1956, 2. Quoted in Segev, *Seventh Million.*

34. D. Rabikowitz, "You Don't Kill a Baby Twice," in *True Love,* trans. Haim Watzman (Tel Aviv: Hakibbutz Hameuchad, 1987), 64.

35. Amos Oz, "Mr. Prime Minister, Hitler Is Already Dead," *Yediot Ahronot,* June 21, 1982, 6. In Hebrew.

36. Segev, *Seventh Million,* 401.

37. Bar-On and Selah, "The Vicious Circle."

38. Segev, *Seventh Million,* 4.

39. http://www.haaretz.co.il/news/education/1.1848141.

40. D. Rosenblum, *Israeli Blues,* trans. Alon Gratch (Tel Aviv: Am Oved, 1998), 95. In Hebrew.

41. Ibid.

42. Dina Porat, *An Entangled Leadership: The Yishuv and the Holocaust, 1942–1945* (Tel Aviv: Am Oved Publishers, 1987), 65–66. In Hebrew.

43. Judd Ne'eman, "The Tragic Sense of Zionism: Shadow Cinema and the Holocaust," *Shofar: An Interdisciplinary Journal of Jewish Studies* 24, no. 1. (Fall 2005): 22–36.

44. Daniel Boyarin, *Unheroic Conduct: The Rise of Heterosexuality and the Invention of the Jewish Man* (Berkeley: University of California Press, 1997).

45. Raz Yosef, *Beyond Flesh: Queer Masculinities and Nationalism in Israeli Cinema* (New Brunswick, N.J., and London: Rutgers University Press. 2004).

46. Ne'eman, "Tragic Sense of Zionism," 35.

47. Y. Kaniuk, *Adam Ben Kelev,* trans. Alon Gratch (Tel Aviv: Sifriat Poalim, 1969), 177. In Hebrew.

48. Ibid., 176.

49. Adi Hagin, "Israelis in Germany: Choosing to Live in a Country with an Awful History, but Where You Can Survive," trans. Alon Gratch, *Markerweek,* August 9, 2011. In Hebrew.

50. Ibid.

51. Don Handelman, *Models and Mirrors: Towards an Anthropology of Public Events* (Cambridge, England: Cambridge University Press, 1990).

52. Y. Ezrahi, *Rubber Bullets: Power and Conscience in Modern Israel* (Berkeley: University of California Press, 1998).

53. Yehuda Elkana, "For Forgetting," trans. Tom Segev, *Haaretz,* March 2, 1988. In Hebrew.

54. Segev, *Seventh Million,* 504.

5. Anatomy of a Cliché: Sabras at War

1. D. Grossman, *Death as a Way of Life: From Oslo to the Geneva Agreement* (New York: Picador, 2004), 8.

2. Ibid., 7.

3. Ibid., 30.

4. Ibid., 43.

5. Ibid., 44.

6. D. Grossman, *To the End of the Land* (New York: Knopf, 2010), 633.

7. R. Cooke, "David Grossman: 'I cannot afford the luxury of despair,'" *Observer,* August 29, 2010.

8. Avraham Balaban, "The Unquenchable Bereavement of Losing a Child," *Haaretz,* October 9, 2011.

9. David Grossman, *Falling out of Time,* trans. Alon Gratch (Tel Aviv: New Library, 2011), 120, 138–39. In Hebrew.

10. Moshe Amirav, *Jerusalem Syndrome: The Palestinian-Israeli Battle for the Holy City.* (Eastbourne: Sussex Academic Press, 2009).

11. Oz Almog, *The Sabra: The Creation of the New Jew* (Berkeley: University of California Press, 2000).

12. Oz Almog, *Farewell to "Srulik": Changing Values Among the Israeli Elite* (Tel Aviv: Zmora-Bitan, 2004).

13. David Brooks, "A Loud and Promised Land," *New York Times,* April 16, 2009.

14. A. Falk, *Fratricide in the Holy Land: A Psychoanalytic View of the Arab-Israeli Conflict* (Madison WI: University of Wisconsin Press, 2004).

15. Grossman, *Death as a Way of Life.*

16. Falk, *Fratricide in the Holy Land.*

17. E. Shalit, "The Relationship Between Aggression and Fear of Annihilation in Israel," *Political Psychology* 15 (1994): 415–34.

18. O. Grosbard, *Israel on the Couch: The Psychology of the Peace Process* (New York: State University of New York Press, 2000).

19. Y. Ezrahi, *Rubber Bullets: Power and Conscience in Modern Israel* (Berkeley: University of California Press, 1998), 251.

20. Grossman, *To the End of the Land*, 592.

21. Grossman, *Falling out of Time*, 99.

22. Dalia Karpel, "He Will Return (or Not)," *Haaretz Magazine*, October 22, 2002. In Hebrew.

23. Almog, *The Sabra.*

24. Yaron Peleg, "Heroic Conduct: Homoeroticism and the Creation of Modern, Jewish Masculinities," *Jewish Social Studies* 13, no. 1 (Fall 2006): 31–58.

25. Yoram Kaniuk, *1948* (Tel Aviv: Miskal—Yediot Ahronot Books and Chemed Books, 2010), 113–21. In Hebrew.

26. Karpel, "He Will Return (or Not)."

27. Dan Senor and Saul Singer, *Start-Up Nation: The Story of Israel's Economic Miracle* (New York: Twelve, 2009).

28. Almog, *The Sabra*, 234.

29. Bruno Boccara, "Policy Making and Its Psychoanalytic Underpinnings," Socio-Analytic Dialogue Working Paper 1, www.socioanalyticdialogue.org.

6. There's No Place Like Masada

1. T. Segev, *1967, Israel, the War, and the Year That Transformed the Middle East*, trans. Jessica Cohen (New York: Metropolitan Books, Henry Holt, 2005), 494.

2. Ibid., 501.

3. Ethan Bronner and Isabel Kershner, "Israelis Facing a Seismic Rift over Role of Women," *New York Times*, January 14, 2012.

4. Yael S. Feldman, *Glory and Agony: Isaac's Sacrifice and National Narrative* (Stanford, Calif.: Stanford University Press, 2010).

5. A. Falk, *Fratricide in the Holy Land: A Psychoanalytic View of the Arab-Israeli Conflict* (Madison WI: University of Wisconsin Press, 2004).

6. Ilan Kutz and Sue Kutz, "How Trauma Takes Its Toll on Us: Two Therapists Tell How Israelis Are Trapped Between Vigilance and Numbness," *Time* magazine (European ed.), April 8, 2002.

7. A. B. Yehoshua, "From Myth to History," *AJS Review* 28.1 (2004): 210.

8. Feldman, *Glory and Agony,* 141.

9. Ibid.

10. Haim Be'er, "Haesh Vehaetzim," in *Al Tishlah Yadkha el Hana'ar,* ed. Ben-Gurion (Jerusalem: Keter, 2002), 11. In Hebrew.

11. Jeffrey Goldberg, "Among the Settlers: Will They Destroy Israel?" *New Yorker,* May 31, 2004.

12. Evyatar Banai, "Avot Ubanim," trans. Alon Gratch, NMC Music Ltd., 1997. In Hebrew.

13. Sigmund Freud, "Remembering, Repeating and Working-Through," in *Standard Edition of the Complete Psychological Works of Sigmund Freud* (London: Hogarth Press, 1953–74), 12:147–56.

14. Robert Stoller, *Perversion: The Erotic Form of Hatred* (New York: Pantheon, 1975).

15. Falk, *Fratricide in the Holy Land,* 19.

16. T. Friedman, http://www.nytimes.com/2014/01/29/opinion/friedman-why-kerry-is-scary.html?hp&rref=opinion&_r=0.

17. D. Grossman, *Death as a Way of Life: From Oslo to the Geneva Agreement* (New York: Picador, 2004), 41.

18. Avener Falk, *Moshe Dayan, the Man and the Legend: A Psychoanalytical Biography* (Tel Aviv: Sifriyat Maariv, 1985). In Hebrew.

19. Feldman, *Glory and Agony,* 145.

20. *Meduzot,* written and directed by Etgar Keret (Tel Aviv: Lama Films, 2007).

21. Joseph Hodara, "*Does Israel Have a Future? In-Depth and Clear,*" trans. Alon Gratch, *Haaretz,* February 20, 2012. In Hebrew.

Conclusion: Saying No, Getting to Yes

1. R. Patai, *The Arab Mind* (Long Island City, N.Y.: Hatherleigh Press, 2002).

2. A. Falk, *Fratricide in the Holy Land: A Psychoanalytic View of the Arab-Israeli Conflict* (Madison, WI: University of Wisconsin Press, 2004).

3. O. Grosbard, *Israel on the Couch: The Psychology of the Peace Process* (New York: State University of New York Press, 2000).

4. Mira M. Sucharov, *The International Self: Psychoanalysis and the Search for Israeli-Palestinian Peace* (Albany: State University of New York Press, 2006).

5. Sefi Rachlevsky, "Netanyahu Must Not Demolish the Strategic Alliance with U.S.," *Haaretz*, February 21, 2012.

6. Ethan Bronner, "Israel Senses Bluffing in Iran's Threats of Retaliation," *New York Times*, January 26, 2012.

7. Thomas Friedman, "Bibi and Barack, the Sequel," *New York Times*, December 3, 2013, http://www.nytimes.com/2013/12/04/opinion/friedman-bibi-and-barack -the-sequel.html?hp&rref=opinion&_r=0.

8. Jeffrey Goldberg, "The Crisis in U.S.–Israel Relations Is Officially Here," *Atlantic*, October 28, 2014, http://www.theatlantic.com/international/archive/2014/10/ the-crisis-in-us-israel-relations-is-officially-here/382031/.

9. Meron Benvenisti, *Intimate Enemies: Jews and Arabs in a Shared Land* (Berkeley: University of California Press, 1995).

10. Shmuel Rosner, "The One-State Problem," *New York Times*, March 6, 2012, http:// latitude.blogs.nytimes.com/2012/03/06/one-state-solution-conference-at -harvard-is-a-distraction-from-ending-the-israeli-palestinian-conflict/?ref =opinion.

11. Sucharov, *International Self*.

12. Thomas L. Friedman, "Lessons from Tahrir Square," *New York Times*, May 24, 2011.

13. Jeffrey Goldberg, "Goldblog Is a Pro–J Street Blog," *Atlantic*, March 28, 2011, http://www.theatlantic.com/international/archive/2011/03/goldblog-is-a-pro-j -street-blog/73009/.

14. Peter Beinart, *The Crisis of Zionism* (New York: Times Books, Henry Holt, 2012).

15. Theodore Sasson, *The New American Zionism* (New York and London: New York University Press, 2014).

Epilogue: Dinner in Jerusalem

1. Roger Cohen, "The Goldstone Chronicles," *New York Times*, April 7, 2011.

INDEX

absence, 182. *See also* dissociated
absence
accusations, of anti-Semitism, 99, 122,
227
achievements, 26, 61–63, 77
action, 170
fight-or-flight response, 44, 139
Nazi-Israeli comparison, 136–44,
146–47, 150–52
Adam Ben Kelev (Kaniuk), 126–27
adaptable-passionate archetype, 47–50
Adiv, Udi, 169, 170
affliction, ideology of, 94
Agassi, Shai, 48–49
aggression, 102, 156, 173
anxiety and, 108–9, 174
gender and, 176–77, 192–93
guilt and, 101, 151
helplessness and, 148–49, 207
Holocaust and, 143, 207
identification with aggressor, 138–39,
142–43, 149–50, 153, 157
retreat and, 135–36
Aharonovich, Yitzhak, 189–90
Ahmadinejad, Mahmoud, 212
allies, 105. *See also* enemies
Almog, Oz, 31, 98, 107, 172, 183

Altalena, 39–40
American Jewish community
generational shift in, 235–40
with guilt, 230–31
identity, 239–40
Modern Orthodox families, 232–34
right wingers supported by, 228–32
role, 226–27, 238–39
secularism in, 232, 235
unassimilated Jews in, 234–35
Zionists in, 234, 235
Amichai, Yehuda, 87
Amir, Yigal, 188
Amirav, Moshe, 167–69
"Among the Settlers: Will They Destroy
Israel?" (Goldberg), 199
anger-and-fear response, 44, 135, 139
annexation, of holy sites, 70
anti-Semitism, 99–101, 103, 122, 227. *See
also* racism
anxiety, 26, 117, 173. *See also* fear
aggression and, 108–9, 174
casualties, 73–74
death, 102–3, 108–9, 130, 132–34,
156–57, 159–81, 215, 223, 245
apartheid, 71, 146–47, 226, 230
Appelfeld, Aharon, 124

the Aqedah, 194, 196–98, 200
al-Aqsa Mosque, 196
Arab Israelis. *See* Israeli Arabs
Arab Jews (Oriental Jews), 76–77, 151
Arab Spring, 23, 58, 105, 157
Arab-Israeli conflict. *See* Israeli-
    Palestinian conflict
Arab-Israeli War (Israel's War of
    Independence) (1948), 6, 12, 98–99,
    128–29, 198
Arab-Israeli War (Six-Day War) (1967),
    1–2, 26, 87, 167
    IDF in, 96, 102, 131, 168–69
    Israeli denial of Palestinian
        demographics, 68–70
    "waiting period," 68, 131
Arab-Israeli War (Yom Kippur War)
    (1973), 13, 96, 102, 131–32
Arabs, 9, 96, 194. *See also* Israeli-
    Palestinian conflict
    Arab Jews, 76–77, 151
    with Hebron massacre (1929), 97–98
    Israeli Arabs, 27–28, 71–72, 76, 97, 140
    with Jewish birthrate differential,
        69–71
    media portrayals, 98, 99
    violence against, 144–46
    violence against Zionists, 23, 196–97
Arad, Michael, 182
Arafat, Yasser, 52, 142
archetypes
    adaptable-passionate, 47–50
    Israeli national character, 47–51, 134
    rigid-unstable, 47–49, 51
    Sharon as, 46–48, 134
Arendt, Hannah, 129, 137–38
argumentative. *See* nay saying
Arlosoroff, Haim, 38–39
art, 26, 63, 110, 143, 171–72, 193. *See also*
    films; music; theater
Aryan ideal, 151
Ashkenazi sabras, 30–31
Ashkenazi ultraorthodox, 31
assassinations, 39, 43, 186–88, 225
Assyrian Empire, 38, 62
Auden, W. H., 201
authority, disrespect for, 79–80
auto industry, 48–49
Avishai, Bernard, 28
avoda zara (foreign labor), 96

Avshalom (Prince of Israel), 88
Azuri, Najib, 23

baby, Israel as old, 26–27, 84, 243
Babylonian Empire, 38, 62
Baker, James, 20, 24, 214, 218–20
Balaban, Avraham, 164
Balfour Declaration, 9
Banai, Evyatar, 200
Bar Kokhba rebellion (132–35 CE), 37,
    89, 98
Barak, Ehud, 52, 167
Barnea, Nahum, 163
Bastiaans, Jan, 117–18
BDS (Boycott, Divestment and
    Sanctions) movement, 238–39
Bedouins, Israeli, 146
Begin, Menachem, 108, 141–42, 153
    Holocaust and, 40, 103, 132–33
    politics and, 3, 41, 57
Beinart, Peter, 230–31, 238
Beitar Yerushalayim, 145
Beit-Hallahmi, Benjamin, 64, 101
belligerence, 173–74, 176–77
Ben-Ari, Eyal, 84
Ben-Gurion, David, 38, 67–68, 121,
    130–31, 176
    with Etzel and *Altalena,* 39–40
    immigration and, 75, 90–91, 122
    reality gap and, 97
Benvenisti, Meron, 218
Bergman, Hugo, 37, 233
Bergmann, Ernst David, 129–30
Berman, Emanuel, 26
Biale, David, 62
Bialik, Hayim Nahman, 77, 87, 193–94
bias, media, 148–49
the Bible, 26, 36–37, 55, 98, 199
    the Aqedah, 194, 196–98, 200
    Chosen People, 61–63, 85, 89–90, 92,
        94, 100
    gender and aggression in, 192–93
bicycle-riding festival, 54
Bilu, Yoram, 84
birthrates, 69–71, 146
Birthright, 237
blame, 149–50
bluffing, 77, 78, 216
Boccara, Bruno, 184
bombings, 8, 10. *See also* 9/11

INDEX

spies with, 211–12
suicide, 31–32, 42, 109, 161, 163,
    199–200
Boruchowitch, Olivier, 205
Botticini, Maristella, 62, 63
boundaries, permeable, 81–82, 107, 160,
    172–73
Boycott, Divestment and Sanctions
    movement. See BDS movement
Brooks, David, 172–73
brothels, 65
bullets, rubber, 156
bullying, 171
business, 26, 35, 48–49, 212

cactus fruit (sabra), 22, 124, 156
Camp David peace accords (1978), 57
Camp David Summit (2000), 52, 70, 220
Carter, Jimmy, 20
casualties, 73–74, 144
cats, dogs and, 107, 108
Cave of the Patriarchs massacre (1994),
    100
censorship, 30, 148–49
change, 62
    with archetypes, 47–51
    fragmentation and, 31, 46–53
    psychology of, 31, 34–35
    transformation and, 26, 73, 77, 84,
        134, 181–82
    war, peace, and cycles of, 31–35, 208,
        217
children, 54–55, 144
    with disrespect for authority, 79–80
    with gender and military culture,
        174–76
    Holocaust and, 115–16, 127, 157–58,
        246
    identification with aggressor and,
        138–39
    immigration policies for, 75
    religion and, 4, 12–13, 96–97
    war and, 4–6, 13–14, 112, 159–60, 161,
        167, 171
    youths, 15, 23, 58–59, 82, 96–97, 105,
        110, 122, 143, 145–49, 151, 157, 167,
        237
Chosen People, 61–62, 85, 89–90
    with compensatory model, 63, 92, 94
    Persecuted People and, 94, 100

Christianity, 64, 70, 76, 97, 141
circle, culture of, 183
citizenship, Israel, 153
"The City of Slaughter" (Bialik), 193–94
Clinton, Bill, 20, 25, 43, 52, 220
collaboration, resistance or, 137–38
collective memories, 27, 55
colonialists, Zionists as, 101, 134
compensatory model, 63, 66, 92, 94
Conference of Presidents of Major
    American Jewish Organizations,
    228–29
conflicts, 192–93. See also Israel-Gaza
    conflict; Israeli-Palestinian conflict
conquest mentality, 92
conservatives. See right wingers
conversions, from Judaism, 97
corruption, 41, 77–78
Cramer, Richard Ben, 31
creativity, trauma and, 181–83
crimes, 25. See also Eichmann, Adolf
The Crisis of Zionism (Beinart), 230
criticism. See self
"Crying for You," 187–88
"crying while shooting," 147–49, 167, 230
culture, 95, 110, 183
    military, 170–71, 174–76, 179–80
    with permeable boundaries, 81–82,
        107, 160, 172–73
    sabras with gender and, 170, 176
curses, 37
cutting corners, 77

da Vinci, Leonardo, 172
Dayan, Assi (son), 171
Dayan, Moshe, 92, 171, 185, 202
death, 88, 90. See also Holocaust
    anxiety, 102–3, 108–9, 130, 132–34,
        156–57, 159–81, 215, 223, 245
    assassinations, 39, 43, 186–88, 225
    with empathy, 91–92, 125
    without empathy, 73–74, 144, 150
    extermination, 37, 131
    Israeli-Palestinian conflict as life and,
        160–63, 173
    massacres, 41, 47, 97–98, 100, 140–41
    murder, 38–39
    politics as life and, 36, 38–39, 41
    revenge killings, 145
    by rubber bullet, 156

death (*continued*)
  slaughter, 22, 123, 149, 193–94
  suicide, 31–32, 42, 109, 161, 163,
    169–70, 199–200, 202, 203
  in war, 185
  as way of life, 105–7, 159–81, 185, 199
Death as a Way of Life (Grossman, D.),
    160–61
defense, 73, 142. *See also* Israeli Defense
    Forces
defense mechanism
  aggression, 138–39, 142–43, 149–50,
    153, 157
  anti-Semitist accusations, 99
  helplessness as, 136–37, 138–39
  heroism, 132
  nay saying as, 21–22, 206–7, 219
DeKoven Ezrahi, Sidra, 85, 87
DellaPergola, Sergio, 71
demographics, denial and. *See*
    populations
denial, 76, 77, 134, 188, 205
  "crying while shooting," 147–49, 167,
    230
  of Nazi-Israeli comparison, 136–44,
    146–47, 150–52
  Palestinian demographics and Israeli,
    68–73, 97, 174, 219, 230
De-Nur, Yehiel. *See* Feiner, Yehiel
dependency, 39, 105, 122, 132
Derrida, Jacques, 62
the Diaspora, 93, 94, 107
  history of, 36–37, 62
  with Jewish fate or *ha-goral ha-yehudi*,
    104–5, 110
  with political divide, 37–38
  timidity of, 22, 26–27, 66, 175, 195, 207
  Zionists and, 64, 150–51
discourse. *See* politics
discrimination
  against Arab Jews, 77
  gender, 191
  against Israeli Arabs, 71–72
  language, 122, 145–46, 147
disdain, for weakness, 75, 80, 81, 122,
    141, 154
displacement, 69, 144. *See also*
    settlements
disrespect, for authority, 79–80
dissociated absence

Holocaust and, 113–17, 121, 155
  mourning and, 164
Does Israel Have a Future? (Laub and
    Boruchowitch), 205
dogs, cats and, 107, 108
Dome of the Rock mosque, 69, 87, 196
Dotan, Shimon, 171
draft avoidance, 11, 14, 187
duality, of trauma, 113–17, 121, 155, 170
dugri (speech under fire), 172–73

Eastern European Jews, 86, 95, 97–98,
    151–52
Eban, Abba, 131, 219
Eckstein, Zvi, 62, 63
economy, 25, 81, 96, 141
  business, 26, 35, 48–49, 212
  Holocaust and financial restitution, 40
education, 63, 166
Egypt, 38, 96, 105, 212, 222. *See also*
    Arab-Israeli War (1967)
Egypt-Israel Peace Treaty (1979), 41, 47,
    57, 220
Eichmann, Adolf, 114–15, 121, 125–26,
    129, 130
*Eichmann in Jerusalem: A Report on the
    Banality of Evil* (Arendt), 137–38
El Al Israel Airlines, 74, 80, 247
Elkana, Yehuda, 157–58
embargo, on Gaza, 103
emotions, 26, 35, 45, 74, 88, 107, 127. *See
    also specific emotions*
  without action, 136
  "crying while shooting," 147–49, 167,
    230
  PTSD, 117, 165–67
empathy
  death with, 91–92, 125
  death without, 73–74, 144, 150
  guilt and, 151–53
  for Holocaust survivors, 132
  love and, 225, 236–37
  narcissism and, 73–76, 92, 141, 206
enemies, 95, 98, 105, 178
  from paranoia, 100–103
  threats, 103, 110, 134, 205, 209–17
England, 39, 95, 130
Eretz Israel (Land of Israel), 84–85, 87
Erlanger, Steven, 46, 128
Eshkol, Levi, 87, 102

Esther (biblical figure), 100
ethnic-religious ideology, 94
Etzel (National Military Organization), 39–40
European Union (EU), 25, 208
evil, 137–38
exile, 89, 122–24, 163
expansion, West Bank settlers and, 78–79
expats, Israeli Jews, 154–55
extermination, 37, 131
extremists. *See* radicals
Ezrahi, Yaron, 52, 53, 100, 157
    on Gaza Strip, 43–44
    on gender and military culture, 174–75
    with rubber bullets, 156

Falk, Avner, 109, 173, 193, 202
    on Arab Jew projections, 76
    mourning and, 85, 88
    repetition compulsion and, 201
Falling out of Time (Grossman, D.), 163–65
family troubles, 81
fate, 104–5, 110
"Fathers and Sons," 200
Faulkner, William, 84
fear, 6, 14–15, 40, 131
    anger-and-fear response, 44, 135, 139
    anxiety, 26, 73–74, 102–3, 108–9, 117, 130, 132–34, 156–57, 159–81, 215, 223, 245
    of gentile world, 96, 104–5, 107
    passivity and, 133–34
Feiner, Yehiel
    as De-Nur, 114–15, 119
    as Holocaust survivor, 113–15, 117–19
    as Ka-Tzetnik, 113–15, 117–19, 125
Feinstein, Meir, 8–9
Feldman, Yael S., 192, 197, 198, 202, 248
few facing many, myths of, 98
Fifty-Day War (2014). *See* Israel-Gaza conflict
fight-or-flight response, 44, 139
films, 155, 171, 177, 180–81, 204
financial restitution, Holocaust, 40
firearms, 9, 11, 42
First Temple, destruction of, 89, 189
Fletcher, Martin, 72, 74, 79
"For Forgetting" (Elkana), 157–58
foreign labor (*avoda zara*), 96

Fox, Eytan, 171
Foxman, Abraham, 230
fragmentation
    change and, 31, 46–53
    tribal, 36
France, 130
fraternal conflicts, 192–93
Fratricide in the Holy Land (Falk), 193
freedom, 15, 39
Freud, Sigmund, 45, 57, 62, 79, 200
Friedman, Thomas, 95, 201, 217, 220, 224
frier (sucker), 80

Gadot, Eli (Gratch, Eli) (brother), 2–3
Gal, Reuven, 165
gap, reality, 97, 162–63
Garbuz, Yair, 104
gas chambers, 131, 133, 146
Gaza Strip, 2, 14, 42, 103, 223–24
    Israel-Gaza conflict (2014), 25, 72, 73, 99, 105, 144
    Jewish and Arab birthrate differential in, 69–71
    landscape and imprinting, 87–88
    Sharon and withdrawal from, 43–44, 48, 57
Gaza-Israel conflict (2014). *See* Israel-Gaza conflict
Gefen, Aviv, 187–88
Geffen, Shira, 204
gender, 90, 170, 191
    aggression and, 176–77, 192–93
    literature and, 85, 171
    military culture and, 174–76, 179–80
generosity, 153, 206
Genius from Vilna, 7, 10
gentile world, fear of, 96, 104–5, 107
geography, of Israel, 82–89
German Jews
    immigration, 90–91, 121–23
    Nazis and transfer agreement for, 38–39
Germany, 40, 110, 120. *See also* Holocaust
    Israeli Jewish expats in, 154–55
    Israeli Jews with German passports, 109
    Nazis, 38–39, 43, 97, 103, 114–15, 118, 121–22, 124, 125–26, 129, 130, 136–44, 146–47, 150–52

Gertz, Nurith, 73, 97, 98–99, 101
Ghetto Fighters Museum, 143
Gillon, Carmi, 195
global stability, 23–26
Glory and Agony: Isaac's Sacrifice and National Narrative (Feldman), 198, 248
God, 194, 200
Goldberg, Jeffrey, 199, 217, 231
Goldmann, Nahum, 228
Goldstein, Baruch, 100
Goldstone, Richard, 244–45
Gordon, A. D., 65
Goya, Francisco, 193
graffiti, hate, 145–46
the grandiose self, 64, 86, 190, 206, 221
Gratch, Alon
  family history, 3–14
  Holocaust and, 120, 123
Gratch, Ariel (brother), 1–2, 17
Gratch, Eli (brother). *See* Gadot, Eli
Gratch, Haya (mother), 15–16
Greenberg, Uri Zvi, 168
Grosbard, Ofer, 99, 108–9, 135, 173, 202
Grossman, David, 28, 94–95
  on aggression and culture, 173
  with death as way of life, 160–65, 170, 175–76
  with Holocaust, 134–35
Grossman, Uri (son), 161–62
Grunzweig, Emile, 41–42
Guardians of the City (Neturei Karta) sect, 7
guilt, 101, 118, 150, 164
  American Jewish community with, 230–31
  empathy and, 151–53
Gur, Mordechai, 87
Guri, Haim, 115, 126

Ha'adama Hazot (This Earth), 197
the Haganah, 10, 11, 39
ha-goral ha-yehudi (Jewish fate), 104–5, 110
Halbertal, Moshe, 100
Halevy, Yehuda, 87
Hamas, 23, 223, 236
  Israel-Gaza conflict (2014), 25, 72, 73, 99, 105, 144
  as threat, 103, 134

Handelman, Don, 156
Hanna (biblical figure), 199–200
Haredim. *See* ultraorthodox
Harkabi, Yehoshafat (General), 188
hate, 145–46, 157–58
  love and, 63, 105–7, 155, 202–3, 225, 236–37
  self-hate, 63, 76–77, 90, 99, 151, 204, 206
Hausner, Gideon, 126
hebraization, of surnames, 3
The Hebrew Republic (Avishai), 28
Hebron massacre (1929), 97–98
helplessness, 134. *See also* weakness
  aggression and, 148–49, 207
  as defense mechanism, 136–37, 138–39
Herod (King of Judea), 189
heroism, 123–24, 132, 169–70, 179, 246
Hertzl, 151
Herzl, Hans (son), 97
Herzl, Theodor, 64–65
Heschel, Abraham Joshua (Rabbi), 235
Heymann, Tomer, 155
high tech, 26, 35, 63, 182–84
history, of the Diaspora, 36–37, 62
Hitler, Adolf, 106, 122, 131, 142
Hodara, Joseph, 205
Hoenlein, Malcolm, 229
Holocaust, 38, 103, 111
  aggression and, 143, 207
  children and, 115–16, 127, 157–58, 246
  financial restitution, 40
  guilt and, 118, 164
  identity and, 127–28, 132, 154–55, 157–58, 204, 247–48
  with intrusive presence and dissociated absence, 113–17, 121, 155
  language of, 123–24, 132
  literature and, 126–27
  in media, 119, 125–26, 128, 135, 157–58
  memories, 114–16, 118–21, 125–27, 132–34, 157–58, 164–65, 247–48
  museum, 113, 127–28, 157
  Native Americans and, 236
  as "other planet," 119, 121, 155
  privatization of, 126–27
  projection and, 124
  reality, 119, 151

silence and, 104, 112–21, 123, 126, 129, 135, 178–79, 210, 246–47
survivors, 22, 112–21, 123–28, 130, 132, 149, 154
holy sites. *See* al-Aqsa Mosque; Dome of the Rock mosque; Temple Mount; Western Wall
holy sites, annexation of, 70
House of Dolls (Ka-Tzetnik), 114
Hussein (King of Jordan), 91–92
Hussein, Saddam, 133, 160

I Shot My Love (film), 155
ideal, Aryan, 151
identity, 51, 56, 170, 239–40. *See also* national character, Israeli
Holocaust and, 127–28, 132, 154–55, 157–58, 204, 247–48
identification with aggressor, 138–39, 142–43, 149–50, 153, 157
"identity seekers," 59
ideology, Zionists, 94–95
IDF. *See* Israeli Defense Forces
Ilan, Uri, 169–70
immigration, 11, 31, 35, 37–39, 86
German Jews, 90–91, 121–23
policies, 75, 121–22
Zionists, 64–66
imprinting, landscape and, 82–89
independence. *See* Arab-Israeli War; freedom
injustice, in legal system, 141
integrity, 108, 109
intermarriage, 64, 232
intifada, Palestinians and non-violence, 224–26
intifada (1987–1993), Palestinian, 42, 133, 136, 143, 222
intifada (2000–2005), Palestinian, 196
death anxiety and, 109, 133–34, 156–57, 223
suicide bombers, 31–32, 109, 161
intrusive presence, 113–17, 121, 155
Iran
with nuclear weapons, 24, 110, 132–33, 209–17
as threat, 103, 110, 205, 209–17
Irgun, with bombings, 8
Iron Dome missile defense system, 73
Islam, 93, 97

Israel, 15, 38, 64, 102, 199, 205, 228. *See also* Arab-Israeli wars; national character, Israeli
citizenship, 153
with denial of Palestinian demographics, 68–73, 97, 174, 219, 230
Egypt-Israel Peace Treaty (1979), 41, 47, 57, 220
El Al Israel Airlines, 74, 80, 247
Eretz Israel, 84–85, 87
geography of, 82–89
as Jewish state, 54
Lebanon invaded by, 41–42, 47, 103, 133, 141
with Nazi-Israeli comparison, 136–44, 146–47, 150–52
nuclear weapons and, 129–30
with nuclear weapons and Iran, 24, 110, 132–33, 209–17
as old baby, 26–27, 84, 243
Palestine's relations with, 25, 36, 75–76, 140
with Palestinians displaced, 69
as psychotherapy patient, 99
subgroups in, 30–31
U.S. relations with, 105, 110, 132, 133, 208, 210–17, 219–22, 231, 242
war-crime charges against, 25
Israel Award, 141
Israel Freedom Fighters (Lechi), 39
Israel Security Agency (Shabak), 81
Israel-Gaza conflict (Fifty-Day War) (2014), 25, 72, 73, 99, 105, 144
Israeli Arabs, 27–28, 71–72, 76, 97, 140
Israeli Bedouins, 146
Israeli Defense Forces (IDF), 5, 12, 15, 78–79, 161, 182–83
in Arab-Israeli War (1967), 96, 102, 131, 168–69
in art, 171–72
draft avoidance, 11, 14, 187
Ilan and, 169–70
Jewish resistance to, 177, 190
library, 29–30
PTSD, 165–67
with rubber bullets, 156
Sabra and Shatila massacre, 41, 47, 141
women in, 176

Israeli Jews. *See also* national character,
Israeli
with Arab birthrate differential, 69–71
expats in Germany, 154–55
with German passports, 109
myths of Israeli identity, 170
Nazi-Israeli comparison, 136–44,
146–47, 150–52
"new Jew," 3, 27, 61, 151, 214
population residing overseas, 89
sabras, 22, 30–31, 41, 47, 103, 124, 132,
141, 151, 156, 170, 176, 194
with secular-religious divide, 53–60,
191–92
stereotypes, 27, 76, 78
with war, peace, and change, 31–35,
208, 217
Israeli-Palestinian conflict
denial in, 68–73, 97, 174, 219, 230
as life and death, 160–63, 173
with non-violent protests, 224–26
prophecies, 23, 37, 67
racism and, 145–47
reasons for, 68, 101, 136
repetition compulsion and, 201
Israeli-Palestinian peace process, 104,
201, 210–17
Camp David Summit (2000), 52, 70,
220
quagmire of, 218–26
turmoil in, 25, 40–43, 52
Israel-Jordan peace treaty (1994), 91
Israel's War of Independence (1948). *See*
Arab-Israeli War

J Street, 228, 231, 237
Jabotinsky, Ze'ev, 9, 38
Jellyfish (film), 204
Jerusalem (Zion), 3, 8, 10, 137–38
holy sites annexed in, 70
Old City of Jerusalem, 87, 167–68,
196
poetics of return to, 87
as symbol, 85–86
"Jerusalem of Gold," 68–69
Jesus, 62, 97
Jewish Agency, 38–39, 95, 121–22
Jewish Defense League, 142
Jewish fate *(ha-goral ha-yehudi)*, 104–5,
110

Jews. *See also* the Diaspora; Holocaust;
Israeli Jews
American Jewish community, 226–40
Arab Jews, 76–77, 151
as Chosen People, 61–63, 85, 89–90,
92, 94, 100
Eastern European, 86, 95, 97–98,
151–52
German, 38–39, 90–91, 121–23
IDF and resistance from, 177,
190
with Israel as Jewish state, 54
Judean, 37
Judenrats, 137–38
Modern Orthodox, 232–34
myth of Romans with exile of, 89
notable, 62
Palestinians and projections of, 76–77,
101, 147–49, 151, 174, 219
Sephardim, 31
ultraorthodox, 31, 53–60, 191–92
Jordan, 3, 10, 91–92
Judaism, 37
conversions from, 97
secular-religious divide and, 53–60,
191–92
Judea, 37, 189
Judean Jews, 37
Judenrats, 137–38
Judenrein, 97
justice, 25, 141

Kadishman, Menashe, 198
Kafka, Franz, 110
Kahane, Meir (Rabbi), 142–43
Kaniuk, Yoram, 110, 126–27, 178–79
on Holocaust, 128–29
with Nazi-Israeli comparison, 151–52
Katz, Elihu, 156
Ka-Tzetnik. *See* Feiner, Yehiel
Keret, Etgar, 110, 204
Kerry, John, 25, 201, 239
Kfar Kassem massacre (1956), 140–41
kibbutz, 65, 73, 198
killings, revenge, 145
"Kinneret Sheli," 83
Kleinstein, Rami, 186
Kluckhohn, Clyde, 51
Kohut, Heinz, 86, 92
Kristallnacht (1938), 75

Kutz, Ilan, 193
Kutz, Sue, 193

labor, 96, 146
"lambs to the slaughterhouse," 22, 123, 149
land, 26, 68, 85, 102, 161–62, 193. *See also To the End of the Land*
  landscape and imprinting, 82–89
  Palestinian refugees and, 71
  transformation of self through, 84
Land of Israel (Eretz Israel), 84–85, 87
language, 172–73
  discrimination, 122, 145–46, 147
  of Holocaust, 123–24, 132
Last Supper, 172
Laub, Richard, 205
leaving with a question *(youtze be-she-ela),* 56–57
Lebanon, 16
  Israel's invasion of, 41–42, 47, 103, 133, 141
  in media, 141–42
Lechi (Israel Freedom Fighters), 39
Leef, Daphni, 177–78
left wingers (liberals), 3
  left-right divide, 36–46, 145–48, 189–91
  with Nazi transfer agreement, 38–39
legal system, injustice in, 141. *See also* trials
legislation, racist, 147
Leibowitz, Yeshayahu, 141
Levin, Hanoch, 198–99
Levine, Alter, 65
LGBT community, 177, 235, 237
liberals. *See* left wingers
Libeskind, Daniel, 182
library, IDF, 29–30
Liebman, Charles, 93–94
lies, 77–78, 163, 216
life
  death as way of, 105–7, 159–81, 185, 199
  Israeli-Palestinian conflict as death and, 160–63, 173
  politics as death and, 36, 38–39, 41
Lifshitz, Uri, 198

literacy, survival and, 62–63
literature, 26, 63, 110, 177
  gender and, 85, 171
  Holocaust and, 126–27
  with Jerusalem as symbol, 85–86
Livni, Tzipi, 146
lobbying groups, 64, 228
London, Yaron, 128
loss, 109
  mourning and, 85–86, 88, 156, 163–65, 182
  transformation of, 181–82
love, 105–7, 155, 202–3. *See also* hate
  empathy and, 225, 236–37
  self-love, 63
LSD, 117–19

Madrid Peace Conference (1991), 220
Manasseh (King of Judea), 37
marriage, 64, 232
martyrdom, suicide bombers and, 199–200
Marx, Karl, 79
Masada, 194–95, 230, 237
masochism, powerlessness as, 140
massacres, 41, 47, 97–98, 100, 140–41
mathematics, 63
media, 98–99, 130, 142, 217
  bias and censorship, 148–49
  Holocaust in, 119, 125–26, 128, 135, 157–58
  with Nazi-Israeli comparison, 140–41, 143, 146
  social media, 145, 210
medicine, 26, 63
Meir, Golda, 148, 176
memorialization, mourning and, 162, 179, 182
memories, 27, 55, 178–79
  Arab-Israeli War (1948), 6, 128–29
  Holocaust, 114–16, 118–21, 125–27, 132–34, 157–58, 164–65, 247–48
mentality, 92, 122–24
Merk, Andreas, 155
Michael, B. (columnist), 146
Middle East, 217
  global stability influenced by, 23–24, 26
  oil, 23, 209, 212, 221

militants, 37, 39. *See also* Etzel; Hamas; Irgun; Jewish Defense League; Lechi
military, 15, 25, 39–40, 73. *See also* Israeli Defense Forces
    culture, 170–71, 174–76, 179–80
    Jewish Agency with British, 95
Millard, David, 67
mirroring, 52
mistrust, 93, 95–96, 104
Modern Orthodox families, 232–34
money, 40, 81
moral superiority, 148, 152
"Moriah complex," 199
mosques, 69, 87, 196
mourning, 68, 140, 157, 176, 187, 238
    dissociated absence and, 164
    loss and, 85–86, 88, 156, 163–65, 182
    memorialization and, 162, 179, 182
Moyne (Lord), 39
Mubarak, Hosni, 105
murder, 38–39
Murray, Henry A., 51
museums, 113, 127–28, 143, 157
music
    achievements in, 26, 63
    songs, 68–69, 83, 104, 186–88, 200
My Promised Land: The Triumph and Tragedy of Israel (Shavit), 102
myths, 62, 89, 97–98, 170

Nachal (pop group), 186
names, 3, 62
narcissism, 61, 63, 80
    Chosen People with, 94, 100
    displays of, 73–75
    empathy and, 73–76, 92, 141, 206
    narcissistic character, 90–91
    paranoia and, 94, 96, 101
    pathological, 86, 92
    phallic-narcissistic character, 81
    projection, 78–79, 90–91, 107, 219
    with symbols over reality, 85–86
    Zionists with, 66, 85–86
narratives, Zionist, 129, 156, 175, 198, 248
Nasser, Gamal Abdel, 130, 131
national character, Israeli
    archetypes, 47–51, 134
    criticisms of, 24, 242–43

defined, 52–53
    description, 19–26
    with disrespect for authority, 79–80
    without empathy, 73–74, 144, 150
    global stability and, 24
    left-right divide and, 36–46, 145–48, 189–91
    narcissism, 61, 63, 66, 73–76, 78–82, 85–86, 90–92, 94, 96, 100–101, 107, 141, 206, 219
    nay saying and, 20–22, 24, 46, 52
    with sabra or cactus fruit, 22, 124, 156
    secular-religious divide, 53–60, 191–92
    self-esteem, 89–92, 107, 206
    for survival, 21–23, 62, 193
    with weakness disdained, 75, 80, 81, 122, 141, 154
National Military Organization. *See* Etzel
Native Americans, 236
native Israelis. *See* sabras
nature hikes *(tiyulim)*, 84
nay saying (argumentative)
    as defense mechanism, 21–22, 206–7, 219
    Israeli national character and, 20–22, 24, 46, 52
    no, as negotiable, 78–79
    oppositional, 56–57, 206, 219, 243
Nazis, 43, 103, 118, 122. *See also* Holocaust
    Judenrats and, 137–38
    Judenrein, 97
    Nazi-Israeli comparison, 136–44, 146–47, 150–52
    with *sabon* or soap, 124
    with transfer agreement for German Jews, 38–39
    on trial, 114–15, 121, 125–26, 129, 130
    Zionism with guilt and, 150–51
Ne'eman, Judd, 150–51
negotiations, 24, 110. *See also* peace
    left-right divide and, 39, 42
    no, as negotiable, 78–79
Neriah, Yuval, 176, 179–80
Nes, Adi, 172
Netanyahu, Benjamin, 163
    Obama and, 100, 213–18, 231
    racism and, 147

INDEX

Neturei Karta (Guardians of the City) sect, 7

"new Jew," Zionists with, 3, 27, 61, 151, 214

Night (Wiesel), 164–65, 247–48

9/11, 17, 153, 182

1948 (Kaniuk), 128–29

1967: Israel, the War, and the Year That Transformed the Middle East (Segev), 26

no, as negotiable, 78–79. *See also* nay saying

non-violent protests, 224–26

Nordau, Max, 64

"Nothing But You," 186

nuclear weapons
    Iran with, 24, 110, 132–33, 209–17
    Israel with, 129–30

Obama, Barack
    Israel and, 221–22
    Netanyahu and, 100, 213–18, 231

oedipal rebellion, of Zionists, 79, 85, 181, 192

oil industry, 23, 209, 212, 221

Old City of Jerusalem. *See* Jerusalem

Olmert, Ehud, 57

One Palestine, Complete (Segev), 75

Oppenheimer, Robert, 62

oppositional. *See* nay saying

Oriental Jews. *See* Arab Jews

orthodox. *See* Modern Orthodox families; ultraorthodox

Oslo Accords, 25, 42–43, 152, 188, 220

"other planet." *See* Holocaust

Oz, Amos, 109, 167, 202–3
    Begin and, 108, 141–42
    with death as way of life, 105–7

Palestine, 3. *See also* Hamas; Israeli-Palestinian conflict; Israeli-Palestinian peace process; Palestinians
    intifada (1987–1993), 42, 133, 136, 143, 222
    intifada (2000–2005), 31–32, 109, 133–34, 156–57, 161, 196, 223
    intifada, Palestinians and non-violence, 224–26
    Israeli denial of Palestinian

    demographics, 68–73, 97, 174, 219, 230
    Israel's relations with, 25, 36, 75–76, 140
    Jewish and Arab birthrate differential in, 69–71
    refugees, 69, 71
    the Yishuv in, 38–39, 68–73, 86, 97, 121–23, 174, 219, 230

Palestine Liberation Organization (PLO), 42, 47, 103, 133, 169, 223

Palestinians, 69, 144
    Jews projecting onto, 76–77, 101, 147–49, 151, 174, 219
    Nazi-Israeli comparison with treatment of, 136–44, 146–47, 150–52
    with non-violent protests, 224–26

panic attack, 73–74

paranoia, 105, 107, 110
    enemies from, 100–103
    mistrust, 93, 95–96, 104
    narcissism and, 94, 96, 101

passionate. *See* adaptable-passionate archetype

passivity, 133–34, 138, 175, 207. *See also* weakness

passports, 109

Patai, Raphael, 51–52

pathology, narcissism as, 86, 92

peace, 236, 237
    Camp David peace accords (1978), 57
    Egypt-Israel Peace Treaty (1979), 41, 47, 57, 220
    Israeli-Palestinian peace process, 25, 40–43, 52, 70, 104, 201, 210–26
    Israel-Jordan peace treaty (1994), 91
    Madrid Peace Conference (1991), 220
    Oslo Accords, 25, 42–43, 152, 188, 220
    Peace Now, 41–42
    "Song for Peace," 186–87
    with war and cycles of change, 31–35, 208, 217

Peleg, Yaron, 177

permeable, boundaries as, 81–82, 107, 160, 172–73

Persecuted People, 94, 100

personal boundaries, permeable, 81–82, 107, 160, 172–73

personality types, 81, 90–91
Petrie, William Flinders, 66
phallic-narcissistic character, 81
Picasso, Pablo, 163
planet, other. *See* Holocaust
PLO. *See* Palestine Liberation
    Organization
Pnini, Tom, 204
poems, 179, 193–94, 201
    Nazi-Israeli comparison, 141
    Zionist, 83, 84, 87
poetics of return, to Jerusalem, 87
policies. *See* immigration
politics, 78
    Begin and, 3, 41, 57
    discourse, 36–38, 45, 248–49
    left-right divide, 36–46, 145–48,
        189–91
    as life and death, 36, 38–39, 41
    lobbying groups, 64, 228
    psychology's role in, 26, 28, 102
    racism in, 142, 146–47
Popper, Karl, 41–42
populations, 144
    Holocaust survivors, 112–13, 128
    Israeli Arabs, 71–72
    Israeli Bedouins, 146
    Israeli denial of Palestinian
        demographics, 68–73, 97, 174, 219,
        230
    Israeli Jews residing overseas, 89
    with Jewish and Arab birthrate
        differential, 69–71
pornography, 29–30
post-traumatic stress disorder. *See* PTSD
power, 38, 41, 90
    myth of, 62
    powerlessness as masochism, 140
    strength and, 93, 101, 102, 143, 174
Praver, Ehud (Colonel), 132
presence. *See* intrusive presence
Price Tag, 144–45
privatization, of Holocaust, 126–27
projection
    of Arab Jews, 76–77, 151
    Jews projecting onto Palestinians,
        76–77, 101, 147–49, 151, 174, 219
    narcissistic, 78–79, 90–91, 107,
        219
    paranoia, 101

    sabras with Holocaust, 124
    splitting and, 44–45
prophecies, 23, 37, 67
protests, 9, 194
    Arab Spring, 23, 58, 105, 157
    non-violent, 224–26
    Peace Now, 41–42
    rebellions, 37, 79, 85, 89, 98, 181, 192
    violence at, 144
psychology
    of change, 31, 34–35
    of fragmentation, 31, 36, 46–53
    the grandiose self, 64, 86, 190, 206,
        221
    ideology of affliction, 94
    personal boundaries, 81–82, 107, 160,
        172–73
    politics and role of, 26, 28, 102
    projection, 44–45, 76–79, 90–91, 101,
        107, 124, 147–49, 151, 174, 219
    PTSD, 117, 165–67
    reaction formation, 45, 57, 115–17
    repetition compulsion, 200–202
    splitting and projection, 44–45
psychotherapy patient, Israel as, 99
PTSD (post-traumatic stress disorder),
    117, 165–67

The Queen of the Bathtub (Levin),
    198–99
question. *See* leaving with a question

Rabikowitz, Dalia, 141
Rabin, Yitzhak, 42, 43, 144, 186–88
Rachel (Zionist poet), 83
Rachlevsky, Sefi, 211
racism
    anti-Semitism, 99–101, 103, 122, 227
    apartheid, 71, 146–47, 226, 230
    in politics, 142, 146–47
    youth and, 96–97, 143, 145–46, 151
radicals (extremists)
    global stability and, 25
    path of, 64, 72, 99
reaction formation, 45, 57, 115–17
Reagan, Ronald, 73
reality
    denial and transforming of, 73, 77,
        134
    gap, 97, 162–63

Holocaust, 119, 151
Israeli-Palestinian conflict, 68–73, 97, 174, 219, 230
narcissism with symbols over, 85–86
rebellions, 37, 79, 85, 89, 98, 181, 192. *See also* protests
Reflecting Absence, 182
refugees, 69, 71, 123
Reich, Wilhelm, 80–81
religion
  children and, 4, 12–13, 96–97
  Christianity, 64, 70, 76, 97, 141
  ethnic-religious ideology, 94
  Islam, 93, 97
  Judaism, 37, 53–60, 97, 191–92
  secular-religious divide, 53–60, 191–92
  war with support of, 37
Renan, Ernest, 120
Repeat Dive (film), 171
repetition compulsion, 200–202
resistance, 137–38, 177, 190
retreat, aggression and, 135–36
return. *See* poetics of return, to Jerusalem
revenge, 100, 145, 178, 209, 212
right wingers (conservatives), 3
  American Jewish community and, 228–32
  Etzel, 39–40
  with firearms, 9, 11, 42
  Lechi, 39
  left-right divide, 36–46, 145–48, 189–91
  with Nazi transfer agreement, 38–39
  Price Tag, 144–45
rigid-unstable archetype, 47–49, 51
riots, of 1920, 9, 194
Rivlin, Reuven, 145, 147
Roman Empire, 37, 89, 98, 189, 194–95
Rosenblum, Doron, 148–49
Rosh Hashanah, 54, 197
Rosner, Shmuel, 218
rubber bullets, 156
Russians, 31, 98

sabon (soap), 124
sabotage, 219
sabra (cactus fruit), 22, 124, 156

Sabra and Shatila massacre, 41, 47, 141
sabras (native Israelis), 41, 47, 103, 124, 132, 141
  with Aryan ideal, 151
  Ashkenazi, 30–31
  character, 22, 156, 194
  gender and culture, 170, 176
sacrifice, 194–95, 197–98, 203, 221
Sadat, Anwar, 57, 91, 222, 225
Salamandra (Ka-Tzetnik), 113–14
salaries, for Arabs, 96
sanctions, 103, 212, 238–39
Sasson, Theodore, 235
science, 26, 63
Scroll of Esther, 100
Second Temple, destruction of (70 CE), 37, 62, 85, 89, 189
secularism
  in American Jewish community, 232, 235
  secular-religious divide, 53–60, 191–92
Seeds for Peace, 237
Segev, Tom, 26, 65, 75, 87, 95–96, 115
  on fear and war, 131
  on Hebron massacre (1929), 98
  Holocaust and, 123–24, 127
  on Lebanon, 141
self
  the grandiose self, 64, 86, 190, 206, 221
  land and transformation of, 84
  with privatization of Holocaust, 126–27
  self-criticism, 90
  self-esteem, 89–92, 107, 206
  self-hate, 63, 76–77, 90, 99, 151, 204, 206
  self-love, 63
  self-sabotage, 219
  self-sacrifice, 194–95, 197–98, 203, 221
  self-trust, 104
Senor, Dan, 182–83, 184
Sephardic ultraorthodox, 31
Sephardim, 31
"September 1, 1939" (Auden), 201
settlements
  condemnation of, 218, 231
  dismantling, 41, 43–44, 47, 48, 57
settlers. *See* West Bank settlers
The Seventh Day (Shapira), 131

sex, 29–30, 81, 82, 146, 186
the Sezon, 39
Shabak (Israel Security Agency), 81
Shalit, Erel, 108, 173
Shamir, Yitzhak, 24, 146, 214, 219
Shapira, Avraham, 131
Sharon, Ariel, 2, 43–44, 57, 103, 196
  as archetype, 46–48, 134
  Sabra and Shatila massacre, 41, 47
Shavit, Ari, 102
Shavit, Shabtai, 195
Shemer, Naomi, 68–69
silence. See Holocaust
Sinai campaign (1956), 130, 140
Singer, Saul, 182–83, 184
Six-Day War (1967). See Arab-Israeli
  War
skepticism. See mistrust; paranoia
slaughter, 22, 123, 149, 193–94
"slicks," firearm, 11
soap (sabon), 124
Sobol, Yehoshua, 143
social media, 145, 210
"Song for Peace," 186–87
songs. See music
sovereignty, 26, 27, 85
speech under fire (dugri), 172–73
spies, 64, 130–31, 169–70, 211–12
splitting, projection and, 44–45
Stampfer, Yehoshua, 8
Start-Up Nation (Senor and Singer),
  182–83
stereotypes, 27–28, 45, 76, 78, 97, 122
Stockholm syndrome, 138
Stoller, Robert, 200
strength, 93, 101, 102, 143, 174
subgroups, in Israel, 30–31
Sucharov, Mira, 208, 222
sucker (frier), 80
Suez Canal, 211–12
suffering, 94, 154
suffocation, 15, 58, 81, 108
suicide, 169–70, 199, 202, 203
suicide bombers, 42, 163
  martyrdom and, 199–200
  in Palestinian intifada (2000–2005),
    31–32, 109, 161
superiority, 80, 89, 98–99, 148, 152
surnames, hebraization of, 3
surveys

Chosen People, 89–90
  secular-religious divide, 56
survival
  dependency and, 105, 122, 132
  Israeli Jews with German passports
    for, 109
  literacy and, 62–63
  national character of Israel and, 21–23,
    62, 193
survivors, Holocaust
  empathy for, 132
  judgments about, 22, 123–25, 149, 154
  LSD and, 117–19
  memories, 114–16, 118–21, 125–27, 132
  populations, 112–13, 128
  with two reactions, 115–17
  weakness of, 124–25, 130, 154
Susser, Bernard, 93–94
symbols, 85–86, 128
Szold, Henrietta, 122

A Tale of Love and Darkness (Oz), 105–7,
  202–3
tattoos, 114, 118
Tchernichovsky, Shaul, 84
technology. See high tech
Tel-Chai battle, 194, 237
Temple Mount, 68, 87, 96, 196, 237
temples. See First Temple, destruction of;
  Second Temple, destruction of
terrorism, 10. See also Etzel; Lechi
  9/11, 17, 153, 182
  suicide bombers, 31–32, 42, 109, 161,
    163, 199–200
Teveth, Shabtai, 185
theater, 143, 197–98
The Third Man (film), 180–81
This Earth (Ha'adama Hazot), 197
threats
  Hamas, 103, 134
  Iran as, 103, 110, 205, 209–17
  revenge, 209, 212
timidity. See the Diaspora; Zionists
tiyulim (nature hikes), 84
To the End of the Land (Grossman, D.),
  28, 94–95
  with gender and military culture,
    175–76
  with life and death, 161–62, 170
Tolstoy, Leo, 217, 236

transfer agreements, for German Jews, 38–39
transformation, 26
    of loss, 181–82
    of reality with denial, 73, 77, 134
    of self through land, 84
trauma
    creativity and, 181–83
    duality of, 113–17, 121, 155, 170
    PTSD, 117, 165–67
    repetition compulsion and, 200–202
treaties. See peace
trials, 25
    Kfar Kassem massacre (1956), 140–41
    Nazis on, 114–15, 121, 125–26, 129, 130
Trump, Donald, 81
Trumpeldor, Joseph, 194
trust, 93, 95–96, 104
truth, with lies, 163
Turkish flotilla (2010), 103
Twenty-Five Years of Social Research in Israel (Gratch, H.), 15

ultraorthodox (Haredim)
    Ashkenazi and Sephardic, 31
    with secular-religious divide, 53–60, 191–92
the unfortunate business, 212. See also bombings
United Nations, 22, 110, 244
United States (U.S.), 64, 218. See also Israeli-Palestinian peace process
    American Jewish community, 226–40
    Eastern European Jews and immigration, 86
    Israel's relations with, 105, 110, 132, 133, 208, 210–17, 219–22, 231, 242
    with nuclear weapons and Iran, 24, 110, 132–33, 209–17

victimization, 94, 150
    "crying while shooting," 147–49, 167, 230
    victimizer and, 102, 143, 151–53
Vietnamese boat people, 153
violence. See also terrorism
    against Arabs, 144–46
    "crying while shooting," 147–49, 167, 230

with moral superiority, 148
    non-violent protests, 224–26
    at protests, 144
    against Zionists, 23, 196–97

"waiting period," 68, 131
Walk on Water (film), 171
war, 25, 26, 37, 73, 117, 178. See also Arab-Israeli wars; Israel-Gaza conflict; Sinai campaign; Tel-Chai battle
    children and, 4–6, 13–14, 112, 159–60, 161, 167, 171
    death in, 185
    fear and, 40, 131
    with peace and cycles of change, 31–35, 208, 217
War and Peace (Tolstoy), 217, 236
Watzman, Haim, 170, 176
We Are a Fucked Generation, 187
weakness, 103, 171
    disdain for, 75, 80, 81, 122, 141, 154
    helplessness and, 134, 136–37, 138–39, 148–49, 207
    of Holocaust survivors, 124–25, 130, 154
    passivity and, 133–34, 138, 175, 207
weapons. See bombings; firearms; Iron Dome missile defense system; nuclear weapons
Weizmann, Chaim, 38
Welles, Orson, 180–81
West Bank, 3, 42, 69–71, 228
West Bank settlers
    apartheid and, 146, 230
    EU ban and, 25
    expansion, 78–79
    judgments about, 35, 36, 199, 218
    with settlements dismantled, 44
    as subgroup in Israel, 31
Western Wall, 54, 96, 168, 196
"The Whole World Is Against Us," 103–4
Wiesel, Elie, 164–65, 247–48
Wieseltier, Leon, 105
Wilbushewitz, Manya, 65
Winnicott, D. W., 142
Wolf, Arnold (Rabbi), 235–36
women, 30, 65, 85
    aggression in, 176–77

women (*continued*)
  immigration policies for, 75
  ultraorthodox with, 191

Yaalon, Moshe, 78
Yablonka, Hanna, 120–21, 126
Yad Vashem Holocaust Museum, 113,
  127–28, 157
yang/yin, 57
Yehoshua, A. B., 85, 195–96, 198, 200
yin/yang, 57
the Yishuv, 38–39, 86
  with denial of Palestinian
    demographics, 68–73, 97, 174, 219,
    230
  German Jews and treatment by, 121–23
Yom Hashoa Vehagvura, 127
Yom Kippur War (1973). *See* Arab-Israeli
  War
youths, 82, 122. *See also* children
  Arab Spring, 23, 58, 105, 157
  Birthright and, 237
  "crying while shooting," 147–49, 167
  "identity seekers," 59
  with Jewish fate or *ha-goral ha-yehudi,*
    110
  military and, 15
  racism and, 96–97, 143, 145–46, 151

youtze be-she-ela (leaving with a
  question), 56–57

Ze'evi, Rehavam, 97
Zion, 85–86. *See also* Jerusalem
Zionists, 8, 10, 31, 38, 41
  in American Jewish community, 234,
    235
  Arabs with violence against, 23,
    196–97
  as colonialists, 101, 134
  the Diaspora and, 64, 150–51
  exile mentality and, 122–24
  with firearms, 9, 11, 42
  with guilt and Nazism, 150–51
  Herzl, Theodor, and, 64–65
  ideology, 94–95
  immigration, 64–66
  judgments about, 35, 36
  with narcissism, 66, 85–86
  narratives, 129, 156, 175, 198, 248
  "new Jew" created by, 3, 27, 61, 151,
    214
  oedipal rebellion of, 79, 85, 181, 192
  poems, 83, 84, 87
  superiority of, 98–99
  with timidity, 22, 26–27, 66, 175, 195,
    207